The Country Journal
NEW ENGLAND
WEATHER BOOK

THE COUNTRY JOURNAL

NEW ENGLAND WEATHER BOOK

by David Ludlum
and the editors of Blair & Ketchum's Country Journal

HOUGHTON MIFFLIN COMPANY BOSTON 1976

To the thousands of people of New England whose daily devotion to the scientific duty of weather observing has made this book possible.

CONSULTANT
Robert A. Lautzenheiser, New England climatologist

Library of Congress Cataloging in Publication Data

Ludlum, David McWilliams, 1910–
   The Country journal New England weather book.

   1. New England—Climate. I. Country journal.
II. Title.
QC984.N35L8   551.6′9′74   75-45184
ISBN 0-395-24299-1
ISBN 0-395-24402-1 pbk.

Printed in the United States of America

P 10 9 8 7 6 5 4 3 2 1

C O N T E N T S

I. *"The Dazzling Uncertainty of It"*

Origins of New England Weather

New England Weather Month by Month

II. *"The Weather Is Always Doing Something"*

New England Storms

Weather's Sumptuous Variety

III. *"Weather Enough, but Weather to Spare"*

A Meteorological Guide

Storm Warnings and Safety Rules

IV. *"Weather Is Necessary to a Narrative of Human Experience"*

MARK TWAIN ON THE NEW ENGLAND WEATHER

I reverently believe that the Maker who made us all makes everything in New England but the weather. I don't know who makes that, but I think it must be raw apprentices in the weather-clerk's factory who experiment and learn how, in New England, for board and clothes, and then are promoted to make weather for countries that require a good article, and will take their custom elsewhere if they don't get it. There is a sumptuous variety about the New England weather that compels the stranger's admiration—and regret. The weather is always doing something there; always attending strictly to business; always getting up new designs and trying them on the people to see how they will go. But it gets through more business in spring than in any other season. In the spring I have counted one hundred and thirty-six different kinds of weather inside of four-and-twenty hours. It was I that made the fame and fortune of that man that had that marvelous collection of weather on exhibition at the Centennial, that so astounded the foreigners. He was going to travel all over the world and get specimens from all the climes. I said, "Don't you do it; you come to New England on a favorable spring day." I told him what we could do in the way of style, variety, and quantity. Well, he came and he made his collection in four days. As to variety, why, he confessed that he got hundreds of kinds of weather that he had never heard of before. And as to quantity—well, after he had picked out and discarded all that was blemished in any way, he not only had weather enough, but weather to spare; weather to hire out; weather to sell; to deposit; weather to invest; weather to give to the poor. The people of New England are by nature patient and forbearing, but there are some things which they will not stand. Every year they kill a lot of poets for writing about "Beautiful Spring." These are generally casual visitors, who bring their notions of spring from somewhere else, and cannot, of course, know how the natives feel about spring. And so the first thing they know the opportunity to inquire how they feel has permanently gone by. Old Probabilities has a mighty reputation for accurate prophecy, and thoroughly well deserves it. You take up the paper and observe how crisply and confidently he checks off what to-day's weather is going to be on the Pacific, down South, in the Middle States, in the Wisconsin region. See him sail along in the joy and pride of his power till he gets to New England, and then see his tail drop. *He* doesn't know what the weather is going to be in New England. Well, he mulls over it, and by and by he gets out something about like this: Probable northeast to southwest winds, varying to the southward and westward and eastward, and points between, high and low barometer swapping around from place to place; probable areas of rain, snow, hail, and drought, succeeded or preceded by earthquakes, with thunder and lightning. Then he jots down this postscript from his wandering mind, to cover accidents: "But it is possible that the programme may be wholly changed in the mean time." Yes, one of the brightest gems in the New England weather is the dazzling uncertainty of it. There is only one thing certain about it: you are certain there is going to be plenty of it—a perfect grand review; but you never can tell which end of the procession is going to move first. You fix up for the drought; you leave your umbrella in the house and sally out, and two to one you get drowned. You make up your mind that the earthquake is due; you stand from under, and take hold of something to steady yourself, and the first thing you know you get struck by lightning. These are great disappointments; but they can't be helped. The lightning there is peculiar; it is so convincing, that when it strikes a thing it doesn't leave enough of that thing behind for you to tell whether —Well you'd think it was something valuable, and a Congressman had been there. And the thunder. When the thunder begins to merely tune up and scrape and saw, and key up the instruments for the performance, strangers say, "Why, what awful thunder you have here!" But when the baton is raised and the real concert begins, you'll find that stranger down in the cellar with his head in the ash-barrel. Now as to the *size* of the weather in New England—lengthways, I mean. It is utterly disproportioned to the size of that little country. Half the time, when it is packed as full as it can stick, you will see that New England weather sticking out beyond the edges and projecting around hundreds and hundreds of miles over the neighboring States. She can't hold a tenth part of her weather. You can see cracks all about where she has strained herself trying to do it. I could speak volumes about the inhuman perversity of the New England weather, but I will give but a single specimen. I like to hear rain on a tin roof. So I covered part of my roof with tin, with an eye to that luxury. Well, sir, do you think it ever rains on that tin? No, sir; skips it every time. Mind, in this speech I have been trying merely to do honor to the New England weather—no language could do it justice. But, after all, there is at least one or two things about that weather (or, if you please, effects produced by it) which we residents would not like to part with. If we hadn't our bewitching autumn foliage, we should still have to credit the weather with one feature which compensates for all its bullying vagaries—the ice-storm: when a leafless tree is clothed with ice from the bottom to the top—ice that is as bright and clear as crystal; when every bough and twig is strung with ice-beads, frozen dewdrops, and the whole tree sparkles cold and white, like the Shah of Persia's diamond plume. Then the wind waves the branches and the sun comes out and turns all those myriads of beads and drops to prisms that glow and burn and flash with all manner of colored fires, which change and change again with inconceivable rapidity from blue to red, from red to green, and green to gold—the tree becomes a spraying fountain, a very explosion of dazzling jewels; and it stands there the acme, the climax, the supremest possibility in art or nature, of bewildering, intoxicating, intolerable magnificence. One cannot make the words too strong.

"Speech on the Weather" was given at the New England Society's seventy-first annual dinner, in New York City on December 22, 1876. (From *The Family Mark Twain*, New York: Harper & Row, 1975.)

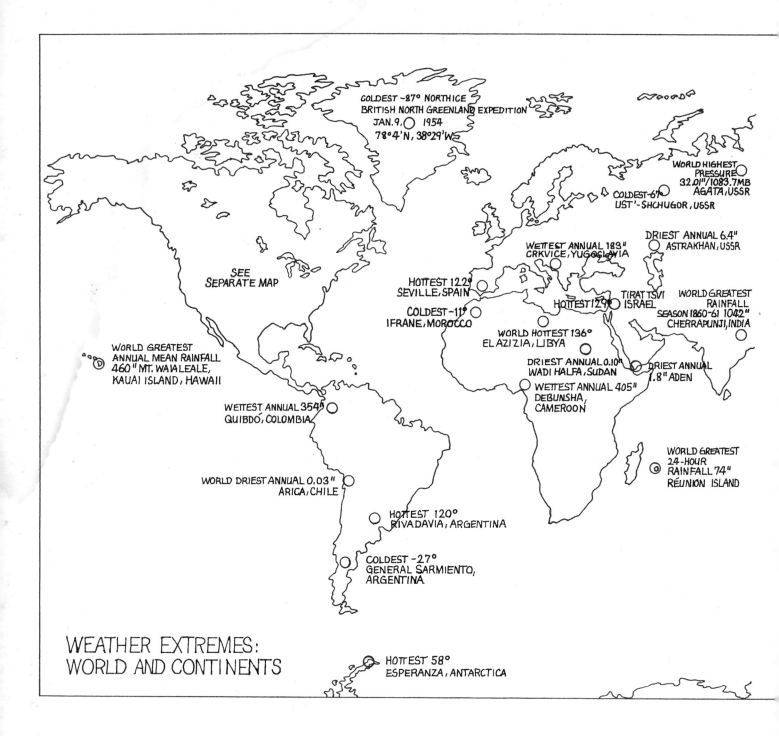

WEATHER EXTREMES:
WORLD AND CONTINENTS

Map labels:

COLDEST ~87° NORTH ICE
BRITISH NORTH GREENLAND EXPEDITION
JAN. 9, 1954
78°4'N, 38°29'W

WORLD HIGHEST
PRESSURE
32.01"/1083.7MB
AGATA, USSR

COLDEST -6°
UST'-SHCHUGOR, USSR

DRIEST ANNUAL 6.4"
ASTRAKHAN, USSR

WETTEST ANNUAL 183"
CRKVICE, YUGOSLAVIA

HOTTEST 122°
SEVILLE, SPAIN

HOTTEST 129°

TIRAT TSVI
ISRAEL

WORLD GREATEST
RAINFALL
SEASON 1860-61 1042"
CHERRAPUNJI, INDIA

COLDEST -11°
IFRANE, MOROCCO

WORLD HOTTEST 136°
EL AZIZIA, LIBYA

DRIEST ANNUAL 0.10"
WADI HALFA, SUDAN

DRIEST ANNUAL
1.8" ADEN

WORLD GREATEST
ANNUAL MEAN RAINFALL
460" MT. WAIALEALE,
KAUAI ISLAND, HAWAII

WETTEST ANNUAL 405"
DEBUNSHA,
CAMEROON

WETTEST ANNUAL 354"
QUIBDO, COLOMBIA

WORLD GREATEST
24-HOUR
RAINFALL 74"
RÉUNION ISLAND

SEE
SEPARATE MAP

WORLD DRIEST ANNUAL 0.03"
ARICA, CHILE

HOTTEST 120°
RIVADAVIA, ARGENTINA

COLDEST -27°
GENERAL SARMIENTO,
ARGENTINA

HOTTEST 58°
ESPERANZA, ANTARCTICA

WEATHER EXTREMES: THE WORLD, NORTH AMERICA, AND NEW ENGLAND

× 48-STATE HIGHEST PRESSURE
31.40"/1063.3MB HELENA, MONT.

+ 48-STATE COLDEST -69.7°
ROGERS PASS, MONT.

GREENLAND COLDEST -87° NORTHICE
BRITISH NORTH GREENLAND EXPEDITION
JAN. 9, 1954
78°4'N, 38°29'W

ALASKA COLDEST -79.8°
ENDICOTT MOUNTAINS

ALASKA HOTTEST - 100° FORT YUKON
CANADA HIGHEST PRESSURE
31.535"/1067.9MB
MAYO LANDING, Y.T.

CANADA COLDEST
-81° SNAG, Y.T.

CANADA WETTEST 262"
HENDERSON LAKE, B.C.
WORLD GREATEST SNOWFALL
SEASON 1971-72
1122" MT. RAINIER, WASH.
U.S. GREATEST SINGLE STORM SNOWFALL
189" MT. SHASTA, CALIF.
U.S. HOTTEST 134°
DEATH VALLEY, CALIF.
U.S. DRIEST 1.63"
DEATH VALLEY, CALIF.

CANADA HOTTEST 113°
MIDALE AND
YELLOW GRASS, SASK.
⊗
⊕
U.S. 42-MINUTE
RAINFALL
12.00" HOLT, MO.

U.S. GREATEST
24-HOUR SNOWFALL
76" SILVER LAKE, COLO.

MEXICO DRIEST
1.2" BATEQUES

CANADA LOWEST PRESSURE
27.94"/946.3 MB
GANDER, NFLD.

U.S. FASTEST 5-MINUTE WIND
188 MPH
MT. WASHINGTON, N.H.

U.S. 1-MINUTE RAINFALL
1.23"
UNIONVILLE, MD.

U.S. GREATEST 24-HOUR
RAINFALL 38.70"
YANKEETOWN, FLA.

U.S. LOWEST PRESSURE
26.35"/892.3MB
MATECUMBE KEY, FLA.

COLDEST -90°
VERKHOYANSK AND
OIMEKON, USSR

WORLD LOWEST PRESSURE
TYPHOON IDA SEPT. 24, 1958
U.S. AIR FORCE
25.90"/877.1 MB
19°N, 135°E

HOTTEST 128°
CLONCURRY, QUEENSLAND
DRIEST ANNUAL
4.05" MULKA,
SOUTH AUSTRALIA
COLDEST -8°
CHARLOTTE PASS,
NEW SOUTH WALES

WETTEST ANNUAL
179" TULLY,
QUEENSLAND

WORLD COLDEST -127° VOSTOK, ANTARCTICA
78°27'S, 106°52'E

MAINE COLDEST -48°
VAN BUREN JAN. 19, 1925

WORST FOREST WINDFALL
ALLAGASH, AUG. 15, 1958

(MT. WASHINGTON DATA
NOT INCLUDED)

WORST DOWN EAST BLIZZARD
DEC. 30-31, 1962

N.H. COLDEST -46° PITTSBURG
JAN. 28, 1925

COLDEST MONTH -0.8° JAN., 1970
COLDEST ANNUAL MEAN 37.3°
FIRST CONNECTICUT LAKE, N.H.

NEW ENGLAND COLDEST
-50° BLOOMFIELD, VT.
DEC. 30, 1933

SNOWIEST 24 HOURS
56" RANDOLPH, N.H.
NOV. 22-23, 1943

WORST DROUGHT-FIRE HOLOCAUST
BAR HARBOR OCT., 1947

HIGHEST PRESSURE 31.14/10545MB
NORTHFIELD, VT. JAN. 31, 1920

SNOWIEST PINKHAM NOTCH, N.H.
STORM 77" FEB. 24-28, 1969
MONTH 130" FEB., 1969
SEASON 323" 1968-69

GREATEST FREEZE-UP
ALL HARBORS FROZEN JAN.-FEB., 1780

DEADLIEST FLOOD
NOV. 3-4, 1927

MOST WIDESPREAD
ALL-NEW ENGLAND FLOOD MARCH, 1936

WORST BLIZZARD MARCH 12-13, 1888

GREATEST 24-HOUR RAINFALL
18.15" WESTFIELD, MASS. AUG. 18-19, 1955

WETTEST YEAR 78.53"
BURLINGTON DAM, 1955

DEADLIEST
TORNADO
JUNE 9, 1953

HOTTEST MONTH 78.6° LOWELL, MASS., JULY, 1955

NEW ENGLAND HOTTEST 107°
CHESTER AND NEW BEDFORD, MASS.
AUG. 2, 1975

WETTEST MONTH 27.70"
TORRINGTON, CONN. AUG., 1955

MOST COSTLY FLOOD
HURRICANE DIANE
AUG. 18-19, 1955

DRIEST YEAR 21.76"
CHATHAM, MASS., 1965

WARMEST ANNUAL MEAN 51.9°
BRIDGEPORT, CONN.

DEADLIEST HURRICANE TIDE
RHODE ISLAND SEPT. 21, 1938

LOWEST PRESSURE 28.04"/949.5 MB
HARTFORD, CONN. SEPT. 21, 1938

I

The Dazzling Uncertainty of It

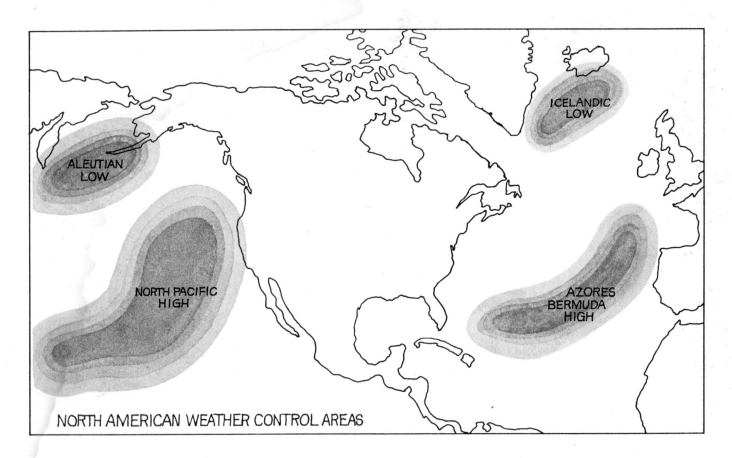

NORTH AMERICAN WEATHER CONTROL AREAS

CHAPTER 1
Origins of New England Weather

New England weather brings daily frustration to those who have to cope with its intricacies. Mark Twain once discerned 136 varieties in one day, but not being a scientist, he greatly underestimated the true situation. Even the modern computer has not been programmed to comprehend the full scope of the region's weather possibilities. The complexity of atmospheric behavior over the six states is probably the reason why no book on the subject exists. Although Yankees talk constantly about the weather, none has had the temerity to write at length about it. So may my human presumption in attempting to present a summary of New England meteorology in such short compass be tolerated until a mechanical brain is prepared to do so.

The General Circulation

New England may be viewed as a vast meteorological mixing bowl where diverse air currents converge and concoct atmospheric situations as varied as tossed salads.

The airstreams meeting over New England and creating local weather have their origins many hundreds and even thousands of miles from the six-state area. They may be conditioned over the arctic tundra of Canada, the cool waters of the North Pacific Ocean, the desert lands of the American Southwest and Mexico, the warm waters of the Gulf of Mexico and tropical parts of the North Atlantic Ocean, or the vast reaches of the cool, subpolar seas.

An airstream's content is known as an air mass in its source region where it acquires distinctive qualities and becomes rather homogeneous at equal elevations in its lateral extent. Air masses may rest many days undisturbed in their source regions until the general circulation of the upper-air currents causes the mass to flow off on a journey that may be hemispheric in extent.

Along its path of hundreds of miles to New England, the qualities of an airstream are usually modified by the varying surfaces traversed and by mixing with other airstreams along the way. Those airstreams with short trajectories traveling over uniform terrain will undergo little modification, while others moving from snow-covered to bare ground or from ocean to land surface will experience major changes. The direction from which an airstream arrives in New England is most important, since it gives an obvious clue to its probable origin and likely characteristics.

Controlling High- and Low-Pressure Centers

On a typical weather map of the Northern Hemisphere two large ridges of high pressure are usually found over the middle latitudes of the Pacific and Atlantic oceans, with an arm of each often adjacent to a coastline of the United States. These semipermanent anticyclonic structures are of considerable depth and horizontal extent and are the dominating features on most surface and upper-air weather charts.

The Pacific High occupies a changing position in the area roughly north and northeast of the Hawaiian Islands covering millions of square miles. The weather crossing the Pacific Ocean, made up of upper-air jet streams and traveling cyclonic disturbances, is steered around the northern periphery of the Pacific anticyclone. The location and strength of the northeastern arm of the Pacific High determines the latitude of entry into North America of all storm systems that cross the Pacific from Japan and Siberia.

In the Atlantic Ocean there is a similar high-pressure feature, but on a smaller scale. It stretches from near the Middle Atlantic coast of the United States, across the ocean in the latitudes of Bermuda and the Azores, toward the coast of Spain. It is known as the Azores High, and its western extension, which affects North American weather, is known as the Bermuda High. It is a migratory body whose shifts northward and southward and extensions eastward and westward determine the tracks pursued by storm centers moving across the eastern United States.

As complements to the oceanic semipermanent high-pressure ridges, there are two major areas of low pressure where semipermanent trough conditions persist at the surface and aloft most of the year. They have great influence on the development and energy of most storm systems moving across the temperate and arctic regions of the hemisphere.

The Aleutian Low occupies a shifting position in the North Pacific Ocean close to the mainlands of Siberia and Alaska where the proximity of cold airstreams from the Arctic and mild airstreams from the tropics mingle and produce a center of maximum storminess. The Aleutian Low is the great storm factory of the world. From time to time, impulses of low pressure—discernible as troughs in the upper-air flow and as cyclonic centers at the surface, separate from the main body and move eastward across the entire continent. They may come as a family of four or five disturbances and affect the weather across North America for a fortnight.

The Icelandic Low, well to the northeast of New England, serves as a storm magnet and attracts traveling disturbances moving off the North American continent. When its position is southwest of normal, near Newfoundland, it exerts a very important influence on the atmospheric circulation over New England and eastern Canada by intensifying offshore storm centers and prolonging periods of northerly gales.

The position and strength of the semipermanent pressure complexes determine the course and speed that surface anticyclones and cyclones will take across the continent, whether they will pass north or south of New England, and whether the region will be dominated by polar air or tropical air or by a modification of each.

3

Air flow at 10,000 feet during west-east flow pattern

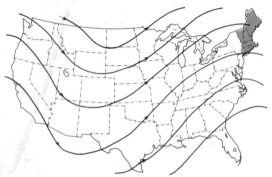

Air flow at 10,000 feet during western trough–eastern ridge pattern

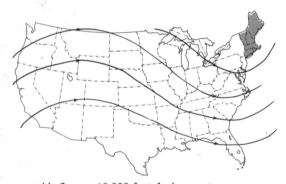

Air flow at 10,000 feet during western ridge–eastern trough pattern

National Weather Map Patterns

When major troughs and ridges in the upper-air flow are absent, a straight west-flow pattern exists across the country with winds blowing roughly along the lines of latitude, varying from west-southwest to west-northwest. The jet stream speeds across central Canada, and weather systems are carried rapidly eastward on their most northerly track across central and southern Canada. This fast air flow hurries them on their way, normally taking about three days for the transcontinental passage. The source region of the original air flow is the North Pacific Ocean, which imparts its qualities of coolness and wetness to the air masses. Most of the moisture is lost in the ascent of the Pacific Coast Ranges and in crossing the elevated plateau, and the air flow is warmed in its descent of the Rocky Mountains, emerging on the Great Plains as mild, dry airstreams. In the central valley of the midcontinent the westerly airstream may mix briefly with polar or tropical streams, but the flow from these regions is quickly cut off by a renewal of the westerly flow as another pressure impulse moves eastward. The modified air mass may travel as far as the Atlantic coast, bringing mild, rather dry conditions as far as New England.

Successive northerly and southerly air flow may be expected when a western trough–eastern ridge pattern prevails. This alignment's feature is a marked north-south trough of low pressure extending from the Arctic—in a position to the west of the Great Plains over either the Rocky Mountains, the intermountain region, or the Pacific coast. To the east of the Mississippi Valley, a large ridge of high pressure stretches with its crest over the Appalachian Mountains or the Atlantic states. This arrangement of the upper-air contours permits a strong persistent flow along the meridians with northwest to north winds sweeping from the polar regions into the western trough, and southwest to south winds from the tropics into the western side of the eastern ridge. Cold weather then is the rule in the West and warm conditions prevail in the East.

Under the western trough–eastern ridge pattern, storms move into British Columbia and Washington and then travel southeast to Colorado, where they regenerate east of the Rocky Mountains and recurve northeastward. When conditions permit a moist airstream from the Gulf of Mexico to be drawn into the circulation, the storms may become good rain and snow producers over the Midwest, the Great Lakes region, and most of New England.

Wind flow directions are reversed across the country when a western ridge–eastern trough arrangement is present. This places a strong ridge of high pressure over the intermountain and Rocky Mountain regions with a low-pressure axis running north and south to the east of the Mississippi River, either along the western slope of the Appalachians or the Atlantic coastal plain. Storms from the Gulf of Alaska move into western Canada. After being steered around the northern periphery of the western ridge, they are carried by the northwest flow aloft into the northern plains and Great Lakes region, often accompanied by a fresh outbreak of cold polar air from northern Canada but with light precipitation. As the upper trough accompanying these reaches the Appalachian Mountains and the Atlantic coast, the following cold air may clash with the tropical air over the Gulf Stream and storm development may take place along the coast from Florida to the Carolinas. The secondary centers move northeastward with driving snow in winter and pelting rain the rest of the year—the famous northeasters of the North Atlantic seaboard. When the storm track passes just offshore, cold air from central Canada is drawn southeastward in the wake of the storm, and the New England states experience some of their severest cold waves in wintertime and refreshing cool spells in summer.

When the length of the waves in the upper-air flow shorten, a western ridge–central trough–eastern ridge pattern appears on the weather maps. It features a well-defined low-pressure axis running south or southwestward from the Hudson Bay region through the Mississippi Valley to Texas and Mexico. There are equally prominent ridges of high pressure to the east along the Atlantic seaboard and to the west over the plateau and Pacific seaboard. The north and south transport of air masses causes sharp contrasts in the central United States. Storm systems move from the Pacific Ocean around the western ridge across Alberta and Saskatchewan, down the northern plains and upper Midwest, and then head eastward or northeastward over the Great Lakes and down the Saint Lawrence Valley. A feature of this type is the tendency of secondaries to form in the southern end of the trough, either in the Texas Panhandle or even in the western Gulf of Mexico, at the same time the primary center is passing over the Great Lakes. The secondary centers move rapidly northeastward along a front separating very cold polar air from very warm tropical air. Heavy precipitation often results, and the eastern United States may experience its most turbulent weather.

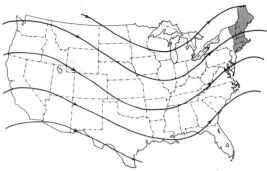

Air flow at 10,000 feet during western ridge–central trough–eastern ridge pattern

Directional Wind Flow

Northwest. The early colonists from England were much impressed with the northwester, since winds from that direction in their homeland had very different characteristics. Here, central and northern Canada—not the North Atlantic—are the home of air masses borne by northwest winds to New England. Characterized by coldness and lack of moisture, Canadian airstreams are drawn southeastward when the circulation pattern is favorable and reach New England with wind flow from north through west according to the weather map situation. Northwest is the most frequent direction, and wintertime is the season when polar air and even arctic air are most prominent on the New England scene. After a storm center passes and the cold front sweeps through, the wind usually shifts abruptly to the northwest; it may become blustery for a while with brief snow or rain showers, and then skies clear and the temperature tumbles ten or twenty degrees or more. A high-pressure system usually moves southeastward, bringing a period of fair weather. The coldest temperatures occur when the center of the high-pressure area is about overhead. Winds subside and the sky remains free of clouds at nighttime. These conditions enable the surface of the ground to radiate heat to outer space and, in turn, cool the layer of air nearest the ground so that its original coldness is reinforced locally by the radiational cooling. If the surface is snow covered, radiation will be at a maximum and temperatures will reach their lowest depths. In summertime, the northwest air flow from a cool, dry source region brings a welcome change from a heat wave or relief from a sultry period, and the combined drop in temperature and humidity brings the comfort index down to bearable levels. In the spring or fall, the arrival of a northwester is a sign to look out for a frost in a night or two.

Southwest. The American Indians thought their Great Spirit resided somewhere in the southwest, since it was from this direction that warming influences most frequently reached them. A southwesterly flow in New England bears air that has been conditioned by a long traverse over land, either from the distant plains and deserts of the Southwest or from the waters of the Gulf of Mexico. From the first source region, the air may still be quite dry when it reaches New England; but air from the second source region often carries a high moisture content. Southwest flow usually follows the passage of the center of a high-pressure area when winds either shift from an easterly direction or back from a northerly direction. It is accompanied by a falling barometer, a gradual warming trend, and rather pleasant conditions. If the southwest flow continues for a number of hours, clouds will soon appear, moving from the west at high levels; they will lower and thicken, and a period of unsettled weather is usually in the offing. If winds shift more to the south, it is usually a sign that a frontal system is approaching from the west and wet weather may be in store. If the shift is to the northwest, it may mean that a dry front has passed through and the weather will take a turn for the better.

Southeast. The true ocean wind from the southeast brings the influences of the sea far into the interior of New England. Its duration may be quite short, as when the light southeast zephyrs blow on the backside of an eastward-moving anticyclone. At other times the southeast wind may be a temporary sea breeze arising in the middle hours of the day and continuing until late afternoon or evening. When these conditions prevail, there is always the possibility of foggy conditions along the immediate shoreline. The southeast wind becomes the bearer of really thick weather when it is part of a low-pressure system moving from the Ohio Valley northeastward across New York State and northern New England. Then the airstream has a long, circular trajectory over the ocean from as far away as Bermuda, the Bahamas, or the southeast Atlantic coast, where the widening Gulf Stream imparts its characteristics to the atmosphere above. A strong southeaster can be a peril to coastal shipping and shore installations and may bring drenching rains that cause streams and rivers to flood within a few hours. The most damaging winds—hurricanes moving northward over central New England—come from a massive southeast flow accompanying the close passage of a center. This is what occurred in the great hurricanes of 1815, 1938, and 1954.

Northeast. Gov. John Winthrop was quick to learn a fundamental rule of New England weather. After only two years in Boston, he wrote in his journal, "When the wind sets in from the east, you can expect rain or snow in great abundance." Most of the region's memorable snowstorms are northeasters, resulting from a coastal storm passing either near or over Cape Cod and adjacent waters. The six-state area is then subject to a flow of moist, cool air from a source over the Atlantic provinces of eastern Canada or the adjacent offshore waters near Newfoundland. Heavy snows in winter and heavy rains in the warm season can be expected with a continued flow of cyclonically curving northeast winds. Another type of northeast flow has a different character, since the winds are diverging from a high-pressure area over Quebec and Labrador and have a very short sea trajectory, if any. These are called dry northeasters. Usually their duration is no more than a day, since the anticyclonic center moves on eastward and the flow contours change. If a dry northeast flow continues longer, it may indicate low pressure to the southward, in which case a storm circulation may develop, changing the dry flow to wet as winds converge around an increasing low-pressure center. Northeast to east winds, even if of local origin, must be watched at any time, especially along the Maine and Cape Cod coasts, since they can bring offshore fog banks over the land in a matter of minutes. New England's unique "backdoor cold fronts," which bring cool air southwestward along the coastline, are propelled by northeast winds blowing out of high pressure building over eastern Canada.

Local Atmospheric Behavior

HORIZONTAL COMPONENT

Airstreams moving across the varied terrain of the United States seldom flow in a straight line; they either converge inward or diverge outward according to the prevailing pressure pattern. If the deviation from straight-line flow is sufficient, the airstream tends to undergo certain physical changes. Wind circulation around a low-pressure system has

6

cyclonic curvature; that is, it is converging inward with the path of its air particles moving counterclockwise and spiraling inward around the center of lowest pressure. This produces a crowding of the air particles and their only escape route from the increasing sideward pressure is upward. The rising air cools through expansion. If the air column rises to a sufficient height and cools to its dew point, or condensation temperature, its moisture will condense, clouds will form, and precipitation may result.

Divergence is a process associated with high-pressure systems whose air circulation tends to flow outward from the center of highest pressure in a clockwise fashion. This is called anticyclonic curvature. The spreading out of the air lessens the pressure between air particles, permitting air from above to move downward. The descending air is warmed by compression, which creates a stable condition in the lower atmosphere. Warming enables the air to hold additional moisture in the invisible water vapor state. Descending air inhibits cloud formation and tends to produce fair weather conditions.

An important consideration in an airstream of polar or tropical origin is the vertical distribution of temperature; that is, the rate of increase or decrease brought on by changing altitude. If the decrease upward is sharp, the air will tend to become unstable. Heating of the surface of an unstable air mass causes the lowest layer to expand. Since it weighs less per unit volume than the cool air above, it becomes buoyant and rises like a balloon filled with hot air. This rising air column creates turbulence in the otherwise stable air, and when the bubble of air has risen sufficiently to cool to its dew point, a small, cumulus-type cloud will form. These clouds can spread over the entire sky, turning a clear day into one that is mostly overcast. If the rising air has enough thermal energy to continue its ascent, the cloud thickens vertically into a swelling cumulus, from which raindrops or snowflakes may fall. In summertime, when great heat energy is present, unstable air may continue its vertical ascent to great altitudes and produce the towering cumulonimbus, or thunderstorm cloud. So a heavy shower or even a hailstorm with thunder and lightning can result from a small amount of surface heating when a moist air mass is affected by a marked decrease of temperature as it gains altitude.

Unstable conditions can also develop when a moving airstream meets a barrier in the form of mountains or another air mass containing colder or denser air. Fresh polar airstreams moving southeastward over the Green and White mountains often become unstable and develop vertical currents that lead to local rain or snow showers. The same thing happens when a warm, moist air mass from the southwest or southeast meets the small barrier posed by the inland hills of Connecticut and Massachusetts. Some of the region's heaviest rainfalls have occurred over these relatively low elevations—the result of lifting a tropical air mass only a few hundred feet.

Stable air tends to prolong the type of weather currently prevailing. Under such conditions the temperature change—even with increasing altitude—is relatively small; the buoyant energy required to produce vertical convective currents is not available. In fact, there may be descending or subsiding air as occurs in a typical anticyclone. Stable air conditions can be significant during a long-continued period of anticyclonic weather, when the presence of warm air aloft over cool air at the surface puts an effective lid over the lower atmosphere, trapping impurities there. This is called a temperature inversion. Without any vertical motion to vent air impurities upward, dust, smoke, and particulate matter collect in the lower atmosphere, causing pollution. This pollution or smog will usually continue until a new airstream of fresh air arrives, destroys the inversion, and introduces a period of unstable conditions.

VERTICAL COMPONENT

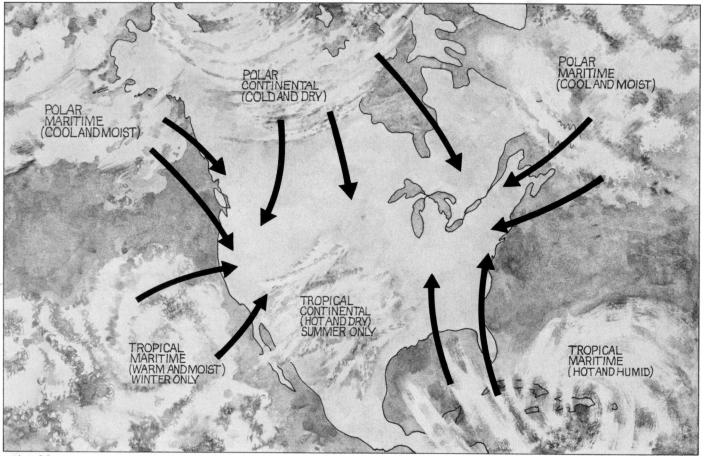

AIR MASSES

An air mass is defined as a large body of air possessing generally similar qualities of heat, moisture, and stability at equal elevations above the surface of the earth. Throughout the air mass, horizontally, one would find nearly identical temperatures, humidities, and cloud conditions. In certain regions of our hemisphere, such as the frozen tundra of northwest Canada, the vast ocean stretches of the Atlantic and Pacific oceans, and the tropical waters of the Gulf of Mexico, air tends to stagnate for days at a time. Like giant air conditioners, these regions impart their native conditions of temperature and moisture to the air above. Weathermen describe these as source regions, and they can usually be identified on a weather map by the persistence of high pressure for several days in a row. In fact, air masses—at their birth and during their early travels—are usually closely associated with anticyclonic conditions. Later in their journeys they may become greatly modified by moving over varied terrain and by mixing with other air masses in a cyclonic situation.

AIR MASS WEATHER

TYPE	SOURCE REGION	PROPERTIES IN SOURCE	SEASON IN NEW ENGLAND	PROPERTIES IN NEW ENGLAND	WEATHER IN NEW ENGLAND
Arctic	Northern Canada	Very cold, very dry	Infrequent, only in cold outbreaks	Very cold, dry	Fair skies, attends extreme cold waves; produces "sea smoke" when passing over coastal waters
Polar Continental	Northern or central Canada	Cold, dry	Frequent all seasons	Cold for season, usually dry, but may be unstable	Nights clear and cold; daytime cumulus, sometimes with snow or rain showers over mountains
Polar Maritime Pacific	North Pacific south of Alaska	Cool, moist	Infrequent, mainly spring or fall	Modified, usually mild and dry	Mostly fair skies; cool at night, moderate daytime
Polar Maritime Atlantic	Northwest Atlantic Ocean	Cool, moist	Occasional, any season, mainly spring and early summer	Cool, moist all seasons	Low clouds, fog, drizzle on coast; when overrun by Maritime Tropical in northeasters, steady rain or snow develops
Tropical Maritime Atlantic	Gulf of Mexico, Caribbean Sea, adjacent Atlantic	Warm, humid	Frequent all seasons	Warm for season; copious moisture	Low clouds on coast with fog and drizzle; broken clouds inland, fog at night, especially if snow cover; often convective or frontal shower in warm season
Tropical Continental	Southwest U.S. and north Mexico	Very hot, very dry	Infrequent, only in hottest summers	Hot, dry	Fair, hazy skies; attends extreme heat waves

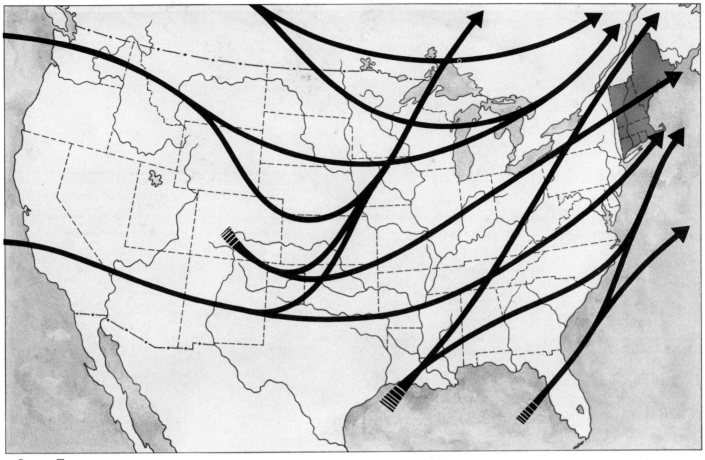

STORM TRACKS

There are three regions in North America where contrasting air masses regularly meet and where storm generation is frequent. The Gulf of Alaska is the home of the semipermanent Aleutian low-pressure area, where cold airstreams from Siberia, Alaska, and Canada mingle with warm air flowing from the central Pacific Ocean. Here is the greatest "storm factory" of the world, where cyclonic activity is at a maximum. The second region, an extension of this Aleutian low-pressure area, runs eastward across British Columbia and southeastward along the crest of the Rocky Mountains. New storm circulations may form at any place along this extensive frontal zone, or old centers moving eastward from the Pacific Ocean may regenerate into active disturbances. Colorado, in the lee of the Rocky Mountains, is the site of frequent cyclogenesis in the cooler months of the year.

A third region favorable for storm generation extends in a sweeping arc from northwest Texas, across the Gulf of Mexico, to the Atlantic Ocean off the Carolinas and Georgia. Tropical air in this region—either from the Gulf of Mexico, the Caribbean, or the North Atlantic—is poised to compete with any outbreak of polar air seeking to invade the tropical seas.

The presence of the jet stream aloft over a cyclogenetic area often contributes to the formation of a low-pressure center. Weathermen keep a close check on its presence and behavior in order to anticipate storm development.

STORM TRACK WEATHER

AREA OF ORIGIN	SEASON	SPEED	PATH NEAR NEW ENGLAND	ASSOCIATED WEATHER IN NEW ENGLAND
Alberta	Frequent all year	Steady travelers; strong westerlies aloft	Well to north	No warm front; preceded by high clouds, low cloud area narrow; light rain or snow; quick clearing
North Pacific	Only in colder months; often in series	Steady travelers	To north with trailing front	Often occluded front only; attended by rain or snow showers
South Pacific	Similar to Texas type			
North Rockies	Similar to North Pacific type			
Colorado	All seasons; mainly cold months	Slow movers at first; then faster on NE track; SW flow aloft	Over Great Lakes, St. Lawrence Valley; secondaries from Ohio may pass over New England	Extensive cloud area; moderate rain producers; warm spell precedes, cold outbreak follows
Texas and West Gulf	Cold months only	Fast movers on NE track; South flow aloft	Close to or over; secondaries form on coast	Good rain or snow producers; extended storm period
East Gulf and South Atlantic	Cold months mainly	Fast movers along coast; occasionally blocked; SSE flow aloft	Mainly vicinity of Cape Cod or eastward	Northeaster with rain or snow, high winds
Tropical	June through November	Speed varies; SSE flow aloft	Usually over or close to coast-line	Can be violent with hurricane force; usually good rain producers with high winds or gales

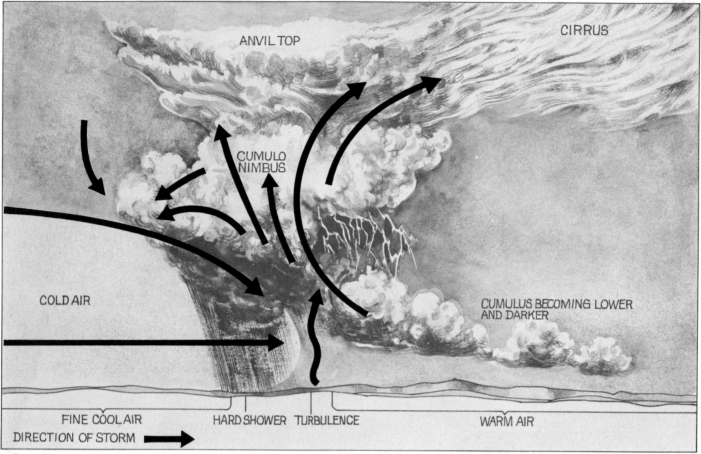

ANVIL TOP

CIRRUS

CUMULO NIMBUS

COLD AIR

CUMULUS BECOMING LOWER AND DARKER

FINE COOL AIR

HARD SHOWER TURBULENCE

WARM AIR

DIRECTION OF STORM →

COLD FRONT

Since a cold front provides the most spectacular action in a low-pressure system, it is the feature of the weather map that must be kept under constant watch by the weather forecaster. The arrival of a cold front in an area not only brings turbulent conditions, but also introduces a complete change of air mass. The cold front's passage signals the concluding phase of cyclonic weather controls and the introduction of anticyclonic or high-pressure controls.

The cold front is the leading edge of a cool or cold air mass that is actively on the move. What furnishes the front's dynamic

energy is cold air—usually consisting of fresh polar or even arctic air from Canada or, less frequently, North Pacific air greatly modified by a transcontinental journey.

No two cold fronts have the same structure or behave in the same manner. Some are active, others create little change. Some are fast moving, others sluggish or even stationary. Some slope steeply to considerable heights, others are shallow with gradual slopes. The characteristics of a cold front may vary from hour to hour or day to day.

COLD FRONT WEATHER

	TEMPER-ATURE	HUMIDITY	BAROMETER	WIND	CEILING & VISIBILITY	WEATHER IN NEW ENGLAND
Pre-frontal	Gradual rise	Gradual rise	Gradual fall	Increasing steadily; gradual veer from SE or S to S or SW	Lowering	Increasing upper and middle clouds
At Passage	Marked drop	Increase; then gradual fall	Fall, then abrupt rise	Gusty with shift to W or NW	Very low; sometimes zero	Low clouds, showers, and thunder in summer; brief rain or snow showers in winter
Post-frontal	Gradual fall	Gradual fall	Rising, then steady	Strong then decreasing, steady from W or NW	Quick improvement	Clearing, unless air very unstable, then continued showers

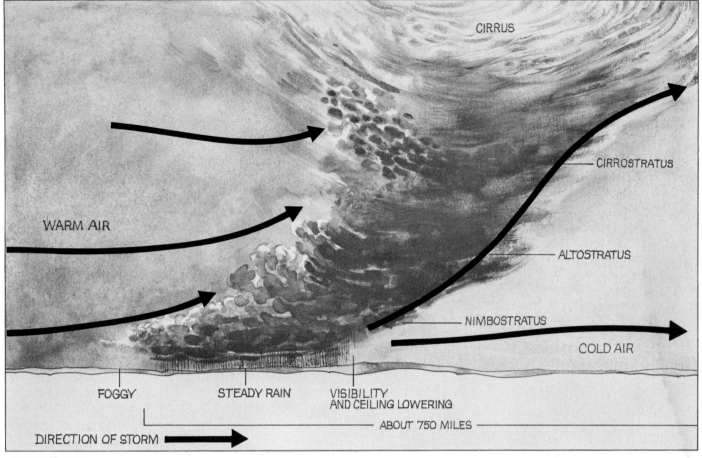

CIRRUS

CIRROSTRATUS

ALTOSTRATUS

WARM AIR

NIMBOSTRATUS

COLD AIR

FOGGY STEADY RAIN VISIBILITY AND CEILING LOWERING

ABOUT 750 MILES

DIRECTION OF STORM

WARM FRONT

The approach of a warm front is a subtle performance, with weather changes coming more gradually than they do with the bustling cold front. A warm front heralds the end of settled conditions and the beginning of an unsettled period when moisture, cloudiness, and precipitation may prevail. Since it marks the commencement of cyclonic controls of the weather, its approach is an important event in the production of local weather conditions.

A warm front is the leading edge of an advancing warm air mass that is displacing a cooler or colder air mass. Since warm air is lighter than cold air, it tends to glide up over the wedge of cold air hugging the surface. While the forward elements aloft speed ahead two or three hundred miles, the main body of the warm air continues to advance along the surface at a slower pace.

The first sign of an approaching warm front appears on the southwest to northwest horizon in the form of cirrus cloud streamers at elevations of six miles or more. These climb to the zenith and in a couple of hours may cover almost the entire sky. Frozen ice crystals composing the cirrus cloud indicate that moist air is arriving on the scene. The cloud sheet gradually thickens and lowers, and middle clouds appear in a few hours. The warm front is the principal rain producer in New England during the cooler season. Since its behavior does not always follow the textbook description, the timing of the onset of precipitation is most difficult to forecast.

WARM FRONT WEATHER

	TEMPER-ATURE	HUMIDITY	BAROMETER	WIND	CEILING & VISIBILITY	WEATHER IN NEW ENGLAND
Pre-frontal	Steady or gradual rise	Gradual rise	Falling slowly	Light, but increasing, veering from NE or SE to SE or S	Lowering	Increasing clouds, first upper then middle, then steady rain with lowering clouds
At Passage	Quick rise	Marked rise	Unsteady	Sometimes gusty, gradual shift to S or SW	Poor, often near zero	Rain ending, often foggy
Post-frontal	Gradual rise or no change	Gradual rise	Steady or falling slowly	Steady from S or SW	Improvement, but usually restricted	Clouds break, sometimes complete clearing; warm and humid for season

CHAPTER 2
New England Weather Month by Month

JANUARY

"As the days lengthen, the cold strengthens"; so goes the old and true proverb. From the southern point of the winter solstice, the sun will climb six degrees higher in the sky and the daylight lengthen by fifty-one minutes by the end of January in central New England. But the thermometer appears reluctant to respond to the increasing solar altitude. During the final week of the month temperatures in most northern sections continue downward to reach the lowest daily means; not until the first week of February does this occur at most southern locations.

The winter-type circulation pattern across North America reaches fullest development in January. The westerly jet stream is found at its most southerly location by the month's end, often dipping as far south as the northern shore of the Gulf of Mexico before trending northeastward toward the Middle Atlantic coast. Storminess is usually at a maximum just north of the path of the jet stream.

The main January storm tracks from the West converge on the Great Lakes from Alberta, Colorado, and Texas, then head east-northeast down the Saint Lawrence Valley, passing into the North Atlantic over southern Labrador or Newfoundland. Another well-traveled storm track is along the Atlantic coast, leading either from the western Gulf of Mexico or from the warm Gulf Stream waters north of the Bahamas to a meeting point near Cape Hatteras. The path then leads northeastward —100 to 200 miles off the New England shore—to the vicinity of Newfoundland.

High pressure favors cold land surfaces and shuns relatively warm bodies of water such as the Great Lakes. This factor divides January anticyclones reaching New England into two types: those originating in the Canadian Northwest and passing east-southeastward between Hudson Bay and Lake Superior; and those traveling southeastward into the Dakotas and then swinging in a gentle curve through the middle Mississippi Valley and the Ohio Valley before heading northeastward over the Middle Atlantic states. The first track usually brings the severest cold to New England, since fresh polar air has a journey of only a few hundred miles from its arctic source region, while the second track's anticyclones have traveled two or three thousand miles and been greatly modified before reaching New England. Though the barometer may stand equally high in each type of anticyclone, the character of its air masses will differ greatly.

Janus was the Roman god of gates and doors whose festival month was January. He is often depicted with two heads looking in opposite directions, an appropriate symbol for the usual January in New England that has periods of severe arctic cold interspersed with the relatively mild periods usually referred to as January thaws. Recent research has demonstrated that the thaw is a reality and most frequently occurs between January 20 and 26. A secondary abnormal rise in temperature has been detected between January 7 and 10. Though the thaw does not come every year, it has put in an appearance often enough to establish its place as a singular factor of the New England climate.

The extreme January readings in New England during this century at non-mountain stations were: 73° at Waterbury, Connecticut, on January 26, 1950, and —48° at Van Buren, Maine, on January 19, 1925.

Caribou   51° 20° / 2°   −32°

Old Town   56° 26° / 5°   −30°

Burlington   64° 26° / 8°   −30°

Mt. Washington   44° 14° / 3°   −47°

Portland   65° 31° / 12°   −26°

Concord   72° 31° / 10°   −35°

Albany   71° 30° / 13°   −26°

Worcester   69° 31° / 16°   −19°

Boston   70° 36° / 23°   −13°

Hartford   70° 33° / 16°   −26°

Providence   68° 36° / 21°   −9°

Nantucket   64° 38° / 25°   −4°

Bridgeport   65° 40° / 23°   −14°

JANUARY DAILY MAXIMUM AND MINIMUM TEMPERATURES:

EXTREMES AND MEANS

RECORD MAX.   MEAN MAX.

RECORD MIN.   MEAN MIN.

A summerish January, a winterish spring.

January

1 1918 Coldest modern New Year's Day: Boston −3°; New Haven −7°; Northfield, Vt., −24°; Bethlehem, N.H., −20°; Van Buren, Maine, −32°.

2 1904 Severe snowstorm commenced: Boston's snowiest January (35.7″); Blue Hill Observatory in Milton, Mass., had 19″ in 24 hours.

3 1913 Extreme low barometer, record for nonhurricane: Burlington, Vt., 28.28″/958mb;* Albany, N.Y., 28.46″/-964mb.

4 1859 Deep snow: 26″ measured at Middletown, Conn., press reported 36″ at Hartford; 30″ fell in 12 hours at Goffstown, N.H.

5 1835 Famous cold morning climaxed cold week: New Haven's all-time low −24°; Hartford −27°; Hanover, N.H., −32°.

6 1856 Deepest snow of Thoreau's "long, snowy winter" provided sleighing until mid-March; 12″ fell at Boston, 18″ at Providence.

7 1770 Early ice breakup caused by heavy rainstorm; 3.80″ fell at Providence; worst floods in 50 years destroyed dams, bridges.

8 1956 Severe glaze storm gave area from Boston north 6–8 hours icing, caused four deaths; melting, then floods, damage $2.5 million.

9 1886 Blizzard of '86: deep storm center on Providence-Boston-Portland line; Boston 64-mph winds; extensive damage on Nantucket.

10 1859 Severe cold, below zero all day except extreme SE: Craftsbury, Vt., −20°; Cambridge, Mass., −4.5° (highs).

11 1894 Thermometers at Fort Kent, Maine, read −45° and −50°.

12 1836 Big Snow of 1836 in Berkshires and Taconics; mixed rain, sleet, snow to the east; 60″ fell in central New York.

13 1914 One of the bitterest days of record in New England: Northfield, Vt., max. −13°, min. −25°; Bloomfield, Vt., low of −44°.

14 1934 Burlington had 24.2″ of snow, greatest 24-hour fall of record.

15 1957 Burlington dropped to −30°, all-time record; Enosburg Falls, Vt., −41°; Blue Hill Observatory, Mass., −16°; Boston −12°.

16 1831 Great Snowstorm of 1831 swept entire Atlantic seaboard: Boston about 24″; New Bedford 36″.

17 1867 Severe gale, snow paralyzed Northeast: Boston 14″, Old Colony R.R. blocked for 10 days.

18 1857 Severely cold day; −4° Providence 2:00 P.M.; snow began at 6:00 P.M., fell to depth of 18″; gales did extensive structural damage.

19 1810 Cold Friday: Portsmouth, N.H., overnight drop from 42° to −13°; NW gales swept countryside; house in New Hampshire blown down, three children frozen.

20 1961 Kennedy Inaugural Storm: dropped 25″ of snow in Connecticut, 24″ in Massachusetts, 25″ in New Hampshire; barometer 28.59″/968mb off Nantucket; high tides.

21 1887 Temperature rose 81 degrees in 42 hours at Windsor, Vt., Jan. 19–21.

22 1754 "A moderate winter, remarkable for an uncommon cold day, cuming up suddenly in which many people out fishing and otherwise exposed perished." Samuel Lane diary.

23 1857 Cold Friday II, bitter day with NW gales: Craftsbury, Vt., morning −34°, afternoon −23°, mean −28°; Providence −14° at sunrise.

24 1857 Coldest morning of nineteenth century: −50° reported in press in Vermont, New Hampshire, Maine; Boston suburbs −25° to −30°; Nantucket −11°.

25 1948 Deepest snow cover of snowy winter: Boston's 22.1″ set January record; east-central Massachusetts had 30″ to 48″.

26 1839 Great southeaster struck all sections with warm rains, spectacular ice breakup, immense damage to bridges, dams, buildings.

27 1888 First Blizzard of '88 struck north only; Vermont railroads blocked for three days; Portland had 21.3″, long a record.

28 1925 Record-breaking cold: −46° at First Connecticut Lake, N.H., state record (nonmountain); −42° Enosburg Falls, Vt.; −39° Van Buren, Maine.

29 1934 Severe on Mount Washington, 25-degree drop in four hours to −47°, wind blowing at 80–95 mph.

30 1894 Severe storm at Eastport, Maine, 78-mph winds, barometer 28.78″/-975mb, nothing like it since 1869 (Saxby's Storm).

31 1780 Coldest month in U.S. history ended; Hartford had January low of −22° and sunrise average of +4.1°.

* Millibar, see glossary.

13

FEBRUARY

Snow is synonymous with February. Most New England locations have more snowy days, average more inches of snowfall per day, and have a snow cover of greater depth in February than in any other month. The reason for the preponderance of frozen precipitation is directly attributable to the increased activity of coastal storms or northeasters. These storm systems raise a vast quantity of moisture from tropical waters and transport it aloft as a southerly airstream to points hundreds of miles northward. At the surface, meanwhile, the spiral of winds in advance of a coastal storm draws a northeast airstream from eastern Canada and the North Atlantic. The northeast flow at the surface supplies the necessary coldness to keep temperatures below freezing, while the southerly current aloft brings the requisite moisture to the scene. As the warm air mass is forced to rise over the cold surface current, it is cooled, condensation of its moisture takes place, and snow descends on the countryside. The highlands and mountains of New England increase the lifting of the moisture-bearing airstreams and thus augment the precipitation process to create the deep snows that fall over higher elevations of the interior.

The typical northeaster is a product of the Gulf of Mexico or the Atlantic seaboard of the Southeast, and February is the time of year of greatest cyclonic activity in these areas. When an old front lies across the Gulf of Mexico and northern Florida and an upper-air trough of low pressure moves eastward across the central United States, cyclogenesis frequently occurs in the southern end of the trough. If the newly formed center follows a storm track west of the Appalachians, it often commences to fade over Kentucky or Ohio and a new secondary center takes form in the vicinity of Cape Hatteras. This soon becomes the principal disturbance. Sometimes a new center may develop independently off the north Florida or Georgia coast and move rapidly northeastward to the Cape Hatteras area. Both types exhibit the same characteristics and often develop great energy in a very few hours when off the New England coast.

Ordinarily, precipitation will fall for six to eight hours in a typical northeast storm during its fast run up the coast. If a blocking high-pressure ridge, lying from Quebec eastward to Newfoundland, is astride the path of the advancing low center, the forward progress of the storm will be slowed or even brought to a standstill in the vicinity of Cape Cod. Then the precipitation continues longer, perhaps for twelve to twenty-four hours or more, with increased snowfall. High-pressure blocking of this type accounted for the immense snows of the Blizzard of '88 and the 100-Hour Snowstorm of February, 1969.

Another prominent feature of February weather maps is the Hudson Bay High. As winter progresses, arctic high-pressure centers have a tendency to generate farther and farther eastward across northern Canada. In late winter and early spring, they may appear in the vicinity of frozen Hudson Bay, remain there for several days while constantly radiating their modest heat content to outer space, and then move swiftly southeastward as a very cold airstream into New England. Since the trajectory from the arctic tundra is short and the terrain usually snow covered, the cold air arrives in pristine state with little modification of frigidity and is capable of dropping thermometers to −30° or more in its advective blast. The famous cold waves on February 8–9, 1934, and February 15–16, 1943, were of this type. Any low-pressure system moving northeastward along the New England coast can draw a polar or arctic airstream southward. If a really vigorous northeaster is raging and a Hudson Bay High of great magnitude builds over eastern Canada, New England will experience its severest weather conditions.

The lowest February temperature of record in New England this century at non-mountain stations is −46° on February 16, 1943, at East Barnet, Vermont; the highest is 77° on February 16, 1954, at Danbury and Waterbury, Connecticut.

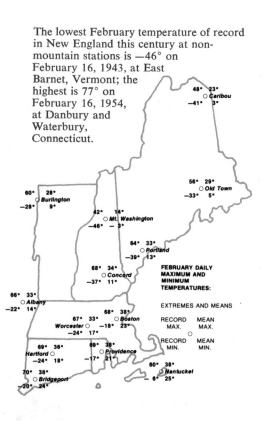

FEBRUARY DAILY MAXIMUM AND MINIMUM TEMPERATURES:

EXTREMES AND MEANS

RECORD MAX.   MEAN MAX.

RECORD MIN.   MEAN MIN.

Warm February, bad hay crop;
Cold February, good hay crop.

February

1 1920 Greatest modern anticyclone: Northfield, Vt., barometer 31.14″/-1054.5mb; Portland, Maine, 31.09″/-1052.8mb, highest ever in U.S. at sea level.

2 1962 Ground Hog Day; extreme cold at Bloomfield, Vt., −40°.

3 1961 Great Snowstorm: Providence 18.8″; Nantucket 14.4″; Boston 14.4″; Worcester 18.8″.

4 1920 Great three-day all–New England snow and sleet storm commenced: 10″ to 15″ fell and froze; 70-mph winds at Block Island; traffic disrupted all month.

5 1918 Coldest in modern records at Nantucket, −6.2°.

6 1855 Famous Cold Tuesday: Burlington, Vt., range −13° to −24°; Boston −5.5° at 2:30 P.M.; West Randolph, Vt., low of −44°.

7 1861 Spectacular temperature drop at Hanover, N.H.: from +40° at noon February 7 to −32° at 7:00 A.M. February 8.

8 1836 Great snow year at Pittsfield, Mass., big storm "making on a level nearly four feet," mail took 38 hours from Northampton.

9 1934 Coldest modern morning in the south: Boston and Providence −18°; Cream Hill, Conn., −26°; Pittsburg, N.H., range −14° to −35°.

10 1857 Severe freshets inundated all New England as very warm February followed very severe January.

11 1780 First general thaw in nine weeks signaled breakup of Hard Winter of 1780, severest in U.S. history.

12 1914 Cold day: Provincetown, Mass., official −8°, some readings there as low as −12°, coldest since 1857.

13 1923 Concord, N.H., 35″ of snow on ground, deepest since 1871.

14 1899 Great Eastern Blizzard ended: Boston's 16″ raised snow cover to 23″, all-time record; Woods Hole barometer 28.86″/977.3mb.

15 1943 Spectacular temperature drops: Portland, Maine, from 32° on the fourteenth to −31° on the fifteenth; Northfield, Vt., range −13° to −34°; −46° in Barnet, Vt.

16 1888 Northfield, Mass., temperature antics: dropped 78 degrees in 40 hours to −29°, rose 68 degrees in 32 hours to 39° on the seventeenth.

17 1791 Rutland, Vt.: "Snow now 60 inches deep." Prof. Samuel Williams.
1958 Great Snowstorm of '58: 30″ fell in interior; Boston's greatest single storm, 19.4″ at Logan Airport, more in suburbs.

18 1952 Two-Tanker Gale: *Pendleton* and *Fort Mercer* broke in two off Cape Cod; 62-mph gusts at Nantucket; total storm fatalities 43.

19 1972 Severe blizzard in the north: 20″ and more fell in interior, gales, roads blocked; great coastal damage; severest this century.

20 1934 Connecticut Blizzard: heaviest snowfall during record cold month; 22″ at New Haven; Block Island barometer 28.73″/972.9mb.

21 1773 Memorable Cold Sabbath: Ipswich, Mass., "Few people at meeting, and most of them were frozen in some of the extremities of the body." Rev. Manasseh Cutler.

22 1802 Great Northeaster wrecked three Indiamen from Salem on Cape Cod; snow depth mounted to 54″ at Epping, N.H.

23 1692 Great Connecticut River flood commenced; highest water until Jefferson Flood in 1801.

24 1862 Severe storm caught 70 fishing schooners on Georges Bank off Nantucket: 13 foundered, 122 men lost making 73 widows and 138 fatherless children.

25 1893 Monroe, Mass., in Berkshires had 53″ of snow in six days; snowiest February of record in the south.

26 1732 "Reckoned as cold a day as has happened here in the memory of the oldest man among us." *New England Weekly Journal.*

27 1952 Cape Cod Blizzard: 18″ at Hyannis; 21.4″ at Nantucket; gusts 70 mph, 10,000 homes without power.

28 1891 Spectacular lightning storm set many buildings afire in the south.

29 1748 End of series of heavy snowstorms of the Winter of the Deep Snow left 30″ on ground at Salem, Mass.

MARCH

March is frequently a wintry month in New England. Not until the close of the month do the chances of a twelve-inch snowstorm or a morning of zero cold diminish to a minimal percentage possibility. One needs only to recall the rugged month of March, 1956, when six storm systems crossed the region, and back-to-back snowstorms on March 17–18 and 20–21 paralyzed the Boston area on the traditional first day of spring. The so-called crown of winter storm often occurs early in the month to raise snow depths to their maximum for the entire winter. The two most famous of all New England snowstorms came on March days: the Great Snow of 1717 and the Blizzard of '88. Temperatures, too, can take a deep tumble during the third month; lows of −40° have been registered in northern sections in the early part of March, with a recording of zero in central Massachusetts as late as March 26.

The storm tracks of winter still prevail. There is less cyclogenesis over the Gulf of Mexico and more over land in Texas, whence disturbances move eastward to the Carolinas where another storm-breeding region is found to the lee of the Appalachians. Anticyclonic blocking in the North Atlantic is a growing influence as spring progresses, and this increasingly affects March storm tracks. Canadian anticyclones tend to originate farther to the east and reinforce the blocking region south of Newfoundland. A new secondary anticyclonic track carries continental high-pressure areas across Ohio to New York and New England.

March and April provide the valleys of New England with the greatest possibility of a snowmelt flood, occasioned by a warm rain falling on a deep snow cover. The extreme example occurred in 1936 when two major rainstorms on March 11–12 and 18–19 dropped from four to eight inches of rain on a snow cover that had from five to ten inches of water content. The enormous runoff resulted in the greatest all–New England flood of record when the stored moisture in the snowbanks was released to join with the rain in a mad dash to the sea. The Connecticut River at Hartford rose to its historic maximum stage of 37.6 feet. Of the seventeen high floods at Hartford since 1692, ten have resulted from a combination of snowmelt and rain in March or April.

The most unpleasant aspect of March and spring weather lies under foot. Mud season—the annual climatic visitor to the New England scene—never fails to put in an appearance sometime in March, though its commencement, duration, and end vary considerably from year to year, much as spells of Indian Summer weather do in the autumn. With the direct rays of the sun again returning to the Northern Hemisphere after the equinox, the hours of sunlight now exceed those of darkness and the heat intensity of solar rays is much increased. Overnight thaws become regular and help to melt ground frost from the surface downward, creating ever-deepening mires of mud. The deeper the winter's frost penetration (sometimes five to six feet in a cold, snowless winter), the longer the mud season will continue. The date of the end of the mud season may vary by four to six weeks, according to latitude and elevation. Baseball may be played in southern Connecticut by April 1 in most years, but it may be mid May before the infield is dry and ready for play in northern Maine.

The extreme March readings in New England at non-mountain stations were: 90° at Providence, Rhode Island, on March 29, 1945, and −40° at Lac Frontière, Maine, on March 9, 1943.

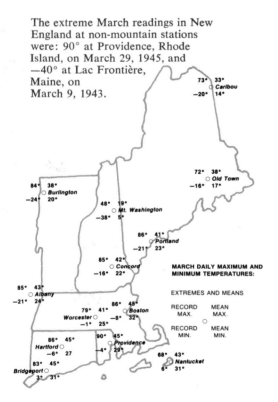

MARCH DAILY MAXIMUM AND MINIMUM TEMPERATURES:

EXTREMES AND MEANS

RECORD MAX.   MEAN MAX.

RECORD MIN.   MEAN MIN.

Lion-like March comes in, hoarse, with tempestuous breath.

WILLIAM DEAN HOWELLS

March

1 **1804** Excessive load of snow crushed the new Hanover-Norwich bridge across Connecticut River.

2 **1833** Severe night with NW gale similar to Cold Friday; mercury at −5° at Boston, −14° at Waltham.

3 **1947** Vermont's deepest modern snowstorm, Readsboro had 50″ in three days; Peru, Mass., nearby had 47″.

4 **1717** Largest contribution to the Great Snow of 1717: two major and two minor storms in nine days deposited about 36″ in Boston area, about 48″ farther north; sheep buried alive for 30 days.

5 **1872** Severest modern March cold wave: Boston −4°, −8°, +2° on successive days.

6 **1723** Famous High Tide of 1723 at Boston, unequaled until 1851; stores, streets inundated while people at church.

7 **1932** Coastal storm, low barometers: Block Island 28.20″/955mb, Boston 28.45″/963.4mb; 53-mph winds at Block Island.

8 **1967** 57″ snow on ground at Readsboro, Vt.

9 **1943** −40° at Lac Frontiere, Maine, coldest ever in March in New England.

10 **1819** Brunswick, Maine, 30″ of snow fell in one day, largest by 10″ in Bowdoin College records, 1807–1859.

22 **1837** Two-day ice storm in Litchfield County, Conn., did $100,000 damage.

23 **1934** Late cold wave: −1° Cream Hill, Conn.; −10° Pittsburg, N.H.

24 **1772** Hartford, Conn.: "The snow on the level is upwards of three feet." *Connecticut Courant.*

25 **1909** Severe easterly storm: Blue Hill Observatory 87-mph winds; "hardest blow in years" in New Hampshire.

26 **1884** Excessive rainfall period March 24–31; totals exceeded 9.00″; damaging floods in Maine and New Hampshire; $12 million in damage.

27 **1846** Four-day rainstorm resulted in greatest ice jam in 100 years at Bangor, Maine.

28 **1913** Ottauquechee River at Woodstock, Vt., reached highest level since 1869.

29 **1945** Climax of hottest March: 90° at Providence; 86° at Boston; only 53° on Cape Cod at Chatham.

30 **1823** Great Northeast Snowstorm swept up coast on Easter; Nantucket barometer 28.83″/976mb; 18″ of snow at Boston; about 24″ at Providence.

31 **1843** End of snowiest March in history at Gardiner, Maine; "Four feet on ground now." (Portland) *Daily Advertiser.*

11 **1936** Rains commenced, leading to the All–New England Flood of 1936, the most widespread and costliest inundation known in region's history.

12 **1888** Blizzard of '88 commenced as coastal low stalled in vicinity of Block Island; 46″ at New Haven, 50″ at Middletown, Conn.; zero temperatures; strong gales.

13 **1963** Snow cover at record modern depths; 73″ at Woodstock, Vt.

14 **1936** Kennebec River crested at Hallowell, Maine, higher than ever known by 3.6 feet.

15 **1871** Connecticut River in high flood at Hartford.

16 **1870** Deep snowstorm blocked 24 trains between Springfield and Albany.

17 **1956** Violent snowstorm struck on St. Patrick's Day; 12.6″ at Blue Hill Observatory.

18 **1936** Second heavy rainstorm commenced; Pinkham Notch, N.H., had 10.97″ in two days; greatest New England flood followed.

19 **1956** Second heavy snowstorm in three days commenced; Blue Hill Observatory had 19.5″ more; Boston 13.3″; snowiest March of record.

20 **1760** Day of Great Boston Fire; wind blowing strong from northwest.

21 **1801** Jefferson Flood in Connecticut Valley; greatest since 1692; so named by Federalists who blamed new president for disaster.

APRIL

Poets in other climes may rhapsodize about the vagaries of April weather, its laughter and tears, but in New England the month has inspired few local bards to lyric praise of the region's early spring weather. With eastern Canada still deep in snow and the coastal waters retaining their wintry chill, northern controls can dominate the meteorological scene with snowfalls and cold lingering through the end of the month. Yet another April might produce a southerly circulation early in the month, bringing blossoms and May flowers well ahead of schedule.

The sun during the thirty days of April will climb more than ten degrees toward the zenith. Mean temperatures, in turn, respond to the increasing solar elevation by rising a full ten degrees along Long Island Sound and thirteen degrees in northern Maine. At the same time the duration of direct sunlight lengthens steadily (in central New England by an hour and twenty minutes). These changes make us more sensible of the progressive amelioration of climate in April than in any other month and hold the promise of better things to come.

"April is the month with the greatest number of storms," according to a recent National Weather Service study. The conclusion applies especially to New England since it remains under cyclonic attack from two directions. First, the storm track from the Gulf of Mexico northeastward along the Atlantic seaboard remains active, while a cyclogenetic area has developed off the Middle Atlantic coast where new storm centers are created and others regenerated. Some of the great North Atlantic storms of history have occurred about mid April when easterly gales, with a long fetch of a thousand miles and more across ocean waters, raise massive waves and drive mighty storm tides onto New England shores. The most spectacular instance was the Lighthouse Storm in 1851 when the newly constructed, cast-iron tower of Minot Ledge Light, rising some eighty-seven feet above the waters and rocks near the entrance to Boston Harbor, fell victim to the raging wind and waves and hurled its two keepers into the sea. The primary winter storm track down the Saint Lawrence Valley continues, meanwhile, to attract storm centers from the Great Lakes and Midwest. Though the disturbances travel farther north, their trailing frontal systems regularly swing across all six states, bringing alternating wind shifts and weather changes.

April is traditionally famous for showers. The records do not show that it has more days with rain than others, though it is near the top in this category. April usually introduces the first samples of summer-type precipitation, caused by local heating of the land surface. This, in turn, heats the surface air layer, which becomes buoyant and tends to rise into the cooler atmosphere aloft. Eventually, when the rising air column is cooled below its dew point, it condenses into visible moisture as cloud. Raindrops form and a shower is born. It may remain small or grow into a towering thunderstorm according to local circumstances. The steadily increasing radiation of the sun supplies the heat energy, while the upper-air currents—still fed from polar sources—provide the cooling agency. The resulting instability of the atmosphere makes precipitation forecasting in April more difficult than usual.

The extreme April readings in New England during this century at non-mountain stations were: 95° on April 20, 1941, at Durham, New Hampshire, and −12° on April 1, 1923, at Bloomfield, Vermont.

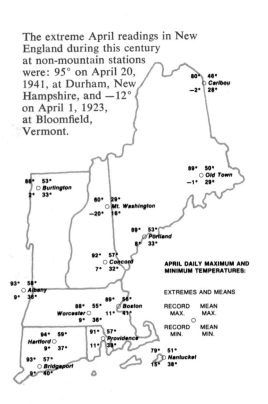

APRIL DAILY MAXIMUM AND MINIMUM TEMPERATURES:

EXTREMES AND MEANS

RECORD MAX.   MEAN MAX.

RECORD MIN.   MEAN MIN.

18

April weather,
Rain and sunshine, both together.

April

1 1807 April Fools' Day Storm: great tide, damage on coast; heavy snow interior; Danville, Vt., 30″ of new snow, depth 60″.

2 1975 Severe storm raged from April 2 to 5; destructive gales all states; 3.00″ of rain in the south; 2–3 feet of snow in the north, great skiing.

3 1904 Harbor at Belfast, Maine, clear of ice, frozen since February 2.

4 1853 First frogs of season heard at Warren, Maine.

5 1874 Temperature 11° at Boston, lowest ever in April.

6 1843 Bangor, Maine, had 15″ of snowfall in final storm of record snowy winter, depth 60″; many lumbermen forced to cease work.

7 1748 Portland, Maine, "Five and a half feet of snow on the ground." Rev. T. Smith.

8 1929 Early heat wave on seventh and eighth: Hartford 90° and 87°; North Grosvenor Dale, Conn., rose from 33° to 87°; Boston 84° both days.

9 1901 Penobscot River, greatest flood; many bridges damaged near Bangor; Bemis, Maine, on the Rangeley Lakes, had 6.00″ of rain in two days.

10 1826 Worcester, Mass., snowstorm all day, 9″ fell. Isaiah Thomas diary.

11 1841 Big late-season snow: New Bedford 16″ compact mass; Boston 18″; Newport 12″; New Haven 10″.

12 1894 Second severe coastal storm, much damage along south shore; Waterbury, Conn., 14″ of snow; Providence 9″.

13 1933 Boston had 5″ of snow on opening day of major league baseball.

14 1953 2.2″ of snow prevented Red Sox from opening baseball season.

15 1854 Severe Easter Weekend Storm raged for four days; easterly gales, intermittent wet snow, raw weather.

16 1851 Famous Lighthouse Storm: great tide, whole gale destroyed Minot Light; Boston tide exceeded legendary 1723 height.

17 1821 Legislature Snowstorm prevented meeting of General Court at Boston; 15″ at Worcester stopped travel.

18 1896 Remarkable early heat wave: 92° at Norwalk, Conn.; 90° at Middletown and Bridgeport.

19 1775 Lexington-Concord Day: crisp anticyclonic morning, 45°, west wind, very fair.

20 1941 95° at Durham, N.H., highest ever in April in New England.

21 1741 Portland, Maine, "Melancholy time, the snow lying, little hay." Rev. T. Smith diary.

22 1696 Dover, N.H.: "About 8 a.m. it begins to snow; by noon the houses and grounds were covered, and at 5 p.m. I saw an isicle seven inches long." Rev. John Pike diary.

23 1852 Lowell, Mass., Merrimack River flood stage of 13.6 feet, highest in 100 years, not exceeded until March, 1936.

24 1700 Boston, "I saw and heard the swallows proaching the spring." Judge Samuel Sewall.

25 1874 Cape Cod, "It snowed every Saturday in April," *Yarmouth Register;* 49″ fell at Woodstock, Vt., in April.

26 1919 Boston 28°, latest reading below 30° in record books.

27 1717 Captain Bellamy of the *Whidnah* wrecked on Cape Cod north of Chatham with loss of 144 pirates, only two survivors.

28 1834 Providence, ground partially covered with snow and sleet.

29 1695 Boston, "A very extraordinary storm of hail, so that the ground was made white with it . . . 'twas as big as pistol and musquet bullets." Judge Samuel Sewall.

30 1812 Backward spring at Salem, Mass., "We cannot refuse to notice an uncommon backward spring. Not a flower to be seen this Maying. . . . It is a Canada season, winter & summer, but no spring." Rev. William Bentley diary.

MAY

The extreme May readings in New England for non-mountain stations are: 101° at North Lewiston, Maine, on May 22, 1911, and 12° at Fort Fairfield, Maine, on May 3, 1903. At the summit of Mt. Washington the thermometer dropped as low as −2° on May 7, 1966.

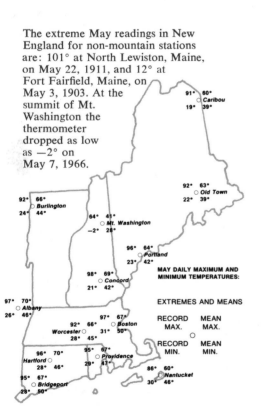

MAY DAILY MAXIMUM AND MINIMUM TEMPERATURES:

EXTREMES AND MEANS

RECORD MAX.   MEAN MAX.

RECORD MIN.   MEAN MIN.

Station	Record Max.	Mean Max.	Record Min.	Mean Min.
Caribou	91°	60°	19°	39°
Old Town	92°	63°	22°	39°
Burlington	92°	66°	24°	44°
Mt. Washington	64°	41°	−2°	28°
Portland	96°	64°	23°	42°
Concord	98°	69°	21°	42°
Albany	97°	70°	26°	46°
Boston	97°	67°	31°	50°
Worcester	92°	66°	28°	45°
Providence	95°	67°	29°	47°
Hartford	96°	70°	28°	46°
Bridgeport	95°	67°	28°	50°
Nantucket	86°	60°	30°	46°

The principal atmospheric changes that take place in May lie in the thermal sphere. The increasing solar radiation heats land surfaces so that they become warmer than bodies of water. The relatively cool Great Lakes, instead of harboring the cyclonic activity of winter, become a seat of anticyclonic formation, as do James Bay and Hudson Bay, forming two associated blocking regions to the west of New England. As a result, the winter cyclone track across the Great Lakes shifts northward into Ontario. Storm passage through the area becomes less frequent and the pace of movement slows, sometimes becoming almost stationary under the blocking influences of slow-moving anticyclones over the Northeast. The storm track along the Atlantic coastal plain decreases in importance, since dry westerlies now dominate the former cyclogenetic areas in the Gulf of Mexico and the South Atlantic coastal region.

Locally, this is the season favoring a sea turn, a term much employed by nineteenth-century writers, especially Henry Thoreau. Webster's Third New International Dictionary defines a sea turn as "a breeze or gale from the sea that often brings mist." This is a totally inadequate definition of the important qualities of what we now refer to as an east wind. Hardly ever a gale, the normal sea turn, or east wind, constitutes a marked shift of wind from a westerly, or land, component to an easterly, or sea, component from northeast through southeast. Sometime during April or May the land surface becomes warmer than the ocean waters. Convective heating of the surface layer of air causes it to expand and rise, lowering the atmospheric pressure. A differential in pressure between the dense cool air hugging the sea surface and the rising lighter air over land causes the heavier sea air to push inland as a vigorous sea breeze. Sometimes the prevailing pressure pattern assists the inauguration of an easterly flow along the New England shore when a backdoor cold front slips down the Maine and Massachusetts coasts, bringing air cooled over the high latitude waters of the North Atlantic into eastern New England. Fog may accompany the onset of an east wind along the immediate shore. The sea turn, east wind, or backdoor cold front is viewed as a climatic blessing by Bostonians, especially since it may bring an abrupt end to an early-season heat wave or in summer ameliorate a spell of uncomfortably high temperature-humidity conditions. A well-developed east wind situation can drop the temperature as much as twenty degrees in about as many minutes.

20

A cold May is kindly
And fills the barn finely.

May

1 1854 Great Connecticut River Flood: stage of 29.8 feet at Hartford not exceeded until March, 1936.

2 1825 Millbury, Mass., "For four hours it snowed fast. Peach trees were in full bloom." Elijah Waters.

3 1903 12° at Fairfield, Maine, lowest ever in New England in May; 13° in New Hampshire; 15° in Vermont.

4 1812 Greatest May snowstorm at sea level: Boston 4"; Waltham 9"; Millbury 12".

5 1951 Relative humidity dropped to 8% at Boston.

6 1833 Greenfield, Mass., late spring snow 12" deep on mountains to west.

7 1930 Early heat wave: Boston had 90° on the sixth and 95° on the seventh, an early-season record; no higher readings have ever occurred in May until May 26.

8 1803 Famous May snowstorm: 6" at Princeton, Mass., with Sabbath sleighing; 2" at New Haven.

9 1956 Bradley Airport near Hartford had 28°, equal to lowest ever in May.

10 1880 Tornado at Island Pond in Northeast Kingdom of Vermont, funnel seen, width 300 feet.

11 1945 Greatest modern May snowstorm inland: covered area from Berkshires to Maine; 26" in New Hampshire; 15" in Vermont and Maine; 10" in Massachusetts.

12 1799 Salem: "This morning we had a flight of snow in all the forms of winter, large, driving, steady." Rev. W. Bentley diary.

13 1866 Barnet, Vt., tornado demolished toll bridge across Connecticut River, tore up trees by roots.

14 1877 Rare Down East Tornado at Eastport, Maine.

15 1834 Great May Snowstorm in interior: 6" in Berkshires to 30" near Newbury, Vt.; 35° in Nantucket.

16 1874 Mill River Disaster in Hampshire County, Mass.; reservoir dam gave way; 138 killed, $1-million loss.

17 1794 Uncommon frost in south, destroyed crops to coastline.

18 1814 Maine rivers in high flood; toll bridge at Brunswick destroyed; much damage along the Saco.

19 1780 Famous Dark Day from Vermont to Cape Cod; darkest at noon, candles required, chickens went to roost; caused by wind-borne smoke and leaf particles.

20 1892 Heavy snow in north; 28" accurately measured at Strafford, Vt.; high winds, much drifting.

21 1806 Dry gale; very strong southwest gales shriveled foliage on trees.

22 1911 101° at Lewiston, Maine, hottest ever in New England in May.

23 1964 Heat wave with 90° or more all six states: Hartford 96°; Concord, N.H., 95°.

24 1962 Tornado at Waterbury, Conn.; 12-mile path; one killed, 70 buildings destroyed.

25 1832 Providence, R.I.: "Snow in morning so as to whiten the ground," Prof. Alexis Caswell.

26 1967 May storm: 6.53" rain at Nantucket in 24 hours; 9" snow fell in southern New Hampshire and Vermont on May 25–26.

27 1880 Two-day heat wave: hottest ever in May at Boston; 97° on the 26th, 96° on the 27th.

28 1775 Keene, N.H.: "Toard Night comes up a Terrible Hurricain Thunder shower. Trees are whirled down in Great Plenty." Abner Sanger diary.

29 1880 Tornado struck Suffield, Conn.; funnel cloud, width 1,000 yards; damage $50,000.

30 1884 Severe frosts: New Haven 32°, latest freeze; Boston 35°, late-season record.

31 1961 Burlington, Vt., dropped to 25°, latest freeze; heavy crop damage interior New England.

21

JUNE

The highest temperature reported in New England during the period of National Weather Service records (1888–1973) was 103° at Turners Falls, Massachusetts, and Falls Village, Connecticut, on June 29, 1933. The lowest was 20° at Fort Fairfield, Maine, on June 1, 1902. On top of Mount Washington, June temperatures in the past forty years have ranged from 71° maximum to 8° minimum.

96° 70°
Caribou
30° 49°

95° 73°
Old Town
31° 49°

96° 77°
Burlington
33° 55°

71° 51°
Mt. Washington
8° 39°

97° 73°
Portland
33° 51°

101° 78°
Concord
30° 52°

100° 79°
Albany
30° 56°

100° 77°
Boston
41° 59°

96° 75°
Worcester
33° 55°

101° 80°
Hartford
37° 56°

95° 76°
Providence
41° 57°

96° 76°
Bridgeport
34° 60°

90° 69°
Nantucket
39° 54°

JUNE DAILY MAXIMUM AND
MINIMUM TEMPERATURES:

EXTREMES AND MEANS

RECORD   MEAN
MAX.   MAX.

RECORD   MEAN
MIN.   MIN.

June at last! No month of the year conjures such pleasant anticipations. Frosty setbacks to summer become a thing of the past, enabling farmers and gardeners to work without fear of a freeze; the woods have dried out sufficiently for hikers and campers to take to the forest trails; and the sun is able to deliver enough heat energy to permit sun-bathing and swimming in comfort. Although thermometers on most clear days will rise into the 80s, the atmosphere appears fresh and stimulating without the debilitating effect of high humidities that come in full summer.

Cyclonic activity declines noticeably with the approach of the summer solstice. Although the principal storm track from the Great Lakes northeastward down the Saint Lawrence Valley remains, fewer storms take this route, and those from Alberta now favor a more northerly route across southern Hudson Bay well north of New England. A storm track continues off the Atlantic seaboard, but coastal storms reach their lowest frequency and intensity of the year; a June tropical storm in these northern climes is a rarity.

In place of large-scale atmospheric controls, local influences emerge as important weather makers. Increased solar input into the lower atmosphere causes convective currents to rise on most days to form the billowy clouds of June. These may range all the way from stray fair-weather cumulus dotting the sky (on the first and second days of polar air flow after a cold front passage) to a giant cumulonimbus thunderhead that proclaims the presence of warm, unstable, tropical air over New England. The crescendo of thunder and the frequency of lightning flashes increase rapidly toward their summer maximum in July.

New England's extreme manifestation of a summer thunderstorm development came on June 9, 1953, when a small cumulonimbus cloud, first detected over the highlands east of the Hudson River, developed gigantic dimensions. It reached upwards of 60,000 feet over the Berkshires and ultimately lowered a funnel to the ground east of Quabbin Reservoir, which then proceeded southeastward in a death sweep through Worcester County. [See page 48.]

The small-to-medium-size thunderstorm is usually welcomed by all, since it serves as an atmospheric engine to transform potential moisture floating aloft into life-giving raindrops. These benefit man and his crops at a time when rain-producing cyclonic storms may be absent for many days in a row. Records show that locations in the northern sections and in the Berkshire–Taconic–Green Mountain range may expect thunderstorms on as many as seven days per month in June and July at the height of the convective season. Along Long Island Sound and the Cape Cod region, where cool onshore winds dampen convective currents, the expectancy of a June thunderstorm drops to four a month, and the same figure applies to the coast of northeast Maine.

Calm weather in June sets corn in tune.

June

1 1812 New Haven's latest blossoming of apple trees on record, 1794–1974.

2 1909 20° at Van Buren, Maine, to equal lowest ever in June in New England.

3 1868 Woodstock, Vt., "slight frost, followed by tornado, with thunder, prostrating trees & even stone walls."

4 1825 Full-fledged hurricane from Cuba swept Atlantic seaboard; great damage to shipping in New England harbors.

5 1859 Famous June frost; vines and some corn killed.

6 1925 Record early June heat wave climaxed at 101° at Waterbury, Conn.

7 1816 Famous June snow covered northern highlands; Danville, Vt., had snow and sleet drifting to 20″; flurries in Connecticut and Massachusetts.

8 1759 June coastal storm did great damage at Salem and Marblehead, Mass., possibly an early-season hurricane.

9 1953 Worcester County Tornado: discontinuous path 46 miles long; 90 killed, 10,000 homeless; damage near $60 million.

10 1816 Last morning of five consecutive freezes, first event in a series of crop calamities.

11 1842 Latest heavy snowfall of record: Irasburg, Vt., 12″; Berlin, N.H., 11″; Bennington, Vt., 4″; Goffstown, N.H., 3″.

12 1802 Lancaster, N.H., "Very cold, a considerable frost." Adino Brackett diary.

13 1802 Hanover, N.H., tornado ripped up trees, shattered buildings.

14 1892 Orono, Maine, tornado blew down chimneys, uprooted trees, unroofed buildings.

15 1662 Salem, Mass., prayers for rain to end drought; "The Lord gave a speedy answer."

16 1964 Trace of snow fell across northern Maine.

17 1775 Battle for Breed's Hill near Bunker Hill, weather: "Serene, dry air, hot—80°—W & WSW winds." Edward A. Holyoke.

18 1875 Severe coastal storm Cape Cod to Nova Scotia; Eastport had 57-mph winds from the east.

19 1907 Bloomfield in Vermont's Northeast Kingdom had 5.51″ of rain in 24 hours.

20 1682 Major Connecticut tornado through Stratford, Milford, Fairfield, and New Haven into Long Island Sound; three barns and one house blown down.

21 1881 Snow covered summit of Mount Washington on the solstice.

22 1906 Destructive hailstorm at Chelsea, Vt., covered area one-by-ten miles; drifts two feet deep; most crops destroyed.

23 1782 Tornado swarm from Berkshires and Taconics into New Hampshire; "It ran in a vein about a half mile wide." *Connecticut Courant.*

24 1816 Thermometer in three-day heat wave rose above 90°: Waltham, Mass., 99° on June 23.

25 1749 Massachusetts, "A general fast on ye account of ye drought." Lt. John Preston diary.

26 1952 Heat wave: Stamford, Conn., 102°; Providence 101°; Hartford and Boston 100°.

27 1808 Newbury, Mass., violent tornado did great damage.

28 1818 Heat wave commenced: Salem, Mass., 98°, reached 100° on June 30.

29 1933 All-time June maximum 103° at Turners Falls, Mass., and Falls Village, Conn.

30 1841 Tornado hit Danvers, Salem, and Marblehead; small fish fell on Boston street.

JULY

"Hot as the Fourth of July" is a time-honored expression in most of America, and in New England it is especially applicable. The former National Weather Service maximum reading of 106° was registered on that day in 1911, and as recently as 1974, many stations recorded their highest temperature of the entire season on July 4. Most New England stations are within a degree or two of achieving their maximum mean temperatures during the first week of July, indicating the influence of the sun's high altitude at this time. New England's hottest weather conditions result from a stagnant weather map situation, with high pressure over the Southeast and low pressure across eastern Canada. Often a high-pressure area becomes stalled over the ocean off Virginia and the Carolinas. This serves as a heat pump to conduct tropical airstreams from the Gulf of Mexico and the subtropical North Atlantic Ocean on a northward journey. When these airstreams reach New England on the wings of a southwest wind, hot and humid conditions prevail inland, while the immediate south shore may be overcast with low fog and temperatures that are much modified by the wind's passage over cool offshore waters.

When the center of the high-pressure area occupies a position farther westward over the middle Appalachians or the Carolinas, the airstreams entering New England will blow from the west or even northwest. These originate over Texas and northern Mexico and follow a long trajectory over the Great Plains and Midwest to reach New England. In passing over the hot, dry land on successive days, they are heated more and more. Upon arrival in the Northeast they may be hotter and drier than the more direct air flow coming from the Gulf of Mexico.

Heat waves normally have a duration of only two to three days before a cold front from Canada brings welcome relief. But on occasion they have endured for as long as ten days, as they did in late June and early July, 1778, during the British retreat across New Jersey that reached a climax in the torrid Battle of Monmouth, or in 1911 when a heat wave lasting from July 2 to 12 brought record maximum temperatures to the three northern New England states.

July can be the foggiest time of the year, as residents of the New England coastal areas well know. Many summer vacationers, attracted by the refreshing coolness of the sea breezes, complain when sea fog obscures the sun and spoils a beach day for sun-bathing and swimming. In July the greatest contrast exists between the relatively cool ocean waters and the hot air masses from the continent. Records show that the foggiest place is Down East in Maine at Moose Peak Lighthouse on Mistake Island, located halfway between Mount Desert Island and Eastport. There are 1,580 hours of heavy fog per year there. Nantucket Island will experience eighty-five days annually with some heavy fog, and fourteen of these will occur in July.

Fog along the New England shore is caused most frequently in summertime by southwest or south winds carrying hot air over inshore waters, which have been cooled by a remnant of the Labrador Current originating far to the north. The air is cooled to its dew point, condenses into visible vapor, and is carried inland by the prevailing wind. This is called advective fog, as differentiated from radiation fog, which forms at inland locations on cool, clear, calm nights. Early morning drivers are familiar with the wispy masses clinging to the ground in valleys while hilltops remain in the clear. On still nights air loses its heat by radiation to outer space. Then it tends to drain downhill, displacing lighter, warmer air, and gathers in low places where it cools still more to its dew point, condenses, and forms ground fog. This is almost always a sign of a good day to come, since the sun in a clear sky will warm the cool air and dissipate the fog pockets in an hour or two after sunrise. Hence the old saying, "When fog appears to disappear into the ground, expect clear warm weather."

The extreme July readings in New England during this century for non-mountain stations are: 106° at Nashua, New Hampshire, and North Bridgeton, Maine, on July 4, 1911, and 29° at West Burke, Vermont, on July 6, 1962.

95° 76°
Caribou
36° 54°

102° 79°
Old Town
40° 55°

100° 81°
Burlington
40° 59°

71° 55°
Mt. Washington
25° 43°

103° 79°
Portland
40° 57°

102° 83°
Concord
35° 57°

104° 84°
Albany
43° 60°

JULY DAILY MAXIMUM AND MINIMUM TEMPERATURES:

EXTREMES AND MEANS

102° 79°
Worcester
44° 61°

104° 81°
Boston
50° 65°

RECORD MAX. — MEAN MAX.

RECORD MIN. — MEAN MIN.

102° 84°
Hartford
44° 61°

101° 61°
Providence
50° 63°

102° 82°
Bridgeport
44° 66°

92° 75°
Nantucket
47° 61°

Dog days bright and clear indicate a good year;
But when accompanied by rain, we hope for better days in vain.

July

1 **1915** Deluge ushered in very wet month: Pawtucket, R.I., had 5.10″ of rain in 24 hours.

2 **1833** Tornado moved through Northeast Kingdom of Vermont, Salem Pond to Norton Pond, about 12 miles long, a half mile wide.

3 **1966** Heat wave: 102° at Concord, N.H., and Hartford, Conn., 98° at Burlington, Vt.

4 **1911** Heat record to date: 106° at Nashua, N.H., and Lawrence, Mass., New England's highest until 1975.

5 **1904** Destructive thunderstorm in Boston Harbor; lightning struck bridge, wharves, and S.S. *Austrian;* damage $1 million.

6 **1682** Ice fall from clouds at Springfield, Mass.; some nine inches in diameter; shingles broken, roofs holed.

7 **1777** Battle of Hubbardton fought in west Vermont on very humid morning.

8 **1788** Canterbury, Conn., hailstorm covered ground 34″ deep; flood followed.

9 **1816** Waltham, Mass., frost in low places on July 8 and 9; 44° at sunrise.

10 **1936** Great heat wave ended: 103° at Waterbury, Conn.; 100° many places.

11 **1874** Cloudburst in Berkshires: dam broke at Goose Pond, water raced down West Branch of Westfield River; $200,000 damage.

12 **1888** Snow fell on Mount Washington almost to base, also on Camel's Hump, Vt.

13 **1897** Southwestern Connecticut deluge: 10.30″ of rain at Southington in 33 hours; 9.39″ at Bridgeport.

14 **1952** Summer storm swept down St. Croix Valley in Maine; struck Eastport at 61 mph on fringe.

15 **1643** Gov. John Winthrop described small tornado at Newbury, Mass., "Through God's mercy it did no hurt, but only killed one Indian."

16 **1879** Violent squall line passed eastward; tornadoes at Pittsfield, Mass., and near Boston; great damage to all region.

17 **1924** Tornado, Templeton, Mass., to Fitchburg, Mass.; 18 miles long; two killed.

18 **1680** Tornado at Cambridge, Mass., described by Rev. Increase Mather; trees uprooted.

19 **1850** Tropical storm brought about 5.00″ of rain to Vermont; high flood.

20 **1890** Calais, Maine, snow fell to appreciable depth during hailstorm.

21 **1916** Ex-hurricane crossed Martha's Vineyard; heavy rains for three days.

22 **1811** Great Vermont Summer Flood: all rivers in high flood; Middletown Springs inundated; spectacular rescues.

23 **1934** Meteorological midsummer; minimum of 57° is the highest for any date in the Boston records.

24 **1830** Three-day rain in Vermont and New Hampshire; flood caused terrible calamity at Bethel, Vt., on White River.

25 **1956** The *Andrea Doria* crashed into the *Stockholm* in fog off Nantucket Lightship, 52 lost.

26 **1819** Extreme cloudburst struck upper Westfield Valley, Mass., about 20.00″ of rain fell in six hours; valley devastated from Otis to Westfield.

27 **1911** Fishing schooner *Nokomis* lost off Nantucket in giant breakers during "sunshine storm."

28 **1891** Coldest July since 1816 culminated in light frosts in Connecticut.

29 **1905** Bridgeport Flood: 11.32″ of rain fell in 17 hours, four dams failed.

30 **1960** Tropical storm Brenda moved on N.Y.C.–Hartford–Concord–Greenville line; heavy rains west, little east.

31 **1839** "Yale Tornado" near West Rock in New Haven; structural damage; studied by Yale faculty.

AUGUST

The lowest August temperature in New England at non-mountain-summit stations is: 25° at South Londonderry, Vermont, on August 31, 1965. The highest is: 107° at Chester and New Bedford, Massachusetts, on August 2, 1975. At the summit of Mt. Washington the thermometer dropped to 20° on August 31, 1965.

95° 73°
O Caribou
34° 52°

101° 78°
O Burlington
35° 56°

98° 77°
O Old Town
32° 53°

71° 53°
O Mt. Washington
20° 41°

100° 78°
O Portland
33° 55°

100° 80°
O Concord
29° 54°

AUGUST DAILY MAXIMUM AND MINIMUM TEMPERATURES:

102° 81°
O Albany
35° 58°

EXTREMES AND MEANS

101° 79°
99° 77° O Boston
Worcester O 46° 63°
38° 59°

RECORD   MEAN
MAX.   MAX.
O
RECORD   MEAN
MIN.   MIN.

100° 82°   102° 80°
O Hartford   O Providence
36° 59°   40° 61°

95° 74°
O Nantucket
39° 61°

101° 80°
O Bridgeport
42° 65°

Heat and drought are the usual concomitants of August. Although the dog days of summer are over early in the month, the cumulative effect of the sun's high altitude and the relatively long duration of sunlight keeps mean temperatures over the land within a degree or two of the summer's maximum attained in late July. The coastal waters continue to store heat and reach their maximum temperatures about a month after the peak readings on land. These thermal conditions cause the earth's surface, both on land and sea, to become unstable. Tornadoes and waterspouts can develop under these conditions, and August has witnessed some of New England's most turbulent outbreaks.

On August 15, 1787, tornadoes spread destruction from Connecticut to New Hampshire. On August 30, 1838, Rhode Island experienced its only major tornado of record. On the twenty-second of the month, in 1851, the Middlesex County Tornado swept the suburban villages only a few miles north of Boston. The town of Wallingford in central Connecticut was shocked by a death-dealing tornado that took thirty-four lives on August 9, 1878. Large waterspouts occurred on August days in 1870, 1880, and 1896 in Vineyard Sound and Nantucket Sound. As recently as 1973 on the twenty-eighth, a sizable tornado spread death and destruction in the vicinity of West Stockbridge in western Massachusetts.

In August the belt of fast westerly winds in the upper atmosphere reaches its farthest north point in its annual migration, lying across southern Canada at about 60°N. Hence there are no principal storm tracks across the conterminous forty-eight states. The main weather activity in New England results from trailing fronts of disturbances moving across central Canada. Sometimes these miss New England altogether or affect only the northern parts. One must now turn a weather eye in another direction, keeping watch to the south, where tropical storm activity accelerates markedly after July 15. A storm track leading from the tropics along the Atlantic seaboard off Cape Hatteras and past Cape Cod poses an increasing threat to New England, though dangerous hurricanes usually postpone their visits northward until the last week in August or later.

In the absence of major cyclonic activity within the United States, high pressure exerts the principal weather controls across the eastern states in August. In fact, the New York–Pennsylvania area has the highest frequency of anticyclones of any place in the Northern Hemisphere. This forms a rather effective block to weather systems moving from the west and accounts for some of the spells of fine weather that August often produces for the benefit of vacationers at the shore and in the mountains.

Dry August and warm
Doth harvest no harm.

August

1 1815 Salem, Mass., "a most wonderful hail storm"; irregular stones five inches in diameter; 20,000 windowpanes broken.

2 1975 New all-time New England maximum: 107° at Chester and New Bedford, Mass.; 104° at Providence set Rhode Island record.

3 1889 Tornado at Middleboro, Mass.; at Provincetown "the most severe of its kind ever experienced."

4 1915 Tropical storm moved on Bridgeport-Hartford-Boston line; 4.00" of rain at Danielson, Conn.; 48-mph winds at Providence.

5 1955 Hottest day of hot month: 103° Windham, N.H.; Boston 100°; Hartford 101° for record August maximum.

6 1931 Hot day in summer of drought: Turners Falls, Mass., 99°; Boston 97°.

7 1918 Hottest day of three-day heat wave: 102° at Vernon, Vt., and Springfield, Mass.

8 1748 Groton, Mass., "We had here a terrible tornado with shocking thunder." Rev. Joseph Emerson.

9 1878 Wallingford, Conn., tornado killed 34, injured 35; 30 homes destroyed, also a church and schoolhouse.

10 1949 Three-day heat wave: Boston 95°, 99°, 101°; equaled all-time August high.

11 1944 Extreme heat wave: Boston 97° or above for seven days, max. 101°; Norwalk, Conn., and Burlington, Vt., record 101°.

12 1778 Hurricane arrival prevented battle off Rhode Island between French and British fleets.

13 1638 One of triple storms of 1638; double tide in Massachusetts Bay; described by Governor Winthrop in journal.

14 1773 Major tornado near mouth of Merrimack River; 200 buildings damaged.

15 1787 Four-state tornado outbreak in Connecticut, Rhode Island, Massachusetts, and New Hampshire; main funnel at Wethersfield, Conn.

16 1777 Battle of Bennington; heavy rain delayed start of battle, enabling reserves to arrive and insure complete victory.

17 1879 Two inches of snow on high ground east of Burlington, Vt.

18 1918 Killing frost at Bloomfield, Vt.

19 1788 Spectacular mini-hurricane did enormous forest damage across western New England.
1896 Remarkable waterspout in Vineyard Sound; spout 3,600 ft. high, 240 ft. wide; formed three times.

20 1955 Extreme floods resulted from deluges of Hurricanes Connie and Diane; Westfield, Mass., 19.76" of rain, $1 billion damage.

21 1925 26° at Somerset, Vt. (elevation 2,096 feet), equals New England August minimum.

22 1746 Salem, Mass., "Some frost so as to kill corn leaves." Lt. John Preston diary.

23 1806 Great hurricane struck Cape Cod and islands; deluges ruined crops; shipping losses.

24 1873 Great Banks Hurricane: 9 Gloucester schooners lost, 32 driven ashore, 138 men drowned; in all, 1,123 vessels wrecked.

25 1635 Great Colonial Hurricane: same stature as 1815 and 1938; track between Boston and Plymouth.

26 1924 Large hurricane brushed Nantucket; barometer 28.71"; trees down, wire systems damaged; 6.36" of rain at Fall River, Mass., in 24 hours.

27 1948 Protracted heat wave, August 24–29: Nantucket 95°; Edgartown, Mass., 98°; Framingham, Mass., 103°.

28 1973 Tornado struck truck stop at West Stockbridge, Mass., 4 killed, 43 injured.

29 1965 Cold spell brought 2" of snow to Mount Washington; 25° in Vermont; 26° in New Hampshire and Maine; 28° in Massachusetts and Connecticut; 33° in Rhode Island.

30 1838 Providence Area Tornado: path 25 miles into Massachusetts as far as Freetown; extensive minor damage, no fatalities.

31 1954 Hurricane Carol: Saybrook, Conn., west of Worcester, Mass., bisected New Hampshire; Providence flooded, 60 killed, $450-million loss.

SEPTEMBER

The extreme September readings in New
England this century for non-mountain
stations are: 103° at Lake Cochituate,
Massachusetts, and Waterbury,
Connecticut, on September
2, 1953, and 12° at
Lac Frontière,
Maine, on
September
22, 1950.

91° 65°
○ Caribou
23° 43°

92° 68°
○ Old Town
27° 44°

95° 70°
○ Burlington
25° 49°

67° 47°
○ Mt. Washington
11° 35°

96° 70°
○ Portland
23° 47°

96° 72°
○ Concord
20° 47°

98° 74°
○ Albany
24° 50°

102° 72°
○ Boston
34° 57°

100° 70°
Worcester ○
26° 52°

96° 75°
Hartford ○
30° 51°

96° 73°
○ Providence
33° 54°

99° 75°
○ Bridgeport
32° 58°

88° 69°
○ Nantucket
35° 56°

**SEPTEMBER MAXIMUM AND
MINIMUM TEMPERATURES:**

EXTREMES AND MEANS

RECORD   MEAN
MAX.   MAX.

RECORD   MEAN
MIN.   MIN.

Meteorological summer (that is, the warmest ninety consecutive days of
the year) ends in early September, but astronomical summer does not
take its leave until the time of the equinox on or about September 22.
Since the sun has completed half of its southward journey, temperatures
commence to drop off rapidly as the month nears its end. In northern
Maine the mean minimum expected drops below 40° by the thirtieth,
and except along the seacoast a heavy frost is a possibility. The passing of the summer season manifests itself through the changing foliage
of the hardwood forests of the northern states, which have taken on
brilliant hues by the end of September.

The September weather maps bear a close resemblance to those of
August. The jet stream is still moving across central Canada, and the
principal North American storm track occupies its summer position at
60°N through Hudson Bay.

The most prominent development this month is the increased frequency of tropical storm formation. A study of this century's tropical
cyclones showed that 35 per cent occurred during the month of September and 14 per cent of the total were active during the first ten days
of September. The Caribbean area, after a midsummer quiet, once again
becomes active in generating storms and sends disturbances northward.
New England is particularly vulnerable to tropical storm landfalls during
September; very destructive hurricanes have smashed across the region
in 1815, 1869, 1938, 1954, and 1960.

September is the month of the supposed occurrence of the equinoctial, or line storm. The time-honored concept of an annual storm in late
September goes back among seafaring men to the middle of the eighteenth century and perhaps earlier. It was believed that a major storm
always occurred at the time the sun crossed the equator, or line; any
storm coming a week before and after was so classified. The mere fact
of the sun's crossing the imaginary line, of course, does not produce a
storm, but September combines the season of maximum tropical storm
activity with the effect of a growing thermal contrast between a rapidly
cooling north and a still-warm south. This is conducive to producing
contrasting air masses and sharp fronts, and the development of winter-
type storms in the temperate region.

Rain in September is good for the farmer but poison to the vine grower.

September

1 1970 Trace of snow at Long Falls Dam, Maine, and about a half inch atop Mount Washington.

2 1953 Extended late-season heat wave peaked at 101° at Hartford, 100° at Boston, 98° at Concord, N.H.

3 1821 Redfield's Hurricane moved on Stamford-Litchfield line in Connecticut; great damage; his studies revealed secret of hurricane circulation.

4 1973 Long heat wave ended: Hartford had 92° and above for nine days, max. 98°.

5 1963 Caribou, Maine, 32° for earliest freeze in recent records, 1939 to present.

6 1881 Famous Yellow Day: smoke aloft filtered out most color rays, leaving a yellow, brassy tinge on verdure and buildings.

7 1881 Hottest September day: 102° at Boston; 100° at New Haven.

8 1869 The September Gale of 1869: Westerly-Milford-Lawrence-Dover path; Providence inundated; structural damage at Boston.

9 1821 The Sunday Tornadoes in Vermont, New Hampshire, Massachusetts; Great New Hampshire Whirlwind moved through Sunapee–Mount Kearsarge–Boscawen, about six killed, great forest destruction.

10 1896 Hurricane crossed Martha's Vineyard and Cape Cod, then through coastal Maine; very destructive, many casualties to shipping.

11 1954 Hurricane Edna cut between Martha's Vineyard and Nantucket, gusts to 100 mph; 8.05″ of rain at Brunswick, Maine, 23 killed, $40 million damage.

12 1960 Hurricane Donna moved on New London–Milford–Lowell path; 92-mph winds at Blue Hill; moderate tides, minor damage, three fatalities.

13 1911 Early cold wave brought frost and falling temperatures—23° at Jacksonville, Vt., and Grafton, N.H., the next morning.

14 1855 Lizzie Bourne died in "wet, cold blasts" only 40 rods from shelter at summit of Mount Washington.

15 1944 Great Atlantic Hurricane crossed Rhode Island and SE Massachusetts; Nantucket had 79-mph winds; very destructive on Cape Cod; 30 fatalities in New England.
1926 Snow fell in Tuckerman Ravine on Mount Washington.

16 1932 Great Rainstorm: total of 12.00″ of rain near Westerly, R.I.; 8.00″ in 24 hours at Durham, N.H.; 7.72″ at Ripogenus Dam, Maine.

17 1933 Hurricane passed 75 miles SE of Nantucket; heavy rain; Provincetown 9.92″ in 24 hours, storm total 13.27″.

18 1908 Smoky atmosphere September 10–18; sun viewed directly without dazzling.

19 1936 Vigorous hurricane moved 40 miles east of Cape Cod; 58-mph winds at Block Island; Provincetown 7.79″ of rain in 24 hours.

20 1845 Great Adirondack Tornado from Lake Ontario, crossed mountains, then Lake Champlain; damage in Burlington, Vt.

21 1938 The New England Hurricane moved west of New Haven, then up Connecticut Valley and across Vermont; Blue Hill had 121-mph winds; record tide inundated Providence, about 600 to 650 fatalities, damage near $400 million.

22 1885 Offshore hurricane passed about 35 miles east of Nantucket, came ashore near Eastport, Maine, where barometer dropped to 28.76″/973.9mb.

23 1815 The Great September Gale: moved over Saybrook, Conn., west of Worcester, Mass., into New Hampshire; great storm tide inundated Providence; extensive structural damage, forest destruction; at least six casualties.

24 1963 Cold wave set date records at Bradley Airport north of Hartford, 36°, 31°, 30°.

25 1696 Salem, Mass., "A black frost. Ye ice on ye side of my house as thick as window glass." John Higginson.

26 1950 Blue sun and moon for several days caused by Canadian forest fires.

27 1947 Dorset, Vt., 15° for lowest ever in New England in September.

28 1836 First of three early-season snows; Ashby Mt. in northeastern Massachusetts had 2″ of covering.

29 1893 Snow fell for 30 minutes at Pittsfield, Mass.; 3″ at New Ashford, Mass.

30 1676 Ephraim Howe in boat blown off Cape Cod by storm; later rescued from island off Nova Scotia by fishing schooner; his sons and three other companions died.

OCTOBER

The extreme October readings in New England this century for non-mountain stations are: 94° at Waterbury, Connecticut, on October 2, 1927, and 1° at Van Buren, Maine, on October 31, 1925.

79° 53°
○ Caribou
14° 35°

84° 57°
○ Old Town
15° 35°

85° 59°
○ Burlington
15° 39°

59° 38°
○ Mt. Washington
−5° 25°

88° 60°
○ Portland
18° 38°

92° 62°
○ Concord
10° 36°

91° 63°
○ Albany
16° 40°

89° 61°
Worcester ○
19° 43°

90° 63°
○ Boston
25° 48°

91° 62°
Hartford ○
10° 36°

90° 64°
○ Providence
21° 43°

90° 65°
○ Bridgeport
20° 49°

82° 61°
○ Nantucket
22° 48°

OCTOBER TEMPERATURE MEANS AND EXTREMES:

EXTREMES AND MEANS

RECORD MAX.   MEAN MAX.

RECORD MIN.   MEAN MIN.

October is the truly autumnal month. The intensity of summer heat has faded, yet the cold sting of winter is still weeks ahead. Warm days, cool nights, and glorious autumn foliage are the normal delightful fare in New England. The number of clear days reaches its annual maximum, winds tend to be light, the horizon is dulled by a blue-gray haze— weather conditions known in American lore as Indian Summer.

The atmospheric controls for this type of weather in New England lie to the southwest. Recent studies have shown that the greatest prevalence of anticyclonic activity in the United States in October is located over West Virginia, where migrating high-pressure areas from the west tend to stall and spread out. This weather map feature has not earned such a distinctive name as the Bermuda High of summer or the Hudson Bay High of winter, but perhaps it should be known as the West Virginia High in view of recent atmospheric developments.

Our grandparents thought of Indian Summer as a favorable period for outdoor activity, but now, when anticyclonic conditions continue for several days in a row, atmospheric scientists have to be on the alert to detect the development of an air pollution threat. The light winds and waning insolation prevailing often combine to create a temperature inversion, a condition occurring when a layer of stagnant warm air aloft puts an effective lid over the lower layer of the atmosphere, preventing man-made pollutants from venting upward in the usual manner. Late September to mid November is the period of greatest threat in New England for the development of a spell of Indian Summer conditions, either of the pleasant old-fashioned kind or the unpleasant modern industrial type.

Land surfaces of the continent cool off at a more rapid rate than water surfaces in October, and this encourages cyclonic formations in the interior United States and Canada, with a diminution of cyclogenesis over the tropical seas and off the Atlantic coast. While the solar radiation decreases, the main storm track shifts across central Canada southward to 55°N, the latitude of northern James Bay and southern Labrador. With disturbances being generated over the northern Great Plains, the storm traffic converging across southern Canada rapidly increases as the month progresses, causing additional frontal sweeps across New England and more changing of air masses than in September. Though the tropical storm season is definitely on the wane by October, the month has produced some mighty hurricanes, as those striking New England in 1804, 1841, 1846, 1878, 1896, and 1954 bear testimony. The Atlantic storm track lies farther east this month, and many storm circulations may miss New England altogether or just brush by Cape Cod and eastern Maine.

*If October bring heavy frosts and winds,
then will January and February be mild.*

October

1 **1959** Ex-hurricane Gracie moved on Albany-Nashua path with only slight damage.

2 **1927** Hottest October day: Waterbury 94°; Hartford 91°; Chestnut Hill, Mass., 91°.

3 **1841** The October Gale: offshore hurricane caught Cape Cod fishing fleet on Georges Bank; 20 wrecks on Nantucket; 57 men lost from Truro, Mass.

4 **1869** Saxby's Gale in Maine and Nova Scotia; great wind destruction; excessive rains over New England; 12.35" at Canton, Conn., record floods.

5 **1638** Maine: "A fearful storm of wind began to rage, called a hurricane," John Jocelyn; many trees blown down, ships wrecked.

6 **1836** Williamstown, Mass., "Mountains white with snow, extended down much more than on Sept. 28th." Ebenezer Kellogg records.

7 **1849** Offshore hurricane brushed SE coast; brig *St. John* wrecked at Cohasset, Mass., 143 perished; Henry Thoreau described scene in *Cape Cod*.

8 **1692** Dover, N.H., "First snow," journal of Rev. John Pike.

9 **1783** Severe tropical storm caused "the fullest tide that has been known these forty years." *Connecticut Journal.*

10 **1804** Famous Snow Hurricane of 1804: destructive winds in the south; heavy snow interior; 36" in Vermont mountains.

11 **1925** Earliest modern snowfall of 6" and more brought out snowplows, impeded traffic on foliage weekend, caused cancellation of football games.

12 **1836** Williamstown, Mass., third early 1836 snow was 3" deep in village, 33°.

13 **1934** Heavy snow in the north: Presque Isle, Maine, 14", York Pond, N.H., 13".

14 **1913** Earliest measurable snowfall at downtown Boston: 0.4".

15 **1954** Hurricane Hazel lashed western sections; 70-mph SE winds at Burlington, Vt.

16 **1877** Waterspout observed in Buzzards Bay near Woods Hole, Mass.

17 **1868** Early snowfall on coast: Boston 2", Steuben, Maine, 4".

18 **1972** Early snowfall in the south on October 18–19; 4.5" at North Scituate, R.I.

19 **1749** October Hurricane of 1749: damage to shipping; seven vessels ashore on Martha's Vineyard alone.

20 **1770** Late Season Hurricane of 1770; accompanied by heavy rain and sleet; high tide at Boston and Newport did damage.

21 **1944** Second hurricane threat of season passed 50 miles SE of Nantucket.

22 **1783** Third coastal storm of month, heavy rains and snowmelt caused greatest flood known in Vermont.

23 **1761** Southeast New England Hurricane of 1761: severest in 30 years at Boston; Providence bridge wrecked; Newport steeple downed.

24 **1785** Greatest flood on Merrimack River after three-day rain; 9.00" and more; extensive damage to bridges and dams.

25 **1925** Tornado at Woburn, Mass., six-mile path, one killed.

26 **1859** Earliest substantial snow in SW New England; New York City had 4".

27 **1764** Rutland, Mass., "Very remarkable storm of snow with high wind, 22 inches." Seth Metcalf.

28 **1879** Offshore hurricane cut from Narragansett Bay to Boston; minor damage.

29 **1793** Measurable snow all New England; East Machias, Maine, 20".

30 **1925** Snowfall in south: 1.3" at New Haven, Yale-Army football game played with snow on sidelines.

31 **1925** Record low October readings: Van Buren, Maine, 1°; Garfield, Vt., 2°; Pittsburg, N.H., 4°.

NOVEMBER

The lowest November temperature of record in New England this century at non-mountain stations is —20° registered in Maine in 1917 and 1933 and in Vermont in 1925. The highest is 84° at stations in Connecticut, Massachusetts, and New Hampshire on November 2, 1950. At the summit of Mt. Washington, in the last 40 years, the thermometer has dropped to a November low of —20°.

68° 38°
Caribou
— 3° 25°

75° 44°
Burlington
— 3° 30°

51° 27°
Mt. Washington
—20° 14°

71° 44°
Old Town
— 1° 26°

74° 48°
Portland
— 6° 30°

80° 48°
Concord
—17° 28°

NOVEMBER DAILY MAXIMUM AND MINIMUM TEMPERATURES.

75° 48°
Albany
—11° 31°

78° 52°
Boston

75° 47°
Worcester
6° 33°

EXTREMES AND MEANS

RECORD MAX.   MEAN MAX.

RECORD MIN.   MEAN MIN.

77° 51°
Hartford
6° 32°

75° 52°
Providence
9° 35°

77° 53°
Bridgeport
8° 39°

69° 52°
Nantucket
15° 40°

Anglo-Saxons called November in Old England the "winde-monath" and their descendants found the designation equally appropriate to New England after experiencing the late autumn's wind behavior here.

Wind movement across the region increases markedly in November, though speeds do not reach their mean monthly maximums until late winter. Individual bursts of speed have been measured at all-time record highs in November at weather stations in New Haven, Hartford, Boston, Portland, Concord, and Burlington, representing practically every corner of the six-state region.

Two of the greatest November windstorms have occurred within relatively recent times. The famous Portland Storm on November 26–27, 1898, stirred the public's morbid fascination as no other storm has ever done, for never have so many New England travelers disappeared so quickly with such mystery surrounding their fate. More recently, the Great Easterly Gale on November 25–26, 1950, spread greater wind damage throughout New England than has any other storm in the non-hurricane class.

The face of November weather maps takes on a wintry aspect as the month progresses. The principal storm track across Canada slips southward from its summer position to about 50°N latitude. Low-pressure centers generating over Alberta or Colorado track eastward on converging paths toward the Great Lakes and then move along a storm highway just north of the Saint Lawrence Valley, reaching the Atlantic north of Newfoundland. The track northeastward along the Atlantic seaboard becomes increasingly active as cyclogenesis makes a seasonal revival in the Gulf of Mexico. Storm centers move over the neck of northern Florida, pass close to Cape Hatteras, brush Cape Cod and Nova Scotia, and cross Newfoundland. True tropical storms become increasingly rare in November, although one out-of-season hurricane in 1888 pounded up the New England coast as late as November 27. With the two principal storm tracks activated and converging on New England, frequent storminess prevails.

Yet all is not wind, cloud, and precipitation this month: the anticyclonic conditions that produce Indian Summer spells in October often reestablish their influence. The main anticyclonic track now follows a course south of the Great Lakes, across the central Appalachians (a West Virginia High if it stalls), and then veers northeastward over southern New England. Of secondary importance is the path followed by polar highs from northwest Canada southeastward across Ontario and then eastward over Maine and the Atlantic provinces. These may bring "squaw winter," described as a brief period of freeze and frost in midautumn, which is succeeded by spells of Indian Summer weather under anticyclonic controls.

If there's ice in November that will bear a duck,
There'll be nothing after but sludge and muck.

November

1 1716 Dark Day in New England; Rev. Cotton Mather sent account to the Royal Society of London.

2 1950 Boston reached 83°, highest by five degrees of any other November reading.

3 1778 H.M.S. *Somerset* grounded in storm on Cape Cod; crew of 480 men captured and marched to Boston.

4 1927 Vermont Flood: tropical low dropped up to 8.00″ of rain on November 3–4 resulting in state's worst weather disaster; 84 dead; $28 million damage.

5 1894 Election Day Snowstorm commenced; about 10″ wet snow along south coast; wires, trees downed.

6 1953 Storm center moved northwest over New York, giving western Connecticut a snowfall of 3″ to 7″.

7 1827 12″ of snow fell at Millbury, Mass., in nine hours.

8 1645 Northeaster with rain beached three ships, damaged wharves.

9 1819 Widespread dark day, rainfall impregnated with burned leaves.

10 1723 "Hurricane" reported in Rhode Island by the *Boston News-Letter*.

11 1835 Southwest gales beached eight ships on Cape Cod during famous windstorm over Northeast.

12 1820 Major snowstorm introduced severe winter of 1820–21; 8″ at New Haven, Conn., and Epping, N.H.

13 1946 General Electric scientists produced snowfall over Massachusetts Berkshires in first modern cloud seeding experiment.

14 1972 Big early-season snowfall dropped 18″ in Vermont and New Hampshire, 12″ in Massachusetts.

15 1740 Snow season of Hard Winter of 1740–41 commenced with 6″ of snowfall.

16 1875 Coastal storm caused gale doing structural damage at Boston and north.

17 1869 First of two big windstorms in three days; mail cars blown from tracks on New York–Massachusetts border, 3 died.

18 1873 Severe northeaster, Portland, Maine, barometer 28.49″/964.8mb; Eastport, Maine, winds at 64 mph, heavy snow and rain.

19 1620 *Mayflower* hit adverse winds on Pollock Rip off Chatham, turned back north to Provincetown.

20 1869 Great windstorm raged over Green Mountains, much damage from SE wind at Middlebury, Vt.

21 1798 Weare, N.H., the famous Long Storm; "Snow fell for three days, in the whole about three feet deep, a tremendous storm." Joseph Philbrook.

22 1641 "A great tempest of wind and rain from the S.E. all the night, as fierce as a hurricane . . . and thereupon followed the highest tide which we have seen since our arrival here." John Winthrop.

23 1931 Late-season heat wave for five days with max. of 77° at Boston.

24 1938 First of two heavy snows in three days; 12″ fell in Connecticut.

25 1950 Great Easterly Gale swept all sections; gusts to 110 mph at Concord, N.H.; 100 mph at Hartford, Conn.; extensive damage.

26 1784 Bennington, Vt., severe gale of wind threw down houses, unroofed barns, tore up trees; coastal damage; similar to November, 1950, storm.

27 1898 The Portland Storm, New England's most tragic: 191 disappeared when S.S. *Portland* foundered off Cape Cod; many other sailors lost on small ships; heavy snow, 27″ at New London, gale damage.

28 1921 Central New England's worst ice storm: 3.00″ and more of frozen precipitation; Worcester area paralyzed; 100,000 trees ruined; heavy snow north.

29 1945 Severe northeaster; Boston averaged 40.5-mph winds for 24 hours, peaked at 63 mph for five minutes; barometer at Block Island 28.38″/-961.1mb; 33 fatalities in region.

30 1875 Lowest November readings of record in cold wave: Eastport, Maine, −13°; Portland −6°; Boston −2°; New Haven +2°.

DECEMBER

"Dark December" is an appropriate description of the twelfth month. Not only does the duration of daylight reach its annual minimum, but cyclonic activity increases to a seasonal maximum, and the resulting overcast skies and frequent precipitation make for gloomy weather conditions. Both the jet stream and the Canadian storm track have slipped southward, now passing over the Great Lakes and continuing eastward slightly north of the Saint Lawrence Valley. Warm fronts from these systems move northward and cold fronts southward over New England in endless succession. The central Great Plains of the United States becomes an active storm breeder, sending disturbances northeastward to the lower Great Lakes and then eastward along the Saint Lawrence Valley route, with an occasional center passing over northern New England. There is an increase of traffic along the storm track leading from the Gulf of Mexico, where cyclogenesis reaches a maximum in December. Northeasters become frequent visitors as the month progresses, and many mighty storms of this type have lashed the New England countryside during the final ten days of December when the days are darkest.

Pressure charts place the center of maximum anticyclonic activity over Quebec and an area of minimum pressure southeast of Nantucket, setting up a strong pressure gradient across the region. Storms moving into this zone tend to slow down or stall, all the while intensifying with increasing winds and precipitation. Temperatures continue their decline toward midwinter lows and daily means drop below freezing everywhere in New England by the end of the month, ranging from 32° along Long Island Sound to 12° in extreme northern Maine.

Much of December's precipitation will fall as snow in northern locations and at higher elevations of the interior. December snowfall in the extreme south may average 5.3 inches, increasing to 7.7 inches in the Boston coastal area, and mounting to 20 inches in the northwest at Burlington. Higher elevations receive much more, as the monthly mean of 39 inches at Mount Washington demonstrates. Precipitation may come in a varied mixture, with snow changing to ice pellets (sleet) or freezing rain (glaze), and then to rain, and again back to snow. Or all types may fall together or alternately—resulting in treacherous going by foot or vehicle.

Some of winter's worst weather has occurred during Christmas week. The famous Hessian Storm on December 25–26, 1778, caused the death by freezing of a number of British mercenaries at Newport and gave all New Englanders one of their cruelest lashings from shifting gales, zero temperatures, and driving snow. The cold storm over Long Island Sound on December 24–25, 1811, drove many ships onto the lee shore in zero cold where their crews froze on the exposed beaches. On December 28, 1839, a fierce storm centered near Nantucket caused great shipping losses in Massachusetts Bay and buried the interior under 30 inches of snow. On the twenty-sixth in 1872 a cold storm lashed the coastline with biting gales and as much as 18 inches of snow. On Christmas Night in 1909 a northeaster raised the mightiest tide experienced at Boston since the Lighthouse Storm in 1851 and brought deep snows to the interior. Many Connecticut residents remember sharing in the deep snow on December 26–27, 1947, which buried New York City under a record 25.4 inches. The recent storm on December 26–27, 1969, in Vermont and New Hampshire blocked all roads and caused great disruption for skiers en route to holiday visits in the ski country.

The severest spell of cold weather in the present century occurred at the end of December in 1917, adding to the wartime woes of a civilian population already suffering from an acute fuel shortage and the beginning of a cruel influenza epidemic. Again at the end of December in 1933 an outbreak of frigid arctic air dropped the temperature at Bloomfield in northeastern Vermont to −50°, the lowest ever registered in New England on an official National Weather Service thermometer.

The extreme December readings in New England this century at non-mountain stations were: 72° at Enosburg Falls, Vermont, on December 5, 1941, and −50° at Bloomfield, Vermont, on December 30, 1933.

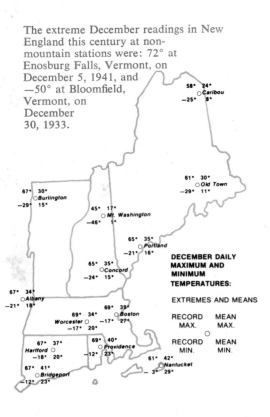

DECEMBER DAILY MAXIMUM AND MINIMUM TEMPERATURES:

EXTREMES AND MEANS

RECORD MAX.   MEAN MAX.

RECORD MIN.   MEAN MIN.

A green December makes a fat churchyard.

December

1 1964 Down East Blizzard: 15″ at Machias, Maine; 13″ at Eastport; 60-mph winds; barometer 28.88″/978mb.

2 1942 Deep cyclonic storm: Caribou, Maine, barometer 28.17″/954mb; severe thunderstorms across south, lightning damage at Boston.

3 1791 Salem, Mass., "Nivis tempestates per totum diem," Wm. Bentley diary.

4 1964 Ice storm over Massachusetts from December 3–6; ice 1″ thick; 50,000 homes without power; worst since 1921.

5 1784 Great Winter Freshet in Merrimack Valley; many bridges floated off.

6 1786 Big December Snowstorm ended; 20″ near Hamden, Conn.; mercury dropped to −9° at Hartford for early season record.

7 1869 Severe northeaster struck Maine coast with heavy snow, gales.

8 1902 Early zeros: Boston −4°; Newport, Vt., −26°.

9 1786 Third major snowstorm in week, total 37″ at Hamden, Conn.; Boston had more snow on ground than for 70 years.

10 1699 Boston, "The rain freezes upon the branches of the trees . . . considerable hurt is done in orchards." Judge Samuel Sewall.

11 1878 Great December floods: rain on snow raised streams almost to 1869 levels; Westfield, Mass., inundated.

12 1960 Prewinter Snowstorm: Nantucket 15.7″; Walpole 19.7″; Boston 13″; "unique, true, severe blizzard."

13 1915 Heavy snow in west, 12″ to 30″, commenced snowiest season in modern record.

14 1677 Plymouth, Mass., "Such a dreadful storme, as hath not bin knowne these 28 years." Rev. John Cotton diary.

15 1839 First of triple storms of 1839: gales swept Massachusetts Bay; 50 Gloucester vessels wrecked in harbor, many lost; Hartford had 24″ of snow.

16 1835 New England's bitterest daylight, at noon: Hanover, N.H., −17°; Williamstown, Mass., −16°; Norfolk, Conn., −15°; Boston −4°, down to −12° by sundown.

1779 "Broke up College & dismissed the students," Pres. Ezra Stiles of Yale; early onset of cold weather, start of the Hard Winter of 1779–80.

17 1740 High floods on Merrimack River; warm rains on deep snow; worst in 70 years; houses floated away.

18 1620 Pilgrim exploring party landed at Plymouth in wild windstorm.

19 1675 Great Swamp Battle near Kingston, R.I.; ice enabled English to cross swamp and dispatch 600 Narragansetts.

20 1942 Early cold wave: Boston −11°; Nantucket −3°; Hartford set four date records.

21 1905 Manchester, Vt., windstorm unroofed buildings, blew barn doors off.

22 1839 Second of triple storms brushed south coast on December 22–23; Providence had 3″ of snow, much drifting.

23 1883 Boston temperature went down to −12°, long a December record until 1917.

24 1966 "Donner and Blitzen" storm in Connecticut as snow-thunderstorm spread 6″ to 8″ for White Christmas.

25 1872 The Cold Christmas: −8° at Boston; Lunenburg, Vt., −45°; unofficial −54° near North Stratford, N.H.

26 1778 The Hessian Storm at Newport; extreme northeaster brought 18″ of snow and zero temperatures; many British mercenaries frozen to death.

27 1947 New York's Big Snow ended, 26″; Danbury, Conn., 22″; Hartford 19″; Boston 9″.

28 1839 Third of triple storms: barometer 28.77″/974.3mb; whole gales swept coast; 24″ of snowfall Hartford to Worcester.

29 1917 Great World War I Cold Wave: Berlin, N.H., −44°; Saint Johnsbury, Vt., −43°; Van Buren, Maine, −37°; Hartford −18°; Boston −14°.

1933 Cold Wave, Boston's −17° lowest ever recorded to this date.

30 1933 Coldest ever in New England: −50° at Bloomfield, Vt., −44° at Pittsburg, N.H., −41° at Woodland, Maine.

31 1962 Down East Blizzard ended: 46″ of snow and 60-mph winds, zero to −15°; many communities isolated.

The Weather

Is Always Doing Something

HURRICANES

Tropical storms are temporary but well-remembered visitors to New England. Their birthplace lies far to the south in the warm waters of the tropical seas. They have generated as far north as Cape Hatteras and to the north of the Bahamas, but usually they originate in the warm tropical section of the North Atlantic Ocean, the Caribbean Sea, or the Gulf of Mexico. In June and again in October the western Caribbean is the favorite birthplace, but in the middle of the season the area to the east of the Lesser Antilles becomes the spawning ground. In September some of the greatest New England hurricanes have developed close to the shore of West Africa and have taken two weeks to cross to the West Indies before recurving and heading northward. Some storms pass well to the north of Puerto Rico before recurving. Several have smashed into eastern Maine and the Atlantic provinces of Canada with devastating effect. New Englanders should remember that a hurricane threat is not over if the storm center passes east of Cape Cod. There is still plenty of coastline Down East for a landfall.

The Nature of New England Tropical Storms

Tropical storms are not all bad in their behavior. Often they bring the copious rainfalls needed to sustain the life and economy of New England. In fact, the absence of tropical storms in the middle 1960s was a major factor in the acute water shortage then prevailing. But they can be monsters, as the accompanying historical record reveals.

Extremes. The highest hurricane wind ever measured in New England was a momentary gust of 186 mph and a sustained five-minute speed of 121 mph at Blue Hill Observatory, Milton, Massachusetts, on September 21, 1938. The greatest hurricane tidal surge occurred along the shores of Rhode Island Sound also on September 21, 1938, when the water level rose seventeen feet above normal and waves were estimated at thirty to forty feet high. The lowest barometric pressure officially re-

CHAPTER 3
New England Storms

Opposite: A couple stranded at Wollaston Beach on Quincy Bay, Massachusetts, during Hurricane Carol, August, 1954. *Above:* These houses in Westbrook, Connecticut, on Long Island Sound, were swept together and destroyed by the great hurricane wave surge on September 21, 1938.

39

corded, 28.04″/949.5mb, was noted at Hartford, Connecticut, on September 21, 1938. Unofficial barometer readings near 28.00″/948.2mb were reported during the passage of Hurricane Edna over Cape Cod and the islands on September 11, 1954. The greatest precipitation from a tropical storm was 19.76 inches at Westfield, Massachusetts, on August 17–19, 1955, during the passage of Diane. The 1938 Hurricane caused more fatalities than any other; they were officially placed at 585, but a recent study estimates the figure close to 650. The most costly was Hurricane Diane with losses estimated at $1.5 billion, almost entirely the result of floods. Hurricane Donna on September 12, 1960, was the last major hurricane to strike New England.

Season. The hurricane season normally extends from June to November. A major hurricane has affected New England as early as June 5 in 1825 and as late as November 28 in 1888. The last week of August and the entire month of September comprise the core of the hurricane season in New England. The most active season of the twentieth century was 1954, when the hurricanes Carol and Edna crossed the New England coastline and Hazel's winds brushed the western portion. The most active season of the past hundred years was 1888, when five tropical storms affected New England. In the thirty-year period from 1871 to 1900, nineteen tropical storms crossed New England and ten others passed near enough to be felt. But in the next thirty years, 1901–1930, only four storms crossed the mainland and an additional four passed nearby. Then, in the thirty-year span from 1931 to 1960, there was a marked pickup in activity: nineteen storms crossed New England and an additional nineteen influenced the local weather. Finally, in the past fifteen years, 1961–1975, there has been a decrease again, with only three crossings and eleven near passages. Over the years one may expect a tropical storm to penetrate the New England mainland once every two years and to cross the land or pass nearby in offshore waters on an average of once each season.

A tropical storm or hurricane is essentially a "heat engine," possessing a central core that is warmer than the surrounding atmosphere and a chimney structure with ascending warm air at its center. The storm derives its vast energies from the condensation of invisible water vapor into water droplets visible as cloud and rainfall. The attendant release of latent heat from this process provides the fuel that drives the storm and creates its vast wind force.

An inward flow of air occurs at levels below 10,000 feet; the middle layer has a predominantly cyclonic circulation (counterclockwise) around the central core; the upper third of the storm (above 25,000 feet) has an outward flow that accounts in part for the reduced atmospheric pressure in the system. At the center, or eye, of the storm, where pressure is lowest, a relative calm area exists. Around this, bands of strong winds circulate. Rising convective currents in these bands create extreme turbulence and the excessive precipitation often accompanying a hurricane. The cloud system may extend upward beyond 40,000 feet with the highest cloud spreading out at the base of the stratosphere. The whole system moves according to the steering currents of the prevailing high altitude wind flow.

Formation. In order to generate, tropical storms require the proper combination of warmth, moisture, and instability of the atmosphere. The exact process has been under intensive study in recent years but is not fully understood. Most are born when an upper-air disturbance, in the form of a tropical easterly wave or polar trough, is superimposed over an area of convection at the warm sea surface. This disturbs the normally homogeneous tropical air mass, causing increased convection and cloud formation. The rotation of the earth provides a deflecting force to the wind flow aloft, convection increases, precipitation takes place, winds accelerate, pressure drops, a central eye takes form at the surface, and a tropical storm is born.

Aftermath of the 1938 hurricane in Middletown, Connecticut

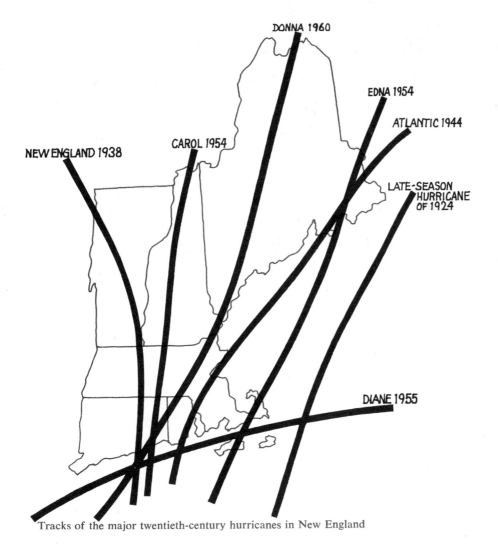

Tracks of the major twentieth-century hurricanes in New England

Hurricanes

THE COLONIAL PERIOD

1635 August 25—Great Colonial Hurricane—Narragansett Bay overland between Boston and Plymouth to Massachusetts Bay; "no storm more dismal"; "thousands of trees torn up by the roots"; 14-foot tide drowned eight Indians; described by Governors Winthrop and Bradford in journals.

1675 September 7—Second Colonial Hurricane—damage reported at New London, in Rhode Island, at Boston; "much loss of corn and hay, multitudes of trees blown down"; described by Rev. Increase Mather in *Remarkable Providences*.

1683 August 23—Hurricane and Flood of 1683—severe at Stonington, Conn., "great storme that blasted all the trees"; Dover, N.H., "exceeding high tide and stormy weather"; Connecticut River rose 26 feet above normal level, damaging flood, probably similar to 1938.

1713 August 30—New London Hurricane—violent storm of rain and wind on the thirtieth was followed by "a Hurrycane wch blew down several buildings & fruit trees such as hath not been known. It blasted or withered ye leaves & like frost, though warm weather." Joshua Hempstead diary.

1727 September 27—"A Great Rain and Horrible Wind" in 1727—struck New London, Stonington, Narragansett Bay, eastern Massachusetts; Marblehead, Mass., "it blew up many trees by the roots"; structural damage at Boston, shipping losses.

1743 November 2—Ben Franklin's Eclipse Hurricane—described at Boston as "worst in years—great damage on land as well as at sea"; tide within four inches of 1723 record flood; by comparing time of lunar eclipse and cloud directions at Boston and Philadelphia, Franklin unlocked secret of movement of northeast storms.

1749 October 19—October Hurricane of 1749—moved short distance offshore; violent on Long Island Sound; drove seven vessels ashore on Martha's Vineyard; at Boston "A violent storm at NE."

1761 October 23–24—Winthrop's Hurricane—path across southeast New England; "most violent storm in 30 years"; "tore up whole trees by the roots"; great shipping losses; described by Prof. John Winthrop in meteorological journal.

1770 October 20—Stiles's Hurricane—reported from New London to Boston; greatest tide at Boston since 1723; at Newport, R.I.: "A violent hurricane. Wind N or NE. Rain violent—hail—vane of church steeple blown off"; described by Rev. Ezra Stiles in weather diary.

1778 August 12–13—The French Storm—major hurricane off Rhode Island damaged French and British warships and prevented start of sea battle, many ships dismasted; on Martha's Vineyard corn crop ruined, hunger followed; heavy coastal shipping damage.

1788 August 19—Western New England Hurricane—this mini-hurricane with small core center did great forest damage for less than 30 minutes' duration over 75-mile-wide track; entered from New York, cut across northwest Connecticut, western Massachusetts, southern Vermont, central New Hampshire, interior Maine; many cattle and several humans killed by falling trees; storm unique in New England annals.

NINETEENTH CENTURY

1815 September 23—The Great September Gale—landfall near Center Moriches, Long Island, bisected New England, Saybrook to Canada; enormous shore damage; extensive structural damage east of track; widespread forest blowdown interior; downtown Providence flooded by storm tide; celebrated in poem by Oliver Wendell Holmes.

1821 September 3—Redfield's Hurricane—storm track from Stamford through the Berkshires into Vermont; extensive shore damage in Connecticut; forest blowdown in the Berkshires, little in Vermont; tree-fall direction studied by William C. Redfield, revealed circular circulation pattern of hurricane.

1841 October 3—The October Gale—severe on Nantucket, outer Cape Cod, offshore waters; 19 vessels stranded on Nantucket where "such a sight was never before or since witnessed"; 57 men lost from Truro alone, many others from nearby towns; Cape Ann also suffered.

1856 August 21—Charter Oak Storm—tropical storm along Long Island to Cape Cod; heavy rains; Hartford's famous Charter Oak, standing for 300 years, snapped off six feet from ground soon after wind shift.

1869 September 8—September Gale of '69—storm track Stonington to Portsmouth; Providence flooded by storm tide; structural damage at Boston and eastern Massachusetts.

New England Hurricane of 1938

The New England Hurricane of 1938 stands unchallenged as the greatest single event in the meteorological history of the region. On that unforgettable afternoon of September 21, the interplay of weather elements over the Atlantic Ocean with those over the nearby continent channeled an atmospheric whirl of massive physical structure and enormous energy onto a path that cut through the heartland of New England. Striking almost without warning and with unprecedented force, the mighty intruder from the tropics snuffed out more lives, temporarily disrupted more living patterns, and destroyed more property than any other natural catastrophe in New England's history.

At sunrise on the fatal twenty-first, a full hurricane of unknown strength was churning northward in the waters off Cape Hatteras. It was expected to follow a normal path by gradually curving northeast away from land and was thought to be moving at a normal speed. Instead, it followed a congenial atmospheric trough of low pressure almost directly northward and accelerated from a normal 30–40-mph rate to a final dash toward land at a pace in excess of 60 mph.

The center of the hurricane smashed ashore on central Long Island at about 3:00 P.M., and an hour later, having crossed Long Island Sound, it was roaring northward in the Milford area of Connecticut about ten miles west of New Haven. The path continued slightly east of north over the Farmington Valley west of Hartford, and then northward, following the central Connecticut Valley. It was close to Hadley, Massachusetts, about 5:00 P.M. Beyond Brattleboro steering conditions in the upper atmosphere carried the center north-northwest and then northwest almost diagonally across the central spine of the Green Mountain State. It passed over Northfield, Vermont, at about 7:30 P.M. and moved very close to Burlington at about 8:00 P.M.

The eye had been much reduced in size and transformed in structure by frictional forces in its passage overland. When passing to the west of Hartford, the diameter was reduced to an estimated ten to fourteen miles. Reaching Northfield, the period of light winds in the eye prevailed for only eighteen minutes. The hurricane made the 260-mile trip through western New England from Long Island Sound to Canada in about five hours at a speed slightly over 50 mph.

Nowhere in New England did the atmospheric pressure fall as low as that registered at Bellport on Long Island, 27.94″/946.2mb. Hartford reported New England's lowest at 28.04″/949.5mb and near the end of the path at Burlington, 28.68″/971.2mb.

Wind blasts along the immediate shoreline exceeded 100 mph on the ground. Block Island recorded a sustained wind for five full minutes of 82 mph, and at Providence—a more elevated exposure—the figure was 87 mph. Boston's Logan Airport, at sea level, had a maximum of 87 mph and a sustained five-minute average of 73 mph. On the crest of Blue Hill, an open exposure south of the city with an anemometer elevation of 681 feet, the funneling effect of the wind over the hill produced a sustained speed of 121 mph with a gust of 186 mph. Atop Mount Washington, when the storm had already lost some of its drive, gusts reached 162 mph with a sustained speed of 136 mph. Top speed at the Burlington anemometer location near ground level was 47 mph.

The greatest amount of damage and the greatest loss of life was caused by the hurricane's tidal surge along the shoreline of Rhode Island and Massachusetts. Along the beaches of Rhode Island facing the open Atlantic, "the series of waves, each higher than the previous one, were lashed into a seething, foaming fury to the height of 30 feet," according to William A. Cawley, a documenter of the storm. Another witness told of mountainous waves, forty feet high, sweeping over the sands, obliterating all man-made structures, and causing major transformation of land forms. In the bays reaching northward and eastward

Downtown Providence, Rhode Island—flooded by

1869 *October 3–4*—Saxby's Gale—struck NE Maine and Bay of Fundy; Eastport hard hit; record tides; low-pressure trough over New England caused extreme floods in all six states.

1878 *October 23–24*—Central New England Hurricane of '78—storm track Albany-Concord-Kennebunkport, Maine; Portland anemometer destroyed; very high tides, harbor damage; tree blowdown inland.

1879 *August 18–19*—Cape Cod Hurricane of '79—landfall at Buzzards Bay; wind lull at Newport, New Bedford, Woods Hole where barometer read 29.05″ and winds were 44 mph; extensive shore damage on islands and Cape Cod.

1888 *November 25–27*—Late-season Hurricane—three-day blow; center off Nantucket at 7:00 A.M. November 27; winds 65 mph at Block Island; wave spray topped Minot Light 114 feet high; 15 vessels wrecked near Boston.

1893 *August 21*—First of three hurricanes in month passed well to the east, giving moderate gales and heavy rain.

1893 *August 24*—Ex-hurricane—storm track Stamford-Pittsfield-Woodstock-Fort Kent; 300 elms downed at New Haven; oyster beds covered; tobacco crop almost ruined in Connecticut Valley.

42

the hurricane of September 21, 1938.

This house in Amherst, Massachusetts, was damaged in the same storm.

1893 *August 29*—Ex-hurricane—crossed west and north; storm track Harrisburg-Bennington-Hanover-Caribou; Northfield barometer 29.34″, Nashua 29.32″; Amherst, Mass., had 66-mph winds.

1893 *October 13–14*—Ex-hurricane in western New England—storm track Washington–central Pennsylvania–west New York; light damage similar to Hazel in 1954.

1896 *October 12–13*—Columbus Day Blow—offshore hurricane at 40°N, 67°W; winds at Block Island 60 mph; "A day practically without precipitation, but with destructive easterly gales, high tides, and an unusually heavy surf on coast," *Climate and Crop Bulletin.*

TWENTIETH CENTURY

1903 *September 16*—New Jersey Ex-Hurricane—unique landfall near Atlantic City, soon dissipated; gave southern New England wind lashing, some damage; New Haven winds 47 mph, highest in 30 years.

1916 *July 21*—July Storm—landfall at Martha's Vineyard; Block Island barometer 29.37″, 40-mph winds; excessive rainfall followed on July 22–23 from tropical air brought northward.

1924 *August 26*—Offshore Hurricane of '24—center within 50 miles of Nantucket; Block Island and Blue Hill had winds at 60 mph; extensive property damage in Rhode Island and Massachusetts; small boat losses; crop damage; 6.36″ rainfall at Fall River.

1933 *September 17–18*—Storm No. 15 of 21 in the most active tropical storm season of modern times passed about 75 miles SE of Nantucket; 54-mph winds, barometer 29.16″/987.5mb; excessive rains, 9.92″ at Provincetown in 24 hours, storm total 13.27″; Boston 5.63″; Woodland, Maine, 3.81″.

1936 *September 18–19*—Storm No. 13 of 16—passed about 40 miles east of Cape Cod; Nantucket barometer 29.27″/991.2mb, winds 45 mph; Block Island 58-mph winds; excessive rains again, Provincetown 7.79″, Kingston 6.46″, New Haven 4.73″.

1938 *September 21*—Great New England Hurricane—landfall near Patchogue, Long Island; track from Milford, up Connecticut Valley, then NW across Vermont to Burlington; lowest barometric pressure in New England 28.04″/949.5mb; Block Island 82-mph winds for five minutes, Blue Hill winds at 121 mph; extreme coastal destruction, downtown Providence flooded by record storm tide; widespread forest blowdown interior;

all western rivers in high flood; 600 or more killed, $306 million damage.

1944 *September 14–15*—Great Atlantic Hurricane—storm track from Point Judith, R.I., to South Weymouth, Mass., 67 miles in 110 minutes; lowest barometric pressure 28.34″/959.7mb; Cape Cod suffered severely; 26 killed in New England, 300 or more at sea, $100 million damage.

1950 *September 11–12*—Hurricane Dog—center 85 miles ESE Nantucket; curved out to sea south of Nova Scotia; Nantucket battered, 72-mph gusts, 4.42″ rain in 24 hours; ships lost; high tide and surf; damage to small boats, sea walls, over $2 million.

1954 *August 31*—Hurricane Carol—storm track from Westhampton on Long Island to Saybrook, Conn., west of Worcester, through central New Hampshire to Quebec; lowest barometric pressure 28.77″/974.3mb; 130-mph gusts on Block Island; 105-mph winds at Providence where downtown flooded by near-record tide; extensive forest damage; 50 killed, $438 million damage.

1954 *September 11*—Hurricane Edna—crossed Martha's Vineyard and Cape Cod; lowest barometric pressure 27.77″/940mb; large marine losses east of track; 21 killed; $40.5 million damage.

From left to right: A stand of pines in Massachusetts decimated by hurricane winds in September, 1938; a derailed train near Stonington, Connecticut — another victim of the 1938 storm; and a scene of chaos in Waterbury, Connecticut, after an August, 1955, hurricane

The Red Cross compiled the following figures for the six states:

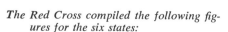

	Deaths	Damage
Maine	0	$ 135,000
New Hampshire	14	22,000,000
Vermont	7	15,000,000
Massachusetts	99	100,000,000
Rhode Island	380	125,000,000
Connecticut	85	125,000,000

from Rhode Island Sound, unprecedented surge heights were reached by the compounded waters in the narrowing estuaries.

At Point Judith and Brenton Point at the entrance of Narragansett Bay, the height of the tide exceeded the normal by seventeen feet. The coincidence of the scheduled high tide and the arrival of the hurricane surge raised levels to record heights. A marker in downtown Providence locates the height of the 1938 water at 13 feet 8.5 inches; this compared with 11 feet 9.25 inches in the previous high, during the Great September Gale of 1815. In Buzzards Bay the increase over normal ranged from nine to twelve feet from the entrance to the head of the bay at Wareham.

The Toll. The exact figures for the loss of life will never be known. Contemporary figures placed it at 585 for New England alone, and this has been rounded off to 600. A recent study by Joe McCarthy in *Hurricane* (1969) concluded: "If an exact count of the deaths resulting from the storm could be made, the total would probably be closer to 700 than to 600. Another 1,754 people were injured, and an estimated 63,000 people, many of them homeless, were forced to seek emergency help and shelter from the Red Cross and various local relief agencies."

Property damage was estimated at $387 million by the Red Cross. The three southern states suffered more than $100 million each. The Red Cross reported that 4,500 homes, summer cottages, and farm buildings were completely destroyed; 15,139 buildings were damaged; and 2,605 boats were lost and 3,369 damaged.

1954 October 15—Hurricane Hazel—passed over New York State; damaging winds in western New England; record 70-mph winds at Burlington; some structural damage and tree losses; one killed, $350,000 damage.

1955 August 17–19—Hurricane Diane—storm track over Long Island east to Cape Cod; rains up to 20″ on soil saturated by Connie a week before; extreme floods all southern New England; 82 killed, $800 million damage.

1960 September 12—Hurricane Donna—broad eye over Long Island Sound moved NE from New London to Maine; New Haven barometric pressure 28.55″/966.8mb; 95-mph winds at Block Island; tides not excessive; some crop losses; three killed.

QUIESCENT PRESENT: 1961–?

1961 Three late-season tropical storms threatened:

Esther reached position 50 miles SSE of Block Island on September 21; winds 83 mph, 7″ to 8″ rain in Connecticut and Rhode Island; then performed a unique clockwise loop south 300 miles to 36°N, then north along 70°W, passing over outer Cape Cod and making landfall again near Rockland, Maine, on September 26; little damage.

Frances moved NNW in Gulf of Maine on October 9, then recurved NE passing over SW Nova Scotia.

Gerda on a NNE track approached within 150 miles of Cape Cod on October 20 but veered NE passing well SE of Nova Scotia.

1962 Alma reached position about 50 miles SE of Nantucket on August 29; winds 37 mph, boat damage; then turned SE performing a loop before moving away to the NE to strike Newfoundland.

Daisy traveled north toward extreme NE Maine on October 7; excessive rains: Wakefield, Mass., 14.25″ total, Portland, Maine, 7.71″ in 24 hours; heavy swell damage and flooding in Massachusetts, New Hampshire, Maine; when SW of Nova Scotia turned NE to cross that peninsula.

1963 Ginny, only storm to approach New England waters, passed 125 miles SE of Cape Cod on October 29; Nantucket winds at 65 mph; crossed S Nova Scotia that night; 100-mph gusts off the Maine coast; 18″ snow interior, 48″ on Mount Katahdin.

1964 Dora on September 14 and Gladys on September 23–24 passed well east of Cape Cod; Nantucket had 42-mph NE winds and heavy rain on the fourteenth; all eastern Massachusetts had heavy rain on the twenty-fourth.

1965 No activity.

1966 Alma, a record early-season hurricane in Florida, moved over Cape Cod and the islands on June 14 as a light to moderate rainstorm.

1967 No activity.

1968 No close activity; Gladys late on October 20 passed SSE of Cape Cod at a distance of 300 miles; moved over Cape Breton Island.

1969 Gerda, most fortunately, proved an historic close miss on September 9; Nantucket Lightship, 75 miles SE of Cape Cod, reported 125-mph winds, gusts to 140 mph, as center passed overhead; Nantucket had only 40-mph winds, gusts to 58 mph; moved over Eastport in evening; Bangor 4.68″ of rain.

1970 No activity.

1971 Three tropical storms threatened:

Beth attained greatest force about 200 miles off Cape Cod on August 15; pressure at center 28.85″/977mb; winds about 87 mph.

Doria crossed coast near JFK Airport on August 28; storm track Litchfield-Keene-Caribou; gusts at Blue Hill to 80 mph, at Mount Washington 98 mph; very heavy rains, floods west of track.

Heidi passed 60 miles east of Cape Cod at noon on September 14, later moved inland near Rockport, Maine; vigorous when offshore in Gulf of Maine, but less than gale force winds at landfall.

1972 Agnes, much weakened and diffuse, moved inland near New York City on NW track on June 22; Bridgeport winds at 37 mph; lowest June pressures of record; moderate rain fell on saturated soil, some flooding; most damaging floods in U.S. history occurred in Pennsylvania and New York.

Carrie passed a short distance east of Cape Cod on September 3; lowest barometric pressure 29.29″/992mb; gusts 100 mph at Cape Cod, 85 mph at Point Judith, R.I.; very heavy rains: 8.55″ at Woods Hole, 7.02″ at Edgartown in 24 hours; disrupted Labor Day land travel, cancelled boat service to islands; landfall near Eastport on the fourth; 7.23″ of rain at Rockport.

1973 No activity.

1974 No activity.

1975 Blanche on north track crossed Nova Scotia on July 28; Gladys turned northeast on October 2, 200 miles off Cape Hatteras and passed 300 miles east of Cape Cod.

TORNADOES

The turbulence necessary for the formation of a tornado is usually associated with a general cyclonic storm moving eastward over New York State and southern Quebec. Preceding the main cold front, an instability line, or squall line, often forms 100 to 150 miles in advance in the warm sector of the storm over New England. These conditions give rise to the development of thunderstorms, and in extreme cases of instability aloft, a tornado funnel may form. Many of these will remain aloft either in the cloud or as a pendant. Only rarely does the funnel extend to the ground.

The atmospheric structure for tornado formation requires the presence of a moist air mass that is warm for the season. The lower winds usually have a southerly component. At intermediate levels a warm, dry stratum exists with a southwesterly air movement. At high levels a strong westerly flow prevails. The exact mechanism that causes a funnel or tornado to form, or not to form under similar conditions, is not fully understood and has been the subject of intense research in recent years by university and government scientists.

The tornado funnel forms in the turbulence aloft and gradually lowers toward the ground. Its rotation is usually counterclockwise. Condensed moisture in the funnel forms the trunklike cloud that is a distinguishing feature of many tornadoes. Funnels in New England differ in appearance from those in the clear, dry atmosphere of the Great Plains; here they may be all but invisible from the ground since the funnel is often imbedded in a dark shower cloud. Dirt and debris picked up from the ground produce a black appearance. The larger New England funnels have been described as pillars of black smoke from an advancing fire. The rotating winds in the funnel have never been accurately measured by an anemometer, but from radar photographs they are estimated to range from 150 mph to 200 mph. Reduced atmospheric pressure prevails in the center of the funnel, giving rise to an explosive action as a tornado passes over a well-insulated or unventilated building.

A waterspout has characteristics similar to a tornado. Its formation is usually over water, though a tornado moving from land to water may continue as a spout as long as its energy lasts. At its base a "bush" of water is raised from the surface. Little of this rises in the column; the water in the funnel results from condensation of atmospheric water vapor caused by the cooling induced by the pressure differential within the spout. Waterspouts usually have short life spans of a few minutes, but several may form and dissipate over a period of an hour or so.

Whirlwinds and dust devils are local phenomena resulting from intense local heating of the surface of the ground, when the rising air takes on a rotary motion. They are common on the afternoon of a hot day. Most have a life span of only a few seconds, but occasionally one may expand sufficiently to lift grass and small twigs into the air as it moves across a field or open country.

Predicting the possibility of tornado occurrence over a 25,000-square-mile area is now made on a routine basis. Tornado watches are issued from one to seven hours in advance. About 50 per cent of tornado watches have been verified in the past five years. Tornado warnings are issued after an actual funnel has been sighted or indicated by radar. [See Weather Warning section for precautions to take when a tornado threatens to occur.]

Tornado Characteristics in New England

Area. Tornadoes may occur anywhere in New England. They have been reported in the Allagash Valley of northern Maine, on Nantucket Island, at Greenwich in southwestern Connecticut, and at Saint Albans in northwestern Vermont. If there is a "tornado alley" in the region, it lies to the east of the Green Mountains and Berkshires in western New Hampshire, central Massachusetts, and central Connecticut. Tornadoes have been more deadly and destructive in this north-south corridor than elsewhere.

Season. Tornadoes, whirlwinds, and waterspouts have been reported in all months. They are rare, however, outside the warm season, and August seems to be the favorite month of occurrence in New England.

Time of day. Most tornadoes occur in the late afternoon or early evening since they are frequently associated with thunderstorms, which develop their greatest severity during the hottest part of the day. The favorite hours for formation extend from 3:00 P.M. to 7:00 P.M.

Direction. About 60 per cent of all tornadoes move from southwest to northeast; west to east is second with about 19 per cent; and northwest to southeast is third with about 10 per cent. The Great Worcester Tornado swept southeastward before turning east and finally heading northeast.

Speed. Forward speed averages between 25 mph and 40 mph, but some have remained stationary and others have moved at a 60-mph clip.

Size. In New England most tornadoes have courses less than one mile long and 100 yards wide. The Worcester Tornado had a path forty-six miles long and a width varying between one-half mile to one mile when fully developed. The Adirondack Tornado in 1845 traveled 275 miles before dissipating at Burlington, Vermont.

Opposite: An artist's conception of the Wallingford Tornado of 1878. *Above:* Worcester Tornado, June 9, 1953

47

Left to right: Homeless victims of the 1953 Worcester Tornado; the remains of houses along the tornado track; and damage to Assumption College in Worcester

The toll in deaths, injuries, and property damage in the towns hit by the main tornado:

| | Deaths | INJURIES | | Damage |
		Major	Minor	
Petersham	0	0	0	$ 128,000
Barre	0	0	0	100,000
Rutland	2	14	30	368,000
Holden	10	36	173	5,000,000
Worcester	62	327	411	32,100,000
Shrewsbury	6	37	156	8,900,000
Westboro	5	12	50	5,000,000
Southboro	5	10	32	547,000
Others	4			

In addition, the Exeter Tornado caused minor injury to five persons and did $100,000 damage. The Sutton-Wrentham Tornado seriously injured two and caused minor injuries to fifteen persons. Total damage in the towns of Sutton, North-bridge, Franklin, and Wrentham amounted to $671,000.

The total deaths on the afternoon of June 9, 1953, have been placed at 94 and the total damage at $53 million.

Worcester Tornado of 1953

For a period of seventy-five minutes on the late afternoon of June 9, 1953, a concentrated destructive force, unprecedented in the annals of New England, swept inexorably southeastward through the Worcester County communities of central Massachusetts. Strangely, its coming was unheralded to those who became its victims, and its very presence was unreported to the officials whose concern such a calamity should be—the police, civil defense authorities, and the weather bureau. In most cases, those suffering injury or loss of homes or property did not know what destructive power had hit them.

Damaging tornadoes had occurred in the Midwest on June 8 in advance of a strong eastward-moving storm system. The storm's sharp cold front lay across central New York State at 2:30 P.M. E.D.T. on June 9 and advanced into western Massachusetts by 5:30 P.M. It was preceded by a squall line that had developed in the early afternoon as heat and moisture were fed into the system. Huge cumulonimbus clouds darkened the skies, crackling with thunder and lightning and spewing hailstones across the countryside.

The first tornado descended from the clouds at Petersham shortly after 4:25 P.M. and moved on a path of forty-six miles to its dissolution in Southboro about 5:45, having a life span of one hour and twenty minutes. A second tornado struck Exeter, New Hampshire, around 5:20 P.M., while a third traveled a twenty-nine-mile path starting in Sutton, Massachusetts, about 5:30 and ending in Mansfield at 6:37. The three storms combined to take 94 lives, inflict over 400 major and

900 minor injuries, and destroy an estimated $53 million in property. All the fatalities, most of the injuries, and the bulk of the property losses were caused by the first tornado, mainly in and around Worcester. Here the funnel attained its greatest intensity and a maximum width of almost one mile.

The first evidence of tornadic activity, so far as contact with the surface of the earth and apparent damage were concerned, came about 4:25 P.M. E.D.T., when a funnel cloud lowered to the ground at a state forest abutting the northeastern shore of Quabbin Reservoir in the southeastern corner of Franklin County. Moving eastward four miles, to a point about a mile southwest of the center of Petersham, the tornado swung southeastward, crossing Routes 32 and 122, on a nearly straight course of six miles to Barre.

By the time it curved southeastward, the tornado had attained major force and expanded to an average width of 500 yards. There were indications that twin funnels moved through the Petersham area, but the second disturbance either dissipated or lifted aloft before reaching Barre. The eastern part of the town was struck about 4:45 P.M. The tornado evidently skipped over the low and swampy country extending to Rutland, since there is little or no sign of damage along the eight-mile stretch intervening. Rutland (hit at about 4:53) suffered most of its damage in a quarter-mile-wide corridor along Main Street from the center of the town eastward to Route 56.

Continuing southeastward eight miles parallel to and about one mile south of Route 122A to Route 31 in Holden, the tornado for the first time reached heavily built-up and populated areas. Simultaneously, in the vicinity of Chaffin Pond near Route 122A, its power increased and its path of destruction began to broaden; thus through the Holden-Worcester-Shrewsbury area, a distance of eight miles, the damage width averaged about three-fourths of a mile and reached a maximum of almost one mile in places. These localities suffered most of the deaths, injuries, and property destruction, and the havoc was virtually indescribable. Holden was struck at about 5:05 P.M., and soon afterward the track cut across the northern extension of Worcester. Trending almost directly southeast, the northern edge followed Mountain

Tornadoes

MAINE

1752 August 12—Portland; "Blew down houses and barns and everything in its way." Rev. T. Smith journal.

1767 July 10—Sebago Lake, Windham, Duck Pond, Portland.

1873 July 26—Between Old Town and Milford; train swept off bridge into Penobscot River, engineer killed.

1892 June 14—Orono; structural damage, trees uprooted; 98 mph on anemometer.

1921 May 22—Searsport near Belfast; one killed.

1929 May 16—Outbreak of tornadoes near Portland; spout on Lake Sebago.

1943 November 5—Outer Casco Bay near Halfway Rock; two spouts seen.

1954 May 11—Near Caribou; plowed up potatoes; one killed, $10,000 damage.

1958 August 22—Allagash Tornado in north; path 20 miles long, 300–400 yards wide through thickly forested area; hardwoods broken, fir and spruce uprooted in swirl fashion.

1971 June 30—Stacyville; intermittent track 12 miles long, occasionally about a half mile wide; machine shop damage.

Street closely, while the southern edge—somewhat wavering and irregular—passed north of Indian Lake and Burncoat Park. At the crossing of West Boylston Street (Route 12) the tornado was between three and four miles north of the green in downtown Worcester.

Maximum damage areas were: in Holden, the residential sections from Main Street east to the Worcester line; in Worcester, the strip southeastward crossing Route 12 (West Boylston Street) between Summit and Greendale to the northern reaches of Lake Quinsigamond, including the Greendale section, the Norton Company plant, Assumption College, the Great Brook Valley Housing Project, and the City Farm; in Shrewsbury, the residential districts on and adjacent to Main Street, Maple Avenue, Crescent Street, Lake Street, Grafton Street, and South Street.

As the tornado entered Shrewsbury at about 5:18 P.M., it swerved eastward momentarily toward the center of the town but soon resumed its previous southeast direction. Crossing the Worcester Turnpike (Route 9) at the intersection with South Street (Route 140), it again swerved and took an eastward path for three miles to Westboro, which was struck at about 5:30 P.M. A three-quarter-mile-wide swath was ripped through the southern part of the town and along Flanders Road, three miles east of Westboro Center.

At this point, the tornado's path began to narrow and curve northeastward, parallel to and about one mile north of the present Massachusetts Turnpike. Damage was still severe, however, in an average quarter-mile-wide band through the Parkerville, Middle, Mt. Vickery, Cordaville, and Break Neck Hills roads area of Southboro. Its path was only 300 yards wide when it recrossed Route 9, smashing the little community of Fayville about 5:40 P.M. A mile and a half beyond, when it was close to the southeastern corner of Sudbury Reservoir and a short distance northwest of the present Framingham Interchange on Route 90, the tornado's track ended. The funnel either lifted from the ground or dissipated.

An 1851 rendering of "Horrors of the whirlwind throughout New England"

MASSACHUSETTS

1643 *July 15*—Newbury; "sudden gust" lifted meeting house with people inside; one Indian killed; described by Gov. John Winthrop.

1680 *July 18*—Cambridge; tree destruction; one killed; described by Rev. Increase Mather.

1759 *July 10*—Leicester; hit house occupied by people; one killed; described by Prof. John Winthrop.

1773 *August 14*—Salisbury, Amesbury, Haverhill; structural damage; several injured; described by Prof. Samuel Williams.

1786 *August 23*—Sturbridge, Southbridge; dark whirling cloud; over 100 buildings damaged; several injured, two killed.

1787 *August 15*—Four-State Outbreak; Barre, Oakham, Rutland, Boylston, Northboro, Westboro, Marlboro, Southboro, Framingham, Sudbury, Wayland, Weston, Malden; moved from Connecticut and Rhode Island; apparently several funnels with skip action.

1811 *August 21*—Northboro; "a most terrifying whirlwind or hurricane"; 1.5-mile path; structural and forest damage.

1821 *September 9*—Franklin County Tornado; Northfield, Warwick, Orange, Royalston; one of an extensive outbreak; ten-mile path; "Sounded like heavy distant thunder and shook the earth to a distance of 2 to 3 miles," *Franklin Herald;* structural damage; debris carried 25 miles; two killed.

1851 *August 22*—Middlesex County Tornado; Wayland, Belmont, Spy Pond in Arlington, Medford; skip action from near Worcester to Rockport; destruction over 12-mile track, maximum width 400 yards; estimated 50-mph forward speed; explosive effect; no deaths, six serious injuries.

1863 *August 20*—Charlestown Navy Yard and East Boston; trees felled, large buildings damaged.

1879 *July 16*—Pittsfield; extensive damage; two killed; tornado-type at Northampton, Fitchburg, Salem, Brockton, Taunton, Woods Hole.

1890 *July 26*—Lawrence Tornado; North Billerica, North Andover, Lawrence; 11-mile path; main damage north end of Lawrence; residences destroyed; 8 killed, 50 injured.

1925 *October 25*—Woburn, Stoneham; one killed.

1927 *July 31*—Rehoboth, North Duxbury; skip action; one killed.

1953 *June 9*—Worcester County Tornado; 46-mile path through settled communities: Petersham, Barre, Rutland, Holden, Worcester, Shrewsbury, Westboro, Southboro, Fayville; explosive effect; extreme structural damage; 90 killed, 1,288 injured, $52.1 million damage.

1953 *June 9*—Norfolk County Tornado; Sutton, Riverdale, Bellingham, Franklin, Wrentham, Mansfield; 29-mile skip path, mainly through woods; 26-mph forward speed; 17 injured.

1958 *September 7*—Duxbury; one killed.

1970 *October 3*—Hardwick, Littleton; discontinuous 35-mile path; one killed.

1972 *August 9*—Needham, Newton, Brookline; seven miles hit-skip path; one killed, six injured in Chestnut Hill section.

1973 *August 28*—From Columbia County, N.Y.; hit truck stop at West Stockbridge; 11-mile path, 350 yards wide; 4 killed, 43 injured.

VERMONT

1782 *June 23*—Wide outbreak; damage at Pawlet, Manchester, Weathersfield, Royalton; some structural damage; forest destruction.

1821 *September 9*—Three-State Outbreak; Pittsford and Brandon area, and Berlin near Montpelier; $20,000 damage.

1829 *August 9*—Peacham, Barnet; tremendous whirlwind; apparently skipped from Essex County, N.Y.; short destructive path, 50–175 yards wide; structural damage; spout on Harvey's Pond.

1833 *July 2*—Orleans–Essex County Tornado; Derby, Salem Pond, Holland, Norton Pond, almost to Connecticut River; about 12 miles long; extensive forest damage.

1845 *September 20*—Adirondack Tornado crossed Lake Champlain as a waterspout; struck downtown Burlington, leveling trees, demolishing chimneys, and unroofing large buildings.

1877 *May 18*—From Cambridge, N.Y., into Bennington County; damage from wind and hail extensive at Shaftsbury and Arlington.

1882 *September 14*—Strafford; four miles long, one-quarter mile wide, buildings damaged, trees uprooted.

1907 *September 30*—Enosburg Falls; funnel seen; five to six rods wide, about one mile long.

1953 *June 21*—Saint Albans; structural damage.

1954 *February 12*—Lake Champlain waterspouts; 40 separate funnels offshore near Burlington.

1957 *June 18*—Franklin, Vt., to West Berkshire, Vt.; $58,000 damage.

1962 *January 4*—Spouts moving north off Burlington.

1962 *May 20*—Series of at least three funnels; Bakersfield, Westfield, Albany, Coventry; farm buildings damaged.

1962 *July 9*—Chester to Weathersfield, 16 miles; Springfield into Charlestown, N.H., eight miles; structural damage.

1970 *August 3*—Saint Albans; five-mile path, 150 yards wide; spout, then tornado; seven injured.

1972 *July 9*—East Fairfield; two-mile path, 50 yards wide; leveled trees, new barn, silo.

1972 *August 9*—Fairlee, Lake Morey, Bradford; four-mile path, 25 yards wide; intermittent damage to cottages.

NEW HAMPSHIRE

1782 *June 23*—Claremont, Croydon; moved from Vermont; one killed.

1787 *August 15*—Four-State Outbreak; Dunbarton, Concord, Rochester.

1814 *May 21*—Merrimack, Londonderry, Chester; 17 miles long; structural damage, forest destruction; one killed.

1821 *September 9*—Great New Hampshire Tornado; Cornish, Croydon, Lake Sunapee, New London, Sutton, Mount Kearsarge, Salisbury, Warner, Boscawen; 23 miles long, 100 feet to a half mile wide; at least five killed.

1877 *July 1*—Gilsum, Sullivan, Nelson; path over Mount Surry; considerable damage.

1880 *July 16*—Hanover; two miles long, about a half mile wide; much damage.

1890 *May 16*—Newmarket; one killed.

1905 *January 7*—Bethlehem; "well-defined tornado" blew down barns, moved a church 18 inches.

1911 *July 24*—Concord; three-mile path, 300 yards wide; numerous buildings wrecked and a great many trees uprooted or broken off.

1929 *May 5*—Berlin; skipping path; $200,000 damage.

1946 *July 23*—Concord; one killed, $60,000 damage.

1953 *June 9*—Exeter; five injured.

1967 *July 12*—Epsom; five injured.

1972 *July 3*—Gilmanton; one mile long, 200 yards wide; ten cottages damaged, two demolished; seven injured.

1972 *July 21*—Three funnels: Canaan, Enfield, Hudson; longest track seven miles.

RHODE ISLAND

1787 *August 15*—Four-State Outbreak; easternmost passed from Connecticut through Gloucester, R.I., into Massachusetts; structural and forest damage.

1838 *August 30*—Cranston, South Providence; spout across Seekonk River into Massachusetts; path 20 miles; some damage; studied by Brown faculty.

1845 Summer—Spout in Narragansett Bay.

1879 *September 11*—Spout near Newport.

1895 *January 26*—Kingston; 400 feet wide; building turned around, barn blown over.

1934 *December 1*—Hope Valley; three-fourths of a mile long, 60 feet wide; considerable damage.

1972 *September 14*—Jamestown to Fort Adams; moved from center of Jamestown into Narragansett Bay as waterspout, then over Fort Adams; two-mile path; small boats damaged.

CONNECTICUT

1682 *June 18*—Norwalk, Fairfield, Stratford, Milford, New Haven; almost universal destruction of all trees; path about 28 miles long, up to a half mile wide; midafternoon occurrence.

1784 *August 17*—Shepaug Dam, Woodbury, Southbury; "a most extraordinary and terrible gale"; path about a half mile wide.

1786 *August 23*—Woodstock, Killingly; one-quarter-mile wide; structural damage, forest destruction; one killed.

1787 *August 15*—Four-State Outbreak; New Britain, Wethersfield, East Hartford, Pomfret, Woodstock, Killingly; skipping action; widespread damage; two killed.

1794 *June 19*—From New York; New Milford, Newtown, Waterbury, Watertown, Branford, Long Island Sound; one or more funnels; skipping action; forest destruction.

1839 *July 31*—Woodbridge, East Rock, Quinnipiac marshes; four miles long, 300 yards wide; six houses, four barns demolished; studied by Yale faculty.

1878 *August 9*—Wallingford Tornado; short track of two miles through north residential area; extensive damage; 34 killed (33 Catholics and 1 Protestant); 100 injured, 28 seriously; $200,000 damage.

1886 *September 12*—Burnside, Ellington, Windermere; 13 miles long, 50–200 yards wide.

1937 *July 26*—Terryville, Bristol; six miles long, 150–200 yards wide.

1951 *August 21*—Litchfield County Outbreak; Kent, New Milford, Washington, Watertown, Bridgewater, Bethlehem, Litchfield; also Bristol in Hartford County.

1962 *May 24*—Middlebury, Waterbury, Wolcott, Southington; 12-mile path; razed 70 structures, heavy damage to 175, moderate to 600; one killed, 50 injured, about $1 million damage.

This contemporary view of the Wallingford, Connecticut, tornado of 1878, was labeled "Junction of clouds over pond of water."

THE WORLD'S GREATEST SLEIGH PARTY.

SNOWSTORMS

At this remove, it would be difficult to dispute the accuracy of the caption above.

Great Snow of 1717

No natural event in colonial New England has achieved such reverential status as the Great Snow of 1717. Accounts appear in many local and regional histories and hardly a diarist fails to mention it. And whenever a contemporary heavy snowstorm was in the news, editors made reference back to 1717. The Great Snow consisted of four successive snowfalls within ten days, from February 27 to March 7, 1717. Two were of major proportions and two were relatively light falls.

Cotton Mather wrote, "As mighty a snow, as perhaps has been known in the memory of man, is at this time lying on the ground." No one left any precise measurements of the depth of each storm, but at its conclusion it was estimated to stand four feet deep at Andover to the north of Boston and three feet deep in the woods of Dorchester just to the south. Dr. William Douglass, a contemporary New England historian, who showed special concern for weather and climate matters, stated that the snow fell "upwards of 3 feet upon a level." Although no such a depth on the ground has been experienced in the modern era in downtown Boston, it is thought meteorologically possible if four storms came in similar quick succession and temperatures remained below freezing. Five feet of snow with drifts of fourteen feet were reported on the Post Road to New Hampshire and Maine.

The *Boston News-Letter* stated, "The snow is so deep that there is no traveling." There were no Sabbath services for two weeks at Mather's church in downtown Boston, and out in Framingham no public meetings could be held until the end of March. Sheep were said to have

52

been buried for twenty-eight days and then dug out alive. It was estimated that 95 per cent of the immobilized deer population was killed by wolves or bears.

An account of the Great Snow was composed by Mather and sent to London for reading before the Royal Society. This later appeared in one of the first publications of the Massachusetts Historical Society.

The Great Snow of 1717

The Blizzard of '88

The Blizzard of '88 remains unrivaled in the annals of modern New England snowstorms. Only the legendary Great Snow of 1717 in colonial times achieved such an enduring reputation. Several storms in the present century have affected particular sections of the six-state region, but none encompassed so much of the area in such deep snow as did the famous storm on March 11–14, 1888. It qualified fully in all three requirements for an eastern blizzard: heavy drifting snowfall, gale-force winds, and bitter, near-zero cold.

The storm concentrated its fury across southern New Hampshire and Vermont and down through central and western Massachusetts and most of Connecticut. Precipitation amounts were greater than three inches of melted water, an excessive amount for a winter storm. Where this fell entirely as snow, depths amounted to 30 inches and in some localities reached 40 and 50 inches. The corner of southeastern New England east of a line from New London to Boston, where temperatures hovered just above freezing, received a sloppy mixture of snow and rain. Boston accumulated nine inches of slush, but on Cape Cod and the islands it was mostly all rain.

The storm center, blocked in its normal northeastward movement up the Atlantic seaboard, stalled in the vicinity of Block Island during the twelfth and most of the thirteenth, all the while increasing its barometric depth and continuing to pump a flow of moist tropical air over the Atlantic Ocean into the interior of New England. There it was opposed by a wedge of very frigid arctic air hugging the land surface and was forced up over the cold air mass, which cooled and condensed its moisture into billions of snowflakes. The snow-making process aloft kept going for over forty-eight hours, with depths on the ground accumulating at a rate of an inch an hour and more. When the snowfall tapered off on the third day, New Haven's official weatherman measured a fall of 46 inches, and nearby Middletown reported 50 inches. Most of the Berkshires, the southern Green Mountains, and the hills of southern New Hampshire westward from the Monadnock area reported 30–36 inches or more. Northern Vermont localities had 20 inches, northern Maine, about 20 inches.

Exchange Place, Waterbury, Connecticut, after the Blizzard of '88

Connecticut's Worst Modern Snowstorm

The coldest month of the past 100 years spawned the worst snowstorm of the twentieth century across the Nutmeg State when a severe northeaster raged for two days during the long, unbroken, frigid period. The center of a coastal storm cut across Rhode Island on a northeastward track during daylight of February 20, 1934. Its severity was attested to by the extremely low barometer reading of 28.73"/972.9mb at Block Island and the 47-mph sustained wind at Providence. Both the northeast winds preceding the center and the northwest following winds gusted to gale force over all of Connecticut. Several stations measured over 2.00 inches of melted precipitation, which amounted to more than 20 inches of snow. Coastal locations such as Bridgeport, Norwalk, and New Haven had 22 inches. Temperatures during the main snow period were close to 30°, but they dropped off rapidly when the winds backed to northwest, and reached 11° at New Haven by midnight of the twentieth and 3° in the north while the snowflakes were still flying. In the extreme southeast much of the precipitation fell as rain; New London reported only 3 inches of snow, but 0.96 inches of precipitation. Before the storm ended, the rapidly declining temperature froze the wet snow solid before it could be removed from streets and highways, causing a serious interruption of traffic. The Hartford press rated the storm as the worst since the Great Eastern Blizzard of February, 1899.

New Hampshire's Most Intense Snowfall

The White Mountains of New Hampshire were never whiter than on November 22–23, 1943, when over 50 inches of pristine snow descended in less than twenty-four hours on the bare valleys of the region, and probably much more covered exposed higher elevations. A coastal storm, stalling for a number of hours in the vicinity of Boston, swept an easterly current of moist air from the warm waters of the central Atlantic Ocean inland over the coastal plain. When forced to ascend over the Presidential Range, its moisture condensed into snow. (As much as 5.00 inches of melted precipitation were caught in snow gauges.) It was heaviest on the northern flank of the range where Randolph, in a deep valley, measured new snow depths of 56 inches and Berlin 55 inches. On the eastern slope, Pinkham Notch at 2,000 feet had 51 inches, and other stations in the vicinity recorded 40 inches or more. But no station on the southern or western slopes reported as much as 20 inches. Temperatures during the big snow period on November 22 ranged from 28° to 32° at Berlin but rose to 40° on the twenty-third.

Rhode Island's Greatest Modern Snowstorm

Snow historians in Rhode Island seem to be at odds as to the state's greatest recent snowstorm. There are several candidates for the title. On February 8–9, 1945, a severe northeaster is said to have deposited 34 inches within twenty-four hours at Foster, located about ten miles west of Providence, though only 14.5 inches, with a water content of 1.58 inches, was measured in the capital. No other station in neighboring states had a snow total much in excess of 20 inches. The Big Snow on February 3–4, 1961, probably deposited a greater mass of snow over the entire state than any other modern storm: Kingston 18.9 inches, Providence 18.3 inches, Block Island 16.9 inches, and Woonsocket 17 inches. The Great Eastern New England Storm on February 24–28, 1969, covered the northeast corner of the state. Woonsocket measured 29.8 inches during the six-day fall, and the ground cover mounted to 38 inches on February 26, a record for the state. At Providence Airport, only twenty miles distant, there was only 15.9 inches and at Block Island only 8 inches on this occasion.

Vermont and Western Massachusetts's Deepest Snowfall

Vermont's deepest single snowfall occurred in the extreme southern end of the state in early March, 1947, when Readsboro (elevation 1,122 feet) measured 50 inches of new snow from the second to the sixth. This raised the depth on the ground to 80 inches. Peru, a short distance to the south in Massachusetts, had a measurement of 47 inches on the same days. Both stations reported over 4.00 inches of melted precipitation. These extraordinary amounts resulted from the unusual path of a very deep storm center that moved slowly up the Connecticut Valley to southern Vermont and then curved northwestward to Lake Champlain

These two sports were photographed while snowshoeing in the Maine woods.

and northern New York State where it stalled for many hours. This trajectory kept a massive flow of very moist air from the Atlantic Ocean riding over the elevated crests of the Berkshires and the Green Mountains for many hours longer than in a normal situation. The higher elevations, where temperatures were just below freezing, received all the precipitation as snow, but in the valleys most of it fell as rain. Highway traffic over the mountains was blocked for many hours, and some communities were isolated for up to four days.

Great Storm of '52 on Cape Cod and the Islands

In 1952 the most spectacular storm to hit the coastal area of southeastern Massachusetts in over half a century dropped over 20 inches of snow that was piled into mountainous drifts by winds of full gale force. All road traffic halted while snow-removal equipment was rushed from the Berkshire towns of western Massachusetts; some 3,000 motorists were stranded on the Lower Cape when Routes 6 and 28 became impassable. An estimated 10,000 homes were without electricity on the Cape when power lines snapped in the near-hurricane force winds.

Snow began at Nantucket about 9:00 A.M. on February 27 and continued until 5:00 A.M. on the twenty-eighth. Some lighter falls came on the night of February 28–29. With the remains of the 10 inches falling on the twenty-first, the depth on the ground increased to 23 inches, the greatest in Nantucket record books. Hyannis, too, had record depths: a fall of 20 inches raised the amount on the ground to 24 inches. Edgartown had received 10 inches on the twenty-first and now had 14 inches more. The storm merely brushed the remainder of southeastern Massachusetts, and away from the Cape amounts diminished: Plymouth 10 inches and New Bedford 11.5 inches. Farther inland, falls were light to moderate: Providence 4.9 inches, Boston 5.2 inches, and Worcester 2 inches.

The storm center remained well offshore, deepening continuously, as a report of a ship's barometer reading of 28.02"/948.9mb indicated.

Above: Digging out a snowbound train.
Below: Clearing a road the hard way

The lowest at Nantucket was 28.79″/974.9mb. Sustained winds of 61 mph were experienced, with gusts as high as 72 mph sweeping Nantucket Airport. The 120-foot Loran tower nearby at Siasconset was toppled by gales at the height of the storm. High tides damaged dwellings in the low ground near Brant Point.

All the ingredients of a blizzard were present except low temperatures. Nantucket had almost identical ranges on February 27 and 28: 36°/27° and 37°/26°. The above-freezing periods caused the snow to settle somewhat, so the storm must be classified as Cape Cod's and the islands' deepest snowstorm of modern times—not a blizzard.

Central Maine's Severest Snowstorm

Severe blizzard conditions set in over most of Maine on December 30, 1962, as a coastal storm performed an unusual maneuver. It had advanced on a normal track along the offshore waters, and near Yarmouth, Nova Scotia, it commenced a counterclockwise loop to the west and then south over central Maine and back again to the northeast toward Nova Scotia. All the while, shifting gales prevailed at the surface, while overhead moist air from the Atlantic continued to glide landward, rising over the disturbed cyclonic whirl at the surface. The result was excessive precipitation driven by strong gales and accompanied by rapidly falling temperatures. The heaviest snowfall was measured at Ripogenus Dam, northwest of Millinocket, where 46 inches fell. The intensity of the snowfall can be gauged by the record 40 inches in twenty-four hours reported at Orono. The shifting gales accompanying the errant storm center piled drifts as high as twenty feet on highways, blocking main roads for three days. The *Bangor Daily News* was unable to publish an edition for the first time in 128 years of operation. The entire state suffered one of its severest wind chills on December 31. Augusta's thermometer sank to −15° on New Year's Eve with gusts of 40 mph in the area. Hundreds of travelers were stranded over the holidays.

The Hundred-Year Storm in One Hundred Hours

In almost 100 years of National Weather Service records, Boston never experienced a single snowstorm of 20 inches or more, though such depths had occurred at many more southerly latitudes in the United States. It required an unprecedented 100 hours of almost steady snowfall in February, 1969, from 1:35 A.M. on the twenty-fourth to 12:10 A.M. on the twenty-eighth, to pile up the current record amount of 26.3 inches. The major deposit of 17 inches fell during the first thirty hours; thereafter, mostly light to occasionally moderate amounts fell. The maximum snowfall measured on the ground was 20 inches at 7:00 P.M. on the twenty-sixth. Neither the twenty-four-hour amounts nor the maximum on the ground constituted records, but the total fall of 26.3 inches goes into the record books as the greatest single snowstorm in Boston in over 105 years.

February, 1969, set a new record for any month with a total of 41.3 inches. The long duration of the snowfall was attributed to the blocking of a surface low near Cape Cod and its convergence with an upper-air low. The combined low-pressure areas then commenced to move slowly eastward offshore, all the while maintaining an easterly flow of moist air on the northern flank where temperatures remained just below freezing. Locations from Rhode Island to central Maine shared in the heavy snowfall. Some Boston suburbs reported over 30 inches; Rockport on Cape Ann combined some sea-effect snowfall with the regular storm to increase the total to 39 inches. Portland, Maine, with 26.9 inches, also set a 100-year single-storm record, as did Portsmouth, New Hampshire, with 33.8 inches. When the moist airstream hit

Bringing in the cows

Abandoned cars jam a highway near Woburn, Massachusetts, in February, 1969.

the White Mountains, some spectacular falls occurred. Pinkham Notch reported daily totals of 21 inches, 24.5 inches, 27 inches, and 4.5 inches from February 25 to 28, for a grand total of 77 inches. Impressive totals were also registered in western Maine where Long Falls Dam set a new state record of 55 inches in a single storm and Old Town Airport had 43.6 inches.

Northwest New England's Greatest Snowstorm

Christmas morning of 1969 dawned cold and clear over Burlington, Vermont, with air movement practically calm. Little did the residents suspect that another twenty-four hours would find the region blanketed by its greatest snowstorm of modern record. At this time a coastal low-pressure area was spreading a variety of weather over the Atlantic coastal plain with very substantial snowfall in the Appalachian highlands. Snow commenced to filter down over northwestern Vermont soon after midnight of the twenty-fifth, when the storm center was off the Delaware coast. There the advancing disturbance came under the influence of a Quebec-Labrador high-pressure area, which slowed its forward progress so much that it required twenty-four hours to move from Long Island to Boston. An upper-air trough was aligned so that it brought a steady southeasterly flow of moist air over all of New England and southern Quebec for three days. The snowfall, continuing at Burlington until 1:25 P.M. on December 28, totaled 29.7 inches, well above the previous single-storm record of 24.8 inches set in January, 1934. The ground accumulation reached 33 inches—just equal to the maximum measurement in February, 1958. Nearby Montpelier reported 34 inches of new snow and a ground cover of 45 inches, and the figures at Saint Albans Bay were 32 inches and 39 inches. Montreal also experienced its greatest snowstorm of all time, with 27.5 inches total. East of the Green Mountains, a severe ice storm succeeded an early moderate snowfall, locking the region in its most damaging ice sheath in many years. In the Saint Johnsbury area the ice lasted most of the winter.

Before the advent of snowplows, New England's roads were packed by horse-drawn snowrollers. This one was in Peacham, Vermont.

57

ICE STORMS

An ice storm occurs when water droplets form in an above-freezing layer of air aloft and fall through a shallow layer of below-freezing air near the surface of the earth. Upon or soon after impact, the water freezes on all exposed objects, coating them with varying thicknesses of ice. If the layer of cold air at the surface of the earth is deep, the droplets will freeze in their descent and form small ice pellets that bounce upon impact and do not adhere to each other. This is technically known as a sleet, or ice pellet, storm as opposed to a glaze storm of freezing rain. Sometimes both ice pellets and freezing rain will occur at different times during a single storm, along with some pure rain and snow, covering the ground with a mixed icy mass and giving exposed objects grotesque shapes.

Ice storms of varying degrees are almost an annual affair in New England. A Connecticut study showed that some glazing occurs during every year, with a mean number of twelve days per season on which ice storms happen somewhere in the state. Sometimes icing will affect only a narrow strip between zones of rain and snow, and sometimes higher elevations will undergo an icing experience while only rain falls in valley locations.

A famous Connecticut ice storm took place on March 22, 1837, when over $100,000 damage was reported in the Litchfield Hills. Early meteorological literature contains the story of three ice storms within a four-week period in late January and early February, 1886. Adjacent areas of Maine, New Hampshire, and Massachusetts were the center of the greatest icing during this period on January 27–30. Connecticut again was visited by a widespread ice storm on February 19–20, 1898, when higher elevations in the northwest received heavy ice coatings while the valleys remained bare. Heavy sleet fell to the north to a depth of 7 inches. Perhaps the most devastating storm of this type in Mas-

sachusetts's history isolated central and eastern sections on November 26–29, 1921, when a combination of rain, sleet, freezing rain, and snow fell for seventy-five hours. A measurement of 4.05 inches of mixed precipitation was made at Clark University in Worcester. Charles F. Brooks wrote in the *Bulletin of the American Meteorological Society,* December, 1921, "Ice on exposed ordinary insulated electric wires of about 0.25-inch in diameter was more than 2.0″ thick, and weighed upwards of 1.3 pounds per foot. It was computed that ice on the side of any dense, unbroken evergreen tree 50 feet high and on the average of 20 feet wide would have weighed 5 tons."

In recent years damaging ice storms have affected central New England in December, 1942; January, 1953; March, 1955; February, 1959; and the Decembers of 1964, 1968, 1969, and 1973.

Pre-Christmas Ice Storm of 1973

One does not need to check further back than December, 1973, for a chilling example of the disruptions that a steady freezing rain of twenty-four hours duration can bring to a modern community. Most of Connecticut and the adjacent sections of Massachusetts and Rhode Island were the hardest hit. On the heels of snow that had been falling since noon, rain commenced at Bradley International Airport on December 16 at 10:00 P.M. with the temperature standing at 25°. During a thirty-six-hour period, 1.39 inches of mixed precipitation were measured, much of which froze on exposed objects. Icy sheaths on branches of trees were estimated to be one-half-inch thick. Some snow and ice pellets fell at the beginning and end of the storm; Hartford measured 2.8 inches and New Haven had 1.3 inches on the ground.

The greatest power outages in New England history resulted. The Connecticut Light and Power Company reported 145,000 of 500,000 customers without power, and the Hartford Electric Company had 103,000 of 280,000 customers cut off by severed lines. The Southern New England Telephone Company was swamped with extra calls; in Hartford the number was up 60 per cent and in Bridgeport up 52 per cent over normal. Tree damage in Connecticut was said to have been greater than what occurred in the Hurricane of 1938. Many homes remained without power or telephone for a week after the storm.

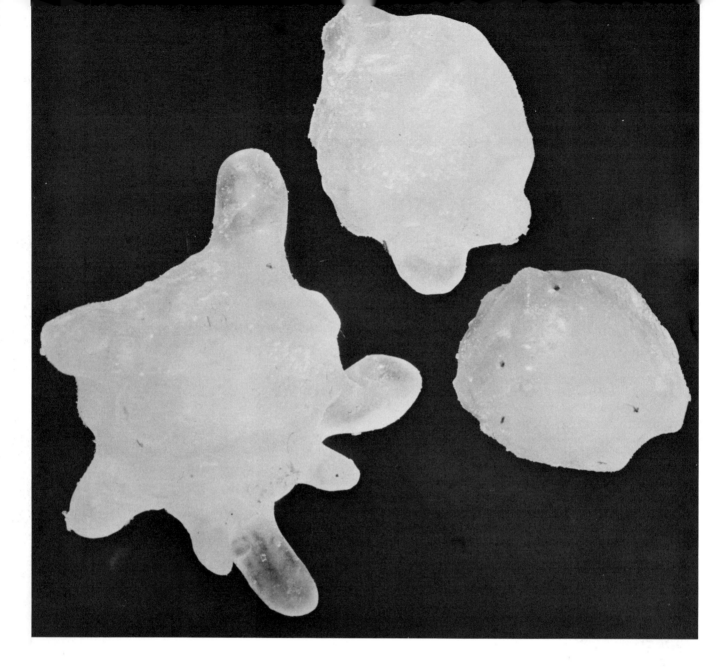

HAILSTORMS

Hailstorms may occur anywhere in New England, though they are less common along the southern and eastern shoreline than a few miles inland. The hilly terrain of western New England in the Berkshires and Green Mountains tend to breed the giant cumulonimbus clouds that develop into thunderstorms. Only the severest of these produce the necessary tremendous updrafts and downdrafts required to create hail. These local storm systems usually travel eastward and reach their maximum development over the lowlands of the Connecticut Valley— above the rich agricultural lands stretching from Middletown, Connecticut, on the south to Bellows Falls, Vermont, on the north. Hailstorms

Above: Three different shapes of hailstones. *Right:* Automobiles riddled by hailstones, 1926

have taken a heavy toll of the valuable crops of tobacco and vegetables grown here.

A hailstone is a warm-season product since its formation requires a cloud of considerable depth and the strong vertical currents characteristic of the chimney-effect cumulonimbus cloud. An individual hailstone is usually spheroidal, though it may become conical or oblate in shape or combine into an irregular mass of ice. The round hailstone generally exhibits a layered interior structure resembling the rings of an onion with alternate layers of clear ice and rime (granular ice) surrounding a nucleus. Hailstones grow by accretion while in the cloud, either in a straight fall from considerable height or in a series of alternate vertical ascents and descents within the cloud. Ice pellets of winter storms are smaller in size and form when raindrops fall from a stratus-type cloud and freeze in a general storm.

Individual hailstones are frequently less than one-fourth of an inch in diameter and weigh less than .01 ounce, but occasionally they may exceed one inch in diameter and weigh from .5 ounce to several ounces in rare instances. Such ice bullets can be highly dangerous to humans and animals and damaging to structures and crops, especially when driven by a high wind. Trees can be stripped of small branches and bark, tobacco leaves pulverized, and whole corn stalks beaten down. Annual losses from hailstorms in Connecticut usually far exceed damage from tornadoes and windstorms.

A hailstorm in early colonial times at Springfield, Massachusetts, was described by Rev. Increase Mather as occurring on July 6, 1682:

> But at Springfield it was most dreadful, where great pieces of ice, some seven, some nine inches about, fell down from the clouds with such violence that the shingles upon some of the houses were broken thereby, and holes beat into the ground that a man might put his hand in, several acres of corn (both wheat and Indian) were beat down and destroyed by the hail.

Judge Samuel Sewall witnessed a hailstorm at Boston on May 9, 1695:

> And about 2 P.M. a very extraordinary storm of hail, so that the ground was made white with it, as with the blossoms when fallen; 'twas as big as pistol and musquet bullets; it broke of the glass of the new house about 480 quarrels [squares] of the front.

The village of Salem on Cape Ann in Massachusetts was struck by a severe local hailstorm on August 1, 1815, and the event was described in the diary of Rev. William Bentley, who served as his community's weather historian:

> Then came the hail and the destruction of Glass in its course was very great. Some houses reckon hundreds of panes in single tenaments. It was little felt in the streets leading to Beverly bridge and hardly at all by the houses in Bridge street. It was about one mile wide and one and ½ in its course. . . . The loss of glass would be a low estimate at 20,000 panes in the hail storm, some say 100,000. Mr. Derby in South Salem lost all the glass of his hothouses and gardens. Col. Pickman's farm house suffered much in the same fields and the whole farm appeared prostrate. The loss of fruit in gardens was great but of property, the glass was the greatest loss. The force with which the hail descended was in several instances to pass through the crown of hats and in one case to knock down and deprive of sense for a moment by the blow. The largest stones I saw were oblate and on their broadest surface one inch. We are told of some weighing above an ounce and being 5 inches in circumference. An accurate observer weighed 10 of the largest he could find, and the mean weight (of each) was 15 pennyweights [15⁄20th troy ounce]. This cannot put aside what otheres saw, but it agrees with my own observations. I had an excellent beverage made from the largest stones I collected, 16 to a lb.

Joseph Felt, a contemporary historian of Salem, estimated that 30,000 panes of glass were broken at a replacement cost of $14,000.

Above: Connecticut broadleaf tobacco damaged by hail. *Below:* Tobacco has long been a major crop in Connecticut. Shown here are 300 hands on a farm in picking season at the beginning of this century.

CHAPTER 4
Weather's Sumptuous Variety

Hot weather usually occurs in New England several times each summer with temperatures rising into the upper 80s and 90s accompanied by uncomfortable humidities. (The temperature-humidity index provides a method of measuring the combined oppressiveness of these elements on a hot day [see page 88].) Heat waves are not a native New England product but are carried to the region by wind flow from southwest and west. The Bermuda High is usually the major factor in introducing and sustaining a heat wave; it causes airstreams from a warm source in the Gulf of Mexico or the southwestern plains to follow a curving trajectory over the dry interior of the continent where the air is further heated each day. If New England skies remain clear by day, the air mass will continue to receive insolation and maintain its heat content. Temperatures of 100° or more have occurred in all sections of New England except parts of northern New Hampshire, interior Maine, and the Down East coast near Eastport.

Hot Sunday of June 29, 1749

"Hot burning season" wrote Rev. Ebenezer Parkman in his diary on June 6, 1749, as a torrid early-summer drought became more firmly established. Thermometers of the day were not noted for accuracy or agreement and few were correctly exposed, but all instruments indicated extreme heat during all of June and most of them pinpointed the twenty-ninth as the hottest day. Professor Winthrop's instrument, though located indoors, reached −13.5° on the Haukesbee, or Royal Society, scale, which he figured was equivalent to 98° on the Fahrenheit scale. The Haukesbee scale employed an inverted numbering, with 0° "extream hott," 65° "frost," and 90° "extream cold." Winthrop reported that the spirits of his thermometer were "in the bulb" (that is, the expansion chamber at the top of the tube) so that he could not make a reading of the highest level attained. A friend of his at Kingston, Massachusetts, whose thermometer was designed for the English climate, saw his glass burst as the expansion of the rising spirits exceeded the capacity of the bulb. The exact outdoor reading on this day in New England cannot be ascertained, but Benjamin Franklin's thermometer in Philadelphia reached an even 100°F, indicating the hottest then experienced in the Quaker City. Peter Kalm, the Swedish traveler and naturalist, later referred to this "hot day in Philadelphia." It so happened that young Ezra Stiles, later to become New England's leading weather recorder, remembered the Hot Sunday very well, for he preached his first sermon from a pulpit that day and never tired of relating the circumstances. Rev. Ebenezer Parkman at Westboro described the day in his diary: "Extreme hot day (so that cakes of chocolate melted on the shelves tho' they lay single)."

A hot day at the beach on Nantucket, 1897

Battle of Monmouth Day: June 28, 1778

The Battle of Monmouth in New Jersey on June 28, 1778, became doubly memorable in the minds of Americans, not only for the claims of a questionable victory, but also for the extreme heat prevailing on that and the following days. No thermometers were close to the battle scene, but from observations at New York City and in New England, one gathers the impression that readings stood in the middle and upper 90s. Timothy Dwight in 1810, when describing the climate of New England, referred back to the time of the Monmouth heat wave: "In the summer of 1778 the heat was intense for 17 days commencing on the 24th of June and terminating on the 10th of July." Rev. Ezra Stiles, who was about to be installed as the president of Yale College in July, set up his thermometer on June 29 and registered successive daily maximums of 94°, 97°, 95°, and 94° through July 2 when a thunderstorm occurred, and a respite of three days followed before the heat wave reestablished its hold. From July 7 through 12 his instrument registered 86.5°, 95°, 95°, 94°, 93°, and 87°. It was hot, too, at Portsmouth, New Hampshire, where the mercury reached 87° or more on every day from June 26 through July 4. Lt. Frederick Mackenzie at Newport declared: "The inhabitants say that they never remember such hot weather on this Island as we have had for some days past."

Summer in the city: Boston, 1952

Hot July in 1825

The outstanding hot month of the period before the organization of a federal weather service in 1870 occurred in July, 1825. Jonathan P. Hall's thermometer on Federal Street in downtown Boston registered a mean of 77.6°, the highest monthly mean in his records from 1821 to 1865. In the modern National Weather Service records since 1871, the warmest month at Boston had a mean of 77.5° in July, 1952. Though means were calculated by different formulae, and the exposure of instruments differed, the two months can be said to represent Boston's weather at its extreme hottest. Hall's thermometer in July, 1825, topped 100° on three occasions with maximums of 102° on July 11 and 12. There were two periods of excessive heat: from July 7 to 12 and 20 to 31. An unusually early heat wave had occurred in June, when Hall's thermometer topped 90° on each day from June 7 to 12, reaching a high of 96° on June 11 and 12.

Fourth of July in 1911

A long-standing record maximum registered on an official thermometer in an approved exposure occurred on July 4, 1911. Weather observers at Lawrence, Massachusetts, and Nashua, New Hampshire, located about fifteen miles apart, recorded maximums of 106° that afternoon. Other state records were established in Vermont, 105° at Vernon; and Maine, 105° at North Bridgton. Boston's 104°, Portland's 103°, and Concord's 102° still stand as the highest ever reached in those cities. The 100-degree isotherm reached as far north as Saint Johnsbury in Vermont and Greenville and Houlton in interior Maine, so nearly all of mainland New England experienced the rarity of a 100-degree day. These absolute maximums marked the peak of a twelve-day heat wave that ranks first for severity and duration in the region's meteorological history. The readings at Keene, New Hampshire, may be taken as representative of valley locations in central New England. The heat wave extended from July first to the twelfth with consecutive readings of 91°, 95°, 104°, 103°, 103°, 101°, 88°, 91°, 99°, 102°, 99°, and 95°.

Early June Heat Wave in 1925

The most remarkable early-season heat wave occurred in June, 1925, when the mercury topped 92° on five consecutive days, June 3 through 7, in the cities of Hartford, Providence, Boston, and Concord, New Hampshire. The Boston readings were 95°, 96°, 95°, 100°, and 92° during the five-day heat wave. The peak figure in New England occurred at Waterbury, Connecticut, on the sixth with 101°. The unusual heat reached far north: the 90-degree isotherm appeared on two days as far north as Burlington (91° and 94°) and Saint Johnsbury (93° and 92°). Northernmost New Hampshire and interior Maine were spared the heat, as were Nantucket and Block Island, and the heat wave ended in dramatic fashion when a sea turn brought cool ocean air over New England. On June 8, Boston's thermometer ranged from a cool high of 62° to a chilly low of 53°.

August, 1948

The late August heat wave in 1948 concentrated its fury along the southern coastal region and on the islands, where new all-time records were set at places that usually escape the worst of a New England heat wave. Edgartown on Martha's Vineyard had 90° or more from August 27 to 30 with a peak reading of 99°. On Nantucket, thirty miles at sea, there were three consecutive days with 90° or more, with a high of 95° on two days. Hyannis set a record with an even 100° on the twenty-eighth and endured four days in the 90s. Inland Providence underwent three consecutive days with 100° or more; a record maximum of 102° was reached on the twenty-sixth. The readings at Logan Airport in Boston from August 25 through 29 were 96°, 99°, 100°, 99°, and 92°. The heat spread northeastward along the Maine coast; Portland had two days with 100°, while the temperature at Eastport climbed to 89°. In the interior, Bellows Falls in the Connecticut Valley of southern Vermont experienced seven consecutive days in the 90s, with a peak of 98° on two days.

The Hottest Modern Month: July, 1955

Never did so many Americans swelter under such high temperatures through such a long summer as did residents of the large industrial cities of the Northeast in July and August, 1955. In southern New England July was the hottest month in eighty-five years of National Weather Service records, and August came close to establishing an all-time record, too. Never did the thermometer exceed 90° on so many days in a single month as in July, 1955. Springfield, Massachusetts, had twenty-four days with 90° or more, and there were five other stations in New England with 90° or more on twenty days. The average temperature in the three southern states exceeded the previous record of July, 1949, by .2 degrees. In the three northern states the mean of 71° was within 1.1 degrees of the record high set in July, 1921. The peak of the hot weather came on July 22 and 23 when Boston recorded 98° and Portland 97°. The heat zone extended into northern Vermont where Saint Johnsbury had four consecutive days with 90° or more. But Nantucket's high during all this was only 85°. In August the heat period continued —the mean in the south came within one degree of the all-time record August, set in 1937. The mercury hit 103° at Windham, New Hampshire, and 100° at Boston on the fifth. Readings did not return to normal until August 24 after the departure of the twin ex-hurricanes Connie and Diane, which had introduced massive flows of hot, moist, tropical air into New England, resulting in disastrous floods when their energy was released over Connecticut and Massachusetts.

A fishing fleet off Cape Cod on a wintry day in 1875.

COLD WAVES

One does not need a weatherman to know which way the wind is blowing, especially if it is a cold wind. Arctic and polar air can arrive in New England on the wings of wind currents from the northeast through southwest, depending on the arrangement of high- and low-pressure areas and the movement of fronts. But it is the northwest wind that most frequently carries the coldest air masses into the region. The tundras of central and northern Canada on either side of Hudson Bay comprise the source region of New England's cold. When the bay is frozen over and the surrounding countryside is snow covered, the bitterest type of winter weather will reach New England. The dynamic agent

The four photographs on these pages were taken during a cold snap in Woodstock, Vermont, in 1940. At left are two views of town meeting—inside and outside the town hall. At right is a farmer who emptied his car radiator every evening and refilled it every morning to save the cost of antifreeze. The horse-drawn sled hauled trash.

is often a Hudson Bay High whose reservoir of cold air remains in that region for several days and nights, while radiating much of its heat content to outer space. Once set in motion by distant pressure changes, the cold air mass flows swiftly southeastward. The short trajectory (only 300–400 miles) and snow-covered terrain insure that the airstream will arrive in northern New England with little modification of its original frigidity. It is capable of dropping temperatures along the U.S.–Canadian border to $-30°$ upon the arrival of its advective blasts. If skies are clear and winds calm on the second night, cold pockets will radiate even more heat and drop readings as low as the -40s in the north and the -20s in the south. The lowest official temperature ever registered in the north was $-50°F/-45.6°C$.

During the early years of the nineteenth century settlement of northern New England was completed and nearly every community came into the possession of thermometers. The extremities of New England's climate became known, and one could measure and compare the degree of severity of each succeeding cold wave. These years marked the culmination of the "Little Ice Age" when temperatures averaged a degree or two colder than now and some outstanding cold weather events occurred.

Eighteenth Century

Three days in the eighteenth century were cold enough to be singled out by weather historian Ezra Stiles as memorable: 1) February 15, 1732, "reconed the coldest day in memory of the oldest man living"; 2) February 22, 1773, "the memorable cold sabbath"; 3) February 5, 1788, known as the "Cold Tuesday." These were days when the mercury stayed below zero all day with a strong northwest wind blowing and causing an extreme chill factor.

Nineteenth Century

Cold Friday. The early morning hours of January 19, 1810, were long remembered in New England for a spectacular overnight temperature descent (at Portsmouth, New Hampshire, from a balmy evening at 41° to a frigid $-13°$ in the morning), and for the extreme wind chill prevailing all day, as a strong northwest gale rushed subzero airstreams across the frigid countryside. Cold Friday entered New England folklore as a result of a family tragedy in Sanbornton, New Hampshire, when the Ellsworth home was demolished by the gale in the early morning hours and three little children were frozen to death while struggling to reach the safety of a neighbor's house. The heart-rending tale was spread widely through newspapers of the region and later told around the fireside while the northwest wind howled outside.

The Cold Week in 1835.   Thermometers on successive nights in early January, 1835, dropped below zero, and on January 5 descended to the lowest figures known since the introduction of thermometers to New England. After a night of intense radiational cooling over a snow-covered terrain, many mercury thermometers in the three northern states congealed at −38.87°F/−39.38°C. Since spirit thermometers were not in general use, the absolute degree of cold could not be determined, but in southern New England some remarkable minimums at urban exposures were reported: New Haven −24°; Waltham (a Boston suburb) −24°; Providence (valley) −26°, (hill) −15°; Hartford −27°; Williamstown −30°; and Northampton −32°.

The Bitterest Daylight.   The most remarkable early-season cold outbreak from the Canadian Arctic swept southeastward across southern New England during December 16, 1835. The early date of its occurrence and the intensity of the daylight wind chill made it one of the most memorable days in the region's meteorological history. At sunrise, thermometers across the northern and western interior were close to −15° and remained near that figure uniformly during the entire day and following night. The core of the cold air, just arriving in the Boston area at daybreak of the sixteenth, reversed the normal trend of temperature by sinking thermometers lower and lower as the sun rose higher and higher. The thermometer of R. T. Paine, weather watcher for the *Boston Evening Traveler,* read exactly zero at sunrise, −6° at 2:00 P.M., and −10.7° at 6:00 P.M. The dome of the densest air passed seaward in the early evening, permitting thermometers to move upward, so the reading rose to −4° by sunrise of the seventeenth. It was the same story at Providence on the sixteenth: −4°, −7°, −12° at the three observation times; skies were clear all day and the wind "piercing from the N.W. all day." The gales were in the vicinity of 40 mph, giving a wind chill equivalent of −70°F. It was the "most nearly insupportable day ever experienced," according to Paine. The day was made doubly memorable for New Yorkers; the greatest fire in the city's history destroyed the major portion of the financial district that windy night.

The Coldest Daylight.   In Boston on February 6, 1855, weather watcher Jonathan Hall's conservative thermometer registered −6° at 7:00 A.M., −5.5° at 2:30 P.M., and −11.5° at 9:00 P.M. for a mean of −7.7°. The mercury remained below zero for about thirty consecutive hours. At Providence the three readings on College Hill were −3° at sunrise, −7° at 1:00 P.M., and −14° at 10:00 P.M. for a mean of −8°. The wind, however, was described as "light from the northwest," so the wind-chill factor on this day was only moderate.

Cold Friday II.   An authentic zero day occurred at Boston on January 23, 1857, with the thermometer remaining below zero from midnight to midnight. The *Boston Evening Traveler*'s thermometer ranged from a high of −0.5° at 2:30 P.M. to a minimum of −11°. At Providence,

Prof. Alexis Caswell's instrument read −14°, −5°, and −10° at the three observation times for a mean of −9.7°, the lowest in his record books: "A very heavy wind from about W.N.W. This has been the coldest day and the severest to be out in, for a period of 25 years." Thermometers in northern New England on the mornings of January 23 and 24 were generally congealed. The press carried reports of readings as low as −50° in Vermont, New Hampshire, and Maine, presumably on spirit thermometers.

Spectacular Temperature Drop in 1861. Cold air began pouring across the Canadian border into Vermont early on the morning of February 7, 1861, to trigger the swiftest temperature change in the New England record books. The leading edge of the cold air mass reached Hanover, New Hampshire, soon after the 1:00 P.M. observation when the Dartmouth thermometer read 37°, but eighteen hours later, at 7:00 A.M. on the eighth, the mercury had plummeted to −32°, a fall of sixty-nine degrees at a rate of almost four degrees per hour. Down in the Berkshires of Massachusetts the change was of even greater degree: West Cummington enjoyed a mild early afternoon of 48° on the seventh before the sudden change arrived and dropped the reading to −32° on the morning of the eighth. Thermometers in the Boston area dropped from 46° to a low of −14° at sunrise on the eighth. The cold wave was short-lived. The thermometer's upward antics during the next three days were almost as spectacular as the previous descent: in the following eighty hours a rise to 60° by the afternoon of February 11 brought Boston's temperature from arctic depths to spring delights.

Twentieth Century

Cold Wave of 1917–18. The only full winter of American participation in World War I produced the most frigid extended cold wave in the modern record books for New England. Many soldiers were housed in flimsy barracks with inadequate heating systems; the civilian population suffered from an acute fuel shortage; and the influenza epidemic of 1918 was soon to take its toll.

Burlington, Vermont, enjoyed a balmy 41° reading at noon on Christmas Day, 1917, but by midnight the thermometer had dropped to 13° and by next sunrise was down to −6°. With below-zero readings following for the next ten nights and no daytime readings above 32° until January 12, this constituted the most prolonged series of extreme readings in the record books.

In northern New England the intensity of the cold congealed mercury thermometers. Berlin, New Hampshire, reported the lowest official reading of −44°, followed by two Vermont stations with −43°. The consecutive minimum figures for a week on the Saint Johnsbury thermometer were impressive: −22°, −43°, −40°, −21°, −35°, and −33°.

The cold air reached the Boston coastal section late on December 26, launching an extended period of extreme cold that appears to have been unmatched since January, 1857. For ten consecutive nights the minimum sank below 10° and on five consecutive nights dropped below zero. It was below zero on the twenty-ninth from 4:00 A.M. to 1:00 P.M., at +1° or +2° for two hours, then zero or below from 4:00 P.M. to noon on the thirtieth, a period of twenty consecutive hours, which constitutes a record that still stands. The temperature on the morning of the thirtieth was −14°, the lowest registered on an official thermometer since the National Weather Bureau was established at Boston in 1871. The mercury finally climbed above freezing on the afternoon of January 6, 1918, to end Boston's longest and bitterest cold wave.

February, 1934. The coldest month in 100 years in southern New England was February, 1934. In the north it was not exceeded until Jan-

In a scene reminiscent of Brueghel, skaters pirouette near a factory in Lowell, Massachusetts.

uary, 1970—and then at a few stations. The entire region showed an average temperature of 11.8°, ranging from 22.6° at Nantucket to 0.4° at Pittsburg, New Hampshire. The extreme reading of the month was −42° at Van Buren, Maine, on the seventh. Cold air commenced moving into the northwest on February second. The first week continued cold with below-zero readings each night, but the figures were not unusual for a February cold wave. When the air mass was reinforced by a stronger, second outbreak on the seventh, thermometers plummeted to record low marks. The eighth constituted a zero day over much of Vermont and northern New Hampshire, resulting in the very low readings that occurred over the snow-covered terrain of the south on the morning of the ninth. Most large cities reached a new absolute minimum: Boston −18°, New Haven −15°, and Providence −17°. The maximum on the ninth at Boston was 2°, Providence 3°, and New Haven 2°, producing the lowest daily means of record since 1871. Out at Nantucket there was a minimum of −4° and a maximum of 5°, the coldest day in its history.

Spectacular Cold Wave in February, 1943. A severe arctic outbreak in mid February, 1943, sent thermometers down to record low levels in many locations, providing the only significant meteorological news in an otherwise uneventful late winter of 1943. The full force of the air behind a sharp cold front struck northern sections early on February 14, driving thermometers downward despite a rising sun. The instrument at Burlington, Vermont, slumped from a morning 21° to −16° by midnight. On the morning of the fifteenth it was down another ten degrees to −26° and rose only to −12° that afternoon. A bitter day prevailed across the north as figures at Newport on the Vermont-Canadian border testify: maximum −19°, minimum −30°, mean −24.5°.

The absolute coldest readings were reached on the morning of February 16, when a night of intense radiation dropped thermometers below −40° at scattered locations in the north. East Barnet, Vermont, reported the lowest at −46°, and nearby Bloomfield was only one degree warmer. The most remarkable readings came at the new Portland City Airport on tidewater: minimums of −31° on February 15 and −39° on February 16. Concord, New Hampshire, was not far behind with −37°. Other locations in the south approached but did not establish new standards: Boston −14°, Nantucket −5°, and New Haven −9°.

January, 1970. The record coldest month for Burlington, Vermont, and Concord, New Hampshire, was January, 1970. Since February of that year ranked among the coldest second months in history, the combination of January-February, 1970, constituted the coldest consecutive months in over 100 years of records at each location.

The thermometer at Burlington went below freezing on December 13, 1969, and did not top 32° until January 28, 1970, and then only for a brief period of twenty-four hours. Through January the mercury dropped below zero every night from the first to the twenty-fourth, the only two exceptions being minimums of 6° and 16°. Daytime highs did not exceed 20° in this span except on three days. With an average minimum of −7.5° and a maximum of 14.6°, the January mean came to 3.6°.

At Concord, New Hampshire, the mean was an even 11°. No above-freezing temperatures were registered until January 26. Maximums were considerably higher in February, but there was only one night at Concord that the mercury did not drop below 32°, and at Burlington only one overnight thaw was experienced. A 16.9° February mean at Burlington and a 22.6° mean at Concord—when averaged with the extreme low January means—made up the coldest two consecutive months of record, even lower than the previous record cold combination of January-February, 1875.

As late as the 1940's, this peddler was delivering hardware and groceries in Vermont.

FLOODS

Floods may occur in New England at any time of the year and under a variety of meteorological situations. The main season comes in early spring, from mid March to late April, when heavy rains fall on deep snow cover and the resulting runoff overflows the banks of streams and rivers. The Great All–New England Flood in March, 1936, was the prime example of this combination of fresh atmospheric moisture and residual ground moisture.

Of all the major floods in the Connecticut Valley, only that of 1862 appears to have been caused by snowmelt alone. Rainfall alone, however, has resulted in major and extreme flooding on numerous occasions, since the atmosphere in the warmer season can supply a much greater amount of moisture. Rainfall floods may occur when a slow-moving cyclonic storm crosses the region from the west and draws on Atlantic Ocean moisture for many hours, or when a tropical storm brings vast amounts of moisture northward from southern latitudes to fall on New England soil. The extreme floods of 1869, 1927, 1938, and 1955 depended on a tropical source for much of their supply of precipitation. The autumn season, from August through early November, is the secondary season for high floods. Winter and early spring floods can be doubly dangerous to life and damaging to property since they come on the wings of a general thaw and ice breakup. Ice floes can be very destructive to bridges and shore installations and may cause jams that greatly accentuate local flood levels. The Great Winter Breakup in late January, 1839, destroyed major and minor bridges in Vermont and New Hampshire.

Maine Rivers. The principal drainage basins—the Penobscot, Kennebec, and Androscoggin—reached their highest levels of record on or about March 19, 1936, when two heavy rainstorms fell on a deeper-than-normal snow cover. The massive runoff caused ice jamming on the rivers and extensive damage through the lower valleys. Other major springtime floods in this century have occurred in April, 1901, June, 1917, May, 1923, April, 1950, and March, 1953. Widespread floods as a result of heavy rainstorms at other seasons came in December, 1901, February, 1907, September, 1909, and November, 1927.

Merrimack Valley. Streams draining into the Merrimack from interior New Hampshire also reached their highest historic marks in March, 1936. All previous marks were exceeded at the Amoskeag Mills at Manchester, New Hampshire, where accurate records have been maintained for over a century. Other floods of note in this century have occurred in March, 1901, November, 1927, September, 1938, and September, 1954.

Connecticut Valley. Flood records have been maintained at Hartford for more than three hundred years. In that long span the highest stage on the Connecticut River was 37.6 feet on March 21, 1936, as the major crest reached the city. No other flood had exceeded 30 feet, though subsequently the 1938 hurricane flood of September 21 rose to a stage of 35.4 feet and in the combination of hurricanes Connie and Diane in August, 1955, the peak at Hartford hit 30.6 feet. Damaging floods have occurred in the northern half of the valley during this century in December, 1901, March, 1913, November, 1927, April, 1928, March, 1936, and December, 1948–January, 1949. In the southern section, floods have struck on the same dates as above, as well as in September, 1938, and August, 1955, when the northern reaches of the valley were not seriously affected.

Crests of Floods at Hartford, Connecticut

Year	Date	Crest
1683	July–August	26.0 feet
1692	February–March	26.2 feet
1801	March 20	27.5 feet
1841	January 9	26.3 feet
1843	March 29	27.2 feet
1854	May 1	29.8 feet
1859	March 20	26.4 feet
1862	April 21	28.7 feet
1869	April 23	26.7 feet
1869	October 6	26.3 feet
1895	April 16	25.7 feet
1896	March 3	26.5 feet
1901	April 9	26.4 feet
1902	March 4	25.5 feet
1913	March 29	26.3 feet
1927	November 6	29.0 feet
1933	April 21	26.0 feet
1936	March 21	37.6 feet
1938	September 23	35.4 feet
1949	January 2	25.2 feet
1955	August 20	30.6 feet
1960	April 7	27.6 feet

This photograph shows the destruction in Montpelier, Vermont, in 1927.

Vermont Flood of 1927

"The flood of November 3, 1927, was the greatest disaster in the history of our beautiful State," declared Gov. John E. Weeks of Vermont. These were words from the heart: the hills and valleys of the land of his birth lay in a state of ruin and his people were suffering a state of mental shock at the magnitude of their losses. Weeks' close associate, Lt. Gov. S. Hollister Jackson, perished in a flood stream raging down an erstwhile highway within sight of his home and at least eighty-three other Vermont residents met similar fates that afternoon and night.

The first drops of rain splattered down on southern Vermont about 9:00 P.M. on the evening of November 2 as a frontal system approached from the west. The rain spread to the Canadian border by midnight but fell lightly, since little moisture was available in the air mass. About daylight, however, a new element entered the situation when a stream of moist air from the tropical North Atlantic Ocean commenced to flow over the hills and valleys of the Green Mountain State. This had been brought northward earlier by a weak tropical storm moving northeastward off the Atlantic seaboard. The low-pressure trough from the west, now over eastern New York State, drew this tropical air into its system, diverting it northwestward over western New England. Moving at a surface speed of 30 mph to 40 mph and much faster aloft, the southeast current, attended by rising temperatures and increasing precipitation, struck a massive barrier composed of two entities: one was the Green Mountain massif, rising to about 4,000 feet; the other was a mass of cold, dense air some 10,000 feet in depth overlying the Champlain and Hudson valleys. In the clash of air masses, the lighter tropical air was forced to glide upward over the heavier polar air and this resulted in greatly increased

71

Boy scouts on emergency duty during the
1927 Vermont flood

A cleanup crew in Jonesville, Vermont,
paused to pose for the photographer.

cooling, condensation, and precipitation, which ultimately loosed a
deluge of unprecedented proportions on Vermont.

During the late morning and afternoon hours of November 3, all
Vermont rainfall records were broken—both for hourly intensity and
for single-storm totals—as the moisture of the oceanic airstream was
wrung from the clouds and dropped over the countryside. It was estimated by a meteorologist that a cubic mile of solid water had been
lifted from the surface of the Atlantic Ocean and deposited on the hills
and valleys of the Green Mountain State. The greatest amount of rain
was measured at Somerset, an elevation of 2,096 feet, where the total
fall was 9.65 inches and amounts up to 15.00 inches may have fallen
on the 4,000-foot mountains. For nine consecutive hours on the third
the rain fell at the valley location of Northfield at a rate of about 0.50
inch per hour. This brought the Dog River to a record crest at about
6:30 P.M., and this level was maintained most of the night.

Masses of water swept down hillsides where no water had flowed
before. When brooks, streams, and rivers were filled to capacity the
water spread over the countryside, submerging venerable landmarks and
setting new high-water marks. Bridges collapsed, highways were washed
out, railroad tracks were undermined, and an undetermined number of
buildings were torn from their foundations and swept downstream, some
carrying hapless victims to a watery grave. In all, Vermont lost eighty-
four residents and suffered at least $25 million in property losses. It
was the greatest catastrophe from a natural cause in the state's history.

All–New England Flood of 1936

The flood of 1936 was an all–New England event, with all six states sharing the disasters and tragedies brought on by a combination of the forces of nature during mid-March of 1936. Alternate periods of rain and thaw earlier in the month softened the great blanket of snow and ice that for many weeks had held the land and rivers of interior New England in a firm icy sheath. This now became a mighty mobile force and by daylight of March twelfth, under the influence of renewed rain, it commenced moving downhill. Massive snowslides occurred at high elevations, and rapid snowmelt began flooding valleys. More melting snow, thawing ice, and rainwater choked the normal channels of brooks, streams, and rivers and the waterways, which were soon ice jammed, were unable to handle the unprecedented volume. Dams gave way and bridges floated off or were smashed by debris; mills and factories were undermined, battered, and demolished; and most means of communications—highways, railroads, and wires—were severed. By the evening of the twelfth it was obvious over all New England that a major spring freshet was under way, but no one realized the magnitude of the mighty force that was moving toward the sea.

Between March 9 and 22, the northeastern United States lay in a vast atmospheric trough reaching from the polar regions to the Gulf of Mexico. In this trough four distinct storm systems formed and moved in a northeasterly direction, their shifting fronts and clashing air masses encompassing all six New England states. The first disturbance formed in the Gulf of Mexico on the ninth, moved northeast to the Carolinas and then directly north over Virginia, Pennsylvania, and central New York. Blocked by a high-pressure system over the Maritime Provinces, a secondary center formed on the eleventh near New York City, and this prolonged and intensified the precipitation over New England. The center of the heaviest rains lay in the White Mountains, where 6.46 inches fell at Pinkham Notch on the twelfth, and many other locations received over 4.00 inches during the two-day downpours.

Another major storm took shape over Texas on the sixteenth, moved to the Atlanta area, and again made the fateful turn directly north, passing over eastern Pennsylvania and eastern New York on the nineteenth. Again a blocking anticyclone slowed its northward journey so that precipitation continued much longer than in a normal storm cycle. The White Mountains, astride the center of all the watersheds of New England, once more received the heaviest amounts: Pinkham Notch had 6.27 inches on the eighteenth and 4.68 inches on the nineteenth. Secondary centers of heavy precipitation of 8.00 inches or more were located over the Worcester area and the Berkshires of western Massachusetts.

These massive amounts of moisture would have created a serious flood problem even if they had fallen on bare ground, and the enormous amount of water locked in the snowbanks raised the March, 1936, storms and floods to catastrophic levels. The snow cover in the White Mountains possessed a density of about 28 per cent; that is, the 33 inches of snow on the ground at Pinkham Notch gave a water equivalent of about 8.00 inches. Adding the snowmelt to the total of 22.43 inches, rainfall during the two storms produced a total of 30.00 inches of available water to drain off the higher elevations. This figure, of course, scaled down away from the White Mountains, but it exceeded 16.00 inches in parts of Vermont and Maine and 10.00 inches in parts of Massachusetts and Connecticut. If one considers that 10.00 inches of water spread over an acre of ground weighs 1,130 tons, the tremendous burden the rivers were called on to discharge comes into hydrologic focus.

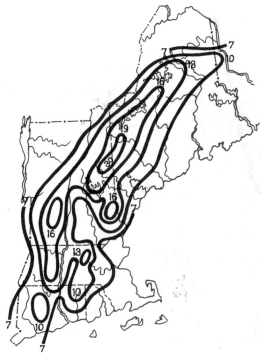

Heights of water levels in the all-New England Flood, March, 1936

73

Ice jams formed in all the Maine rivers and damage there exceeded that of any other recorded flood. As many as eighty-one state highway bridges required reconstruction as a result of flood damage and railroad travel in the interior of Maine was brought to a halt by flood waters.

The floods were especially severe throughout the Merrimack Valley, where all previous records were exceeded except in the northern reaches. The severest washout occurred at Hooksett, New Hampshire, where water 18 to 20 feet deep flowed through the main street. The Amoskeag Mills were severely damaged (a flood marker there indicates that the crest of the 1936 flood was 13.5 feet higher than in any previous flood). The cities of Lawrence, Haverhill, and Lowell suffered great damage from the total inundation of mills and factories; the water at Lowell was 6.4 feet higher than previously recorded.

Record crests were reached in the Connecticut River basin, from the vicinity of Fifteen Mile Falls in the north through the remainder of the valley southward; only in the vicinity of White River Junction was the peak less than in November, 1927. Above Holyoke, Massachusetts, an ice jam formed and for two and a half days diverted the waters of the river across low meadowland for several miles before returning to the normal channel. The flood reached a height of 16.8 feet above the crest of the Holyoke Dam. After the waters had receded it was found that as much as five feet of the dam's granite top had been carried off along 1,000 feet of its length.

The waters at Hartford rose to a stage 8.6 feet higher than any previous flood level recorded since the settlement of the area three hundred years before. A large part of the downtown commercial area was flooded when Connecticut River waters backed up into North Branch Park River, a small stream flowing near the capitol and railroad station.

As a result of timely warnings, loss of life was small, but property damage was estimated to exceed $100 million, making the Flood of 1936 the costliest New England weather experience until the New England Hurricane and Flood of September, 1938, repeated the magnitude of the flood losses and added much wind damage as well.

Is Vernon Dam Holding?

Residents of the Greenfield, Massachusetts, area of the central Connecticut Valley heard the dreaded ten blasts of their fire whistle shortly before 11:00 P.M. on Wednesday, March 18, 1936. The city had just been plunged into darkness as a result of the flooding of the Cabot power station, and the calling out of the militia spread panic through the populace. Radio stations were broadcasting the news that Vernon Dam had broken. Rumors flew through the streets of Turners Falls, the first city below the dam, that a wall of water was approaching and that patients at the Farren Hospital were in imminent danger of being drowned in their beds.

Montague city highway bridge, the Boston and Maine railway bridge at Turners Falls, and the Vermont Central railway bridge at Northfield had gone out earlier in the day, and soon after midnight the weakened Sunderland highway bridge was to go. But had the dam really given way? Had a flood been loosed such as the Connecticut Valley had not seen since the plug of glacial Lake Hitchcock had let go? No one knew. All communication with the flood-isolated New England Power Company's crew at the Vernon dam site had been severed.

Later on, residents of the entire Connecticut Valley below Vernon would give thanks to a small crew of utility workers and a handful of citizens who rushed to the assistance of the beleaguered workers seeking to save the dam. Early on Wednesday it was evident that the dam was in for trouble; ice cakes plunging downstream on the swift current of the rising waters were battering dam and buildings. The main ice run

Sebago Lake flooded this Maine highway in 1936.

had commenced on Tuesday afternoon and continued all night. It was decided to strengthen each end of the dam to prevent the surging waters from outflanking and undermining the anchors of the structure. The New Hampshire abutment was sandbagged, and the Vermont side received new flashboards as well as sandbags. The continued rise of the water during the morning portended possible disaster.

A hurried call for assistance went to Keene, New Hampshire. Two groups quickly assembled. Some twenty-five men from the American Legion post left about 5:00 P.M. equipped with boats, sandbag equipment, and high boots. With the assistance of the Highway Department they made it over back roads to the dam site and immediately joined in the work of strengthening the temporary defenses. Another group of National Guardsmen, whose route to the dam was cut by flooding waters, were forced to wade and walk six miles, and they did not arrive until 5:00 in the morning to relieve those who had held the line all night.

The workers were constantly menaced by huge cakes of ice that battered their man-made barricade. One cut a jagged hole in the abutment but eventually became dislodged and passed over the dam downstream. At this time the water was passing about 10 to 11 feet over the top of the dam, about 2.5 feet higher than in the Great Vermont Flood in 1927. The waters held at this peak for about four hours before commencing to recede shortly after 2:00 A.M.

The high water had started to undermine the towers supporting high-tension wires slung across the river at the dam site, so workers had to climb the towers and cut the main cable with a blow torch. Other smaller towers threatened to tumble into the river and these had to be back guyed. The fight against the river continued all day Thursday, with many volunteers from the surrounding country arriving by rowboat and on foot to save residents of the valley below.

Connie-Diane Floods in 1955

The most recent widespread flooding in southern New England followed a preliminary soaking from hurricane Connie on August 12–13, 1955, and the subsequent deluges within a week of hurricane Diane on August 17–19. At Westfield, Massachusetts, close to the Connecticut border, an incredible 18.15 inches of rain fell on the nineteenth as part of a storm total of 19.75 inches—both figures all-time records for New England. Many dams collapsed under the added pressure, greatly increasing the size of crests on small streams. Downtown Torrington was devastated when the Naugatuck River ran wild through the business section, which was without power or communications for forty-eight hours. It was estimated that 40 per cent of Worcester, Massachusetts, was under water. Woonsocket, Rhode Island, was particularly hard hit; where the Blackstone River is normally seventy feet wide, it spread to one and a half miles. In New England, eighty-two persons died and about five thousand were injured by the torrents. Damage exceeded $800 million for the area's most costly meteorological disaster.

Flash Floods

Extreme heavy precipitation of the cloudburst type has occurred in the upper reaches of smaller streams, causing enormous devastation in the lower valleys where little or no rain fell. The Westfield Valley of southwestern Massachusetts experienced one on July 26, 1819. So much rain fell that in five hours the river swelled to a height twenty feet above normal low water. Every bridge on the Eighth Massachusetts Turnpike was swept downstream along with much of the roadbed from Becket and Chester. No measurement of the amount of rain falling was made, but estimates ran as high as 18 inches.

An artist's conception of a panicky crowd fleeing a Connecticut Valley flood in the nineteenth century.

DROUGHT

New England is normally favored with adequate precipitation that is distributed quite evenly throughout the year. General cyclonic storms provide most of winter's precipitation, while local showers and thunderstorms bring the major portion of rainfall during warmer months. Tropical storms in late summer and early autumn often add considerably to the total rainfall, especially in coastal sections. Conditions tending toward drought usually occur when anticyclonic controls cause a steady westerly wind circulation from the dry interior of the continent. Then agricultural drought sets in, crops of all types suffer, and eventually water supplies reach a critical level.

The early settlers, accustomed to the English climate, complained periodically of droughts in their diaries. Lack of rainfall seriously interfered with the Pilgrims' vital corn crop in two of the first three years at Plymouth. An ambitious climatologist searched the writings of the colonists and found sixteen seasons with serious droughts that affected agricultural crops in the period prior to 1775. The years 1749 and 1762 were singled out as having extreme droughts; field crops caught fire and spread to buildings; and shortages of hay caused imports of that vital commodity from Pennsylvania and England. Public fasts were held and the rains finally came in midsummer to save the late corn crop. There never has been a complete agricultural failure in all New England, even though the combination of drought and summer coldness caused partial failure in the famed summer of 1816.

In the present century a meteorological drought of stubborn endurance commenced in central Connecticut in June, 1929, and continued for thirty-nine months with varying intensity until August, 1932, when a tropical storm definitely ended the long dry period. The duration was even longer in western Massachusetts, not ending until January, 1933—a period that matched the worst years of economic decline in the Great Depression. Other sections of New England experienced droughts of milder intensity and shorter duration in the years 1929–33.

Drought conditions reappeared in the early 1940s, 1948–50, 1956–57, and 1959. The intensity and frequency of these dry periods varies greatly throughout the six states, as does the usual precipitation regime.

The greatest drought of the present century affected all phases of economic life in both urban and rural sections of southern and central New England. Not only did crop yields suffer, but supplies of water for human consumption and industrial use became so depleted that resort was made to conservation and even rationing. The forest fire hazard continued at an extremely high level for many months in a row.

This drought commenced in southern and western sections in July, 1961, though it did not become severe and enduring until early 1963. By September, 1964, the drought reached the extreme stage and remained at that critical level until September–October, 1966. The year 1965 in southern New England was generally the driest year of record since the 1880s, when weather reporting was put on a systematic basis. Precipitation over Connecticut averaged about 65 per cent of normal for the entire year.

Mainly, the absence of coastal storms that normally bring Gulf of Mexico and Atlantic Ocean moisture to New England caused the extreme degree of drought. Not until the soaking northeasters of 1966 on September 14–15 and 21–23 and October 19–20 (each of which brought two to three inches of rainfall) was the water cycle definitely reversed. Shortages ended that autumn.

Good rains at the start of the growing season in April removed the last consequences of the drought and the year 1967 brought normal rainfall to the region. The data at Keene, New Hampshire, illustrated the degree of drought: the precipitation deficit for the years 1963–66 was greater than 25 per cent, and it returned nearly to normal in 1967 and 1968.

By 1966, the water level at Quabbin Reservoir in Massachusetts was far below normal.

This old photograph recalls a sunny day at the beach at Gloucester, Massachusetts.

Sunshine is a vital element, not only for man's physical and psychological well-being, but also for the prosperity of many of his economic enterprises. New England can provide a variety of sunshine regimes, differing by region and terrain and changing with the seasons. The amount of direct solar rays received at the surface of the earth reaches its lowest input over the region in November, when the sunshine recorded at 10 representative stations averages only 41.5 per cent of the amount possible, because of obscuring clouds or particulate matter. December improves to 44.5 per cent and January to 49.4 per cent. Summertime brings the greatest amount of sunshine, both in actual hours and in percentage of the possible. July averages 59.9 per cent of the possible, followed closely by August with 56.5 per cent. As for regional distribution on an annual basis, the mainland stations along the east and south coasts away from the mountains fare best: Portland 58 per cent, Boston 59 per cent, and New York City 59 per cent. The cloudiest locations throughout the year are Eastport, Maine, 50 per cent (where fog is a factor) and Burlington, Vermont, 51 per cent (where lake effect and cyclonic cloudiness play a role). Mountain peaks, of course, often lie in the clouds and experience different conditions from the valleys. Mount Washington receives only 34 per cent of possible sunshine through the year—November's 29 per cent is the lowest, although July and August at 31 per cent are almost as deficient in sun. At lower elevations, November's 30 per cent at Burlington is the least sunny month, while August's 66 per cent at Boston is the sunniest month at the ten stations surveyed.

PERCENTAGE OF POSSIBLE SUNSHINE RECEIVED

	J	F	M	A	M	J	J	A	S	O	N	D	Y
Albany, N.Y. 1938–73	46	51	52	53	55	59	64	61	57	54	36	39	53
Blue Hill 1886–1973	45	49	48	50	52	55	57	58	56	55	47	46	52
Boston 1935–73	54	56	57	56	58	63	65	66	64	61	51	52	59
Burlington 1953–73	43	49	53	51	56	60	65	62	56	50	30	33	51
Concord 1941–73	52	54	52	52	53	57	62	60	55	54	41	47	54
Hartford 1954–73	58	57	56	56	58	58	61	63	60	59	45	49	57
Mt. Washington 1938–73	33	34	34	35	36	32	31	31	36	41	29	31	34
New York City 1876–1973	51	55	57	59	61	64	65	64	63	61	52	49	59
Nantucket 1946–69	42	48	56	56	59	61	60	60	60	58	42	41	55
Portland 1940–73	55	59	56	56	56	60	65	65	61	58	46	53	58
Providence 1954–73	57	56	55	56	57	58	59	60	59	59	48	52	56

FOG

Fog consists of visible, minute, water droplets suspended in the atmosphere near the earth's surface. By technical definition, fog exists when visibility is reduced below one kilometer (0.62 miles). Fogs originate when the temperature and dew point of the air become identical or nearly so. This may occur either when the air is cooled to its dew point (producing advection fog, radiation fog, or up-slope fog), or when moisture is added to the air, thereby elevating the dew point (producing steam fog or frontal fog). Fog seldom forms when the difference between temperature and dew point is greater than four degrees.

Advection fog occurs when a warm body of air passes over a cool surface (cold water or snow-covered land). Radiation fog results when

Fog reduces visibility on a highway near Marshfield, Massachusetts.

the surface is cooled through loss of heat to outer space; the air nearest the ground is cooled to its dew point and a shallow layer of fog called ground fog forms at the surface. Up-slope fog develops when the wind blows over terrain of increasing elevation and the rising air cools to its dew point. Steam fog develops when the vapor pressure of a warm body of water is greater than that of the cooler air above. Steam fog forms over lakes on cool autumn mornings and in winter along coastal waters during a cold wave; it is sometimes called arctic sea smoke. Frontal fog occurs on a frontal approach when rain falls into cold stable air or when sudden cooling of air over a moist surface takes place with a frontal passage.

Inland, the most common type of fog is radiation fog, which forms under the clear skies of anticyclonic conditions during nighttime cooling and usually dissipates by midmorning under the warming rays of the sun. Radiation fog is often patchy, forming in hollows and valleys while higher elevations remain clear. This is a hazard to highway driving in rolling country, especially in the hours before dawn.

Sea fog frequently occurs along the New England coast, making it the foggiest area of the eastern United States. The frequency generally decreases from northeast to southwest. The Labrador Current plays a major role in fog making, since its cool waters in the warm season flow parallel to the Gulf Stream to the east and a warm land surface to the west. The effect of the Labrador Current can be traced southwestward to the waters east of Nantucket, where a cold pool exists. This is attributed to the strong tides and mixing over the shallows of Browns and Georges banks.

The rock-bound coast of Maine has the highest number of hours with fog on the Atlantic coast. Moose Peak Lighthouse on Mistake Island at an elevation of only 72 feet averages 1,580 hours per year of heavy fog. Mistake Island is located about halfway between Mount Desert Island and Eastport, Maine. The latter has sixty-five days on which some heavy fog is observed, while Portland has fifty-five days. Logan Airport on Boston Harbor has only twenty-three days, but Nantucket Island with a full sea exposure has eighty-five days. The foggiest period is during the summer. Mount Washington, New Hampshire (elevation 6,262 feet), is in the clouds much of the time and reports 308 days with fog, almost evenly distributed throughout the year. At the other extreme, Key West, Florida, averages less than one day per year with heavy fog.

Situations favorable for the formation of fog over Cape Cod and the islands almost always are cyclonic in pattern, involving convergence of airstreams at the surface. These may occur (1) in the warm sector of a cyclone, (2) ahead of an approaching cold front, and (3) in association with a semistationary trough along the coast. These conditions develop southwest winds that blow over the cold offshore waters and bring fog over the land. Over the sea there is little variation in fogginess during a twenty-four-hour period, but overland fog tends to dissipate as the day progresses and solar heating warms the atmosphere.

The seasonal variation of fog is marked. At Nantucket, for instance, the late autumn and early winter have the minimum of three foggy days. That number increases to ten in May and to a midsummer peak of fourteen in July. It decreases in August to ten and continues steadily downward to the minimum in November and December.

On July 25, 1956, Italian luxury liner *Andrea Doria* (29,000 tons) was rammed by Swedish liner *Stockholm* (12,644 tons) near Nantucket Lightship, Massachusetts. "The night was mild with thick fog." The *Stockholm* was moving at normal speed of 18 knots "in clear moonlight with stars visible" eastward, while the *Andrea Doria* emerged from the fog across the bow of the *Stockholm*. The former soon lost her stability and slowly sank, making the final plunge twelve hours after the accident. The human toll was fifty-two, either killed by the impact of the crash or drowned before or during rescue operations.

DARK DAYS

Dark days have been a recurring phenomenon in the history of New England. These may be defined as daytime periods when solar rays have been intercepted by atmospheric impurities so as to cause semidarkness and exotic illumination of outdoor objects. Days when candles were required to perform noontime chores occurred in 1680, 1685, 1706, 1716, 1727, 1743, and 1762 during the colonial period.

The most famous of all came on May 19, 1780, at a period when the cause of the American revolutionaries looked dark enough without any unusual atmospheric assistance. The core of the obscuration, first reported in southwestern Vermont at dawn, traveled southeastward during the day and was last reported in the afternoon at Barnstable on Cape Cod. In the Boston area the atmosphere darkened perceptibly after 9:00 A.M. and objects assumed a brassy or light-greenish hue. Midday dinner was served under candlelight, reading of newsprint became difficult even out-of-doors, and fowl were reported to have gone to roost. The darkness lifted somewhat in late afternoon, although the night was reported to have been unusually black.

Rainwater accompanying the early part of the phenomenon had a black, sooty appearance and upon analysis was found to have contained the residue of burned leaves. It was suggested by several "scientific Gentlemen" that forest fires burning in the interior of the continent might put such a mass of incompletely combusted material in the air so as to refract incoming light rays and permit only the yellows and greens to reach the surface of the earth. Others scoffed at such "nonesense" by attributing the phenomenon to Divine action. The superstitious thought it a warning of God's displeasure with the infidelities of the age for the long continuance of the war. Others feared it might be the forerunner of some untold disaster. Church attendance increased perceptibly.

The most famous instance of this phenomenon in the nineteenth century was known as the Yellow Day, September 6, 1881, when for a few hours outdoor objects and foliage took on a yellow or brassy appearance. The occurrence was noticed in the early forenoon at Albany, New York, where artificial light was needed to transact the first hours of business, but clearing took place before noon. At Cambridge, Massachusetts, the greatest effect was noticed in early afternoon; it gradually disappeared after 4:00 P.M. and was not marked in the evening at all. Widespread forest fires in Michigan and Ontario were ascertained to be the source of an obscuring layer of smoke and debris aloft.

In the recent past, the Great Smoke Pall from September 24–30, 1950, caused a blue effect of varying intensity for a full week over the eastern United States. The source of the smoke was traced to a large forest fire in northwestern Canada. It required about forty-eight hours for the obscuring matter, which was confined to a layer between about 8,000 and 15,000 feet, to travel to New England. Horizontal visibility at the surface remained good, and no smell of smoke was evident on the ground. The sun was reported to be tinted with varying shades; the most frequently mentioned were violet, lavender, and blue. It was suggested that large quantities of particulate matter in the atmosphere caused selective scattering that removed certain wavelengths from the solar beam.

The decrease during this century in the frequency of dark or smoky days has been attributed to the forest fire prevention program in the West that was instituted following the Great Idaho Fire in 1910.

It's 10 A.M. on a dark day in Boston in 1947.

80

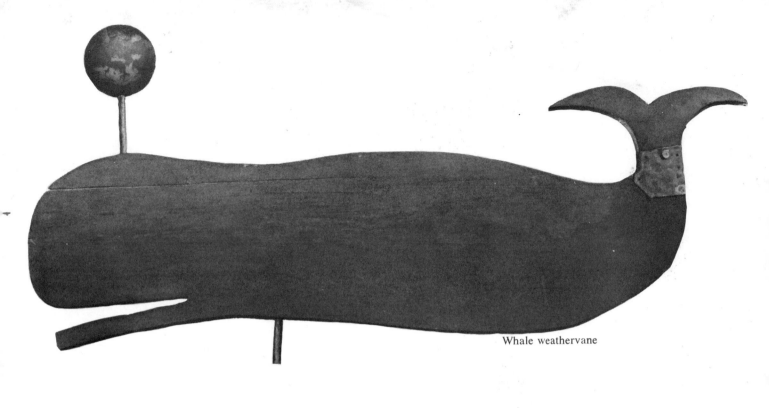

Whale weathervane

The measurement of wind presents many problems to the historian of weather. For one thing, the types of instruments, both anemometers and recorders, have changed several times over the past hundred years. Published measurements prior to 1924 have also been found to have been overestimated by amounts of up to 25 per cent and thus require correction. Furthermore, the exposure of instruments followed no set pattern and depended mainly on local convenience. Although international standards now call for an elevation of 10 meters (33 feet) above the ground, most older records in New England were made at sheltered downtown city locations, while since the 1930s open airport locations have been favored. Thus, wind records at one station or another are not strictly comparable, especially where extremes are being considered.

Other than mountain exposures, the windiest sector of New England appears to be eastern and southeastern Massachusetts, where Boston's 12.7-mph and Nantucket's 13.2-mph mean annual wind speeds lead all stations located near sea level. Blue Hill Observatory, only 11 miles south-southwest of Logan Airport at an elevation of 629 feet, has a mean annual speed of 15.4 mph. Figures drop off in the interior valleys: Concord, New Hampshire, 6.7 mph; Hartford, 9.0 mph; and Burlington and Albany 8.8 mph. Caribou in northern Maine has a mean of 11.2 mph. The months from December to April are generally the windiest.

Again excluding Mount Washington and other peaks, the highest wind speeds in recent years have been reached either in hurricane situations along the coast or at inland locations during the Great Appalachian Storm of November, 1950. Sustained winds have exceeded the hurricane minimum of 73 mph; in the New England Hurricane of 1938, winds in Boston reached 87 mph and in Providence 95 mph. From these figures it seems probable that winds can exceed 100 mph in the maximum wind zone of a hurricane at exposed sea level locations in New England.

WIND

Wind sweeps through the trees lining a
New England road.

The greatest storm in the nonhurricane class of modern times occurred on November 25–26, 1950, when the Appalachian region from North Carolina to Canada was blasted by a mighty cyclonic disturbance. Wind speeds over New England were generally higher inland than along the coast. Hartford had 70-mph winds with gusts to over 100 mph. Putnam, Connecticut, reported gusts to 92 mph. Concord, New Hampshire, set its current record of 72 mph, as did Burlington, Vermont, with the same figure. Sustained winds in excess of 60 mph covered all the New England states, except in northern Maine, for a much longer duration than occurred in either 1938 or 1944. The sweep of the east and southeast gales in 1950 appears to have been the greatest sustained wind force to hit New England since accurate wind measurements commenced.

The highest wind speed ever reported from a station at the surface of the earth occurred on Mount Washington in New Hampshire on April 12, 1934, when a wind gust of 231 mph and a five-minute average of 188 mph were registered. Previously, the highest wind velocity recorded was 140 mph (corrected) in 1876. Weather observations were conducted atop Mount Washington on a year-round basis from 1870 to 1887 and during summer months to 1892. They were resumed in December, 1932, and have been made on a year-round basis to the present. In the recent period, aside from the April, 1934, storm, peak gusts in the winter months are generally in excess of 160 mph; the peak of 180 mph was recorded in March, 1942. The failure of wind measurements

Heavy winds atop Mount Washington

since 1934 to approach the 231-mph figure has caused some to question the world wind-speed record.

The statements of the two people most closely concerned with the record follow:

At noon, April 12, the hourly wind movement had risen to 155 miles with gusts reaching a velocity well above 200 mi./hr. From 12 noon to 1 p.m., while other conditions were comparatively unchanged, the wind attained its extreme force. Between 12:25 p.m. and 12:30 p.m., a 5 minute average wind velocity of 188 mi./hr. was recorded on the Weather Bureau type multiple register. . . . While frequent values of 225 mi./hr., including two-thirds mile at this speed, were obtained, several gusts of 229 mi./hr. were timed, and at 1:21 p.m. the extreme value of 231 mi./hr. for a succession of 3 one-tenth mile contacts were timed twice. This is the highest natural wind velocity ever officially recorded by means of an anemometer on Mount Washington or anywhere else.

Salvatore Pagluica, Weather Observer, July, 1934

Great confidence is justified in the verity of these results, especially the 5-minute travel, because of the character of the automatic record, the sustained movement during the maximum, the excellent fit of the hyperbolic equation to the test observations, and finally, the sound character of the extrapolation of corrections to extreme wind speeds.

Charles F. Marvin, Chief
U.S. Weather Bureau
July, 1934

III

Weather Enough,

but Weather to Spare

Growing Degree Days

CHAPTER 5

A Meteorological Guide

Growing degree days, sometimes called growing units, are an arithmetical accumulation of daily mean temperatures above a certain threshold temperature. They provide a simple means of relating plant growth, development, and maturation to environmental air temperature. Different species of plants have different base, or threshold, temperatures below which they theoretically do not grow. At temperatures above this base, or threshold, value, the amount of plant growth is approximately proportional to the amount of heat or temperature accumulated.

The growing degree day value for any day is easily obtained by subtracting the appropriate base temperature for the specific crop from the mean daily temperature. Thus, on a day with a maximum of 65° and a minimum of 55°, the mean temperature would be 60°. The growing degree days for peas with a 40° base would be 60 minus 40, or 20. The growing degree days for snap beans or sweet corn would be 60 minus 50, or 10.

The growing degree days, to any base, can be computed each day from daily temperatures and can be accumulated over the course of the growing season. Note, however, that negative values are ignored in a summation of growing degree days. Thus, zero is the value assigned to any day when the mean temperature is below the threshold value.

The amount of plant growth is approximately proportional to the amount of heat or temperature accumulated above the base. For each species of plant, and for different varieties, maturity is reached when the growing degree days have accumulated to a certain sum. The various pea varieties, for example, require a range from about 1,200 to 1,800 growing degree days. This means of reckoning the time of maturity has been of much use to the canning industry, since the planting date of peas and other field crops can be scheduled to maintain an orderly supply for processing. The heat unit system is also helpful in selecting crop varieties appropriate to different farming areas. The method has also been used in scheduling the work of fruit orchards. Since insect emergence and development also respond to temperatures, heat sums are often utilized to predict epidemic outbreaks of insects.

Heating Degree Days

Heating degree days are a means of expressing fuel requirements for heating. More simply, they may be called heating degrees for the day. They are calculated day by day when the mean daily temperature is lower than 65°F. They may be totaled for a period or season to express cumulative heating requirements.

Heating degree days are not calculated for days having a mean temperature above 65°, since such days are not considered to require indoor heating.

The heating degree day is determined by subtracting the daily mean temperature from 65°. (The daily mean temperature is one-half the sum of the maximum and minimum temperature for that day.) If the mean temperature is 50°, subtracting that from 65° results in 15 degree days.

The number of heating degree days in New England for the period from 1941 to 1970 varies from 5,395 at New Bedford, Massachusetts, to 10,130 at First Connecticut Lake, New Hampshire.* In other words, the south coast requires only 53 per cent of the fuel that is needed in an average winter in the northern interior. The average number of degree days per heating season at groups of representative stations in each state were: Connecticut 6,334; Rhode Island 5,981; Massachusetts 6,337; Vermont 7,916; New Hampshire 7,734*; and Maine 8,245.

Cooling Degree Days

The cooling degree day provides a means of estimating the energy requirements for air conditioning or refrigeration. It is somewhat similar to the heating degree day, though based on the number of degrees that the daily mean temperature exceeds 65°F. Thus, a mean temperature of 85° would amount to 20 cooling degree days, and for a given period the total daily cooling degree days are accumulated. Southwestern Connecticut has the greatest seasonal number of cooling degree days in New England with 735, while Eastport in the northeast corner of Maine accumulates the trifling amount of 30 in a typical season. Incidentally, there are no air conditioners needed atop Mount Washington, where the cooling degree day total for the season is always zero, since the maximum temperature has never exceeded 72°.

* Without Mount Washington, which has an average of 13,878 heating degree days.

Base temperatures of several economically important plants

Spring wheat	37–40°F
Canning peas	40°F
Oats	43°F
Potatoes	45°F
Sweet corn	50°F
Snap beans	50°F
Lima beans	50°F
Tomatoes	50°F
Field corn	55°F

At the central New England location of Keene, New Hampshire, the monthly percentages of the seasonal heating requirements are:

PERCENTAGES

	MONTHLY	CUMULATIVE
July	0.1	0.1
Aug	0.5	0.6
Sept	2.1	2.7
Oct	6.5	9.2
Nov	11.2	20.4
Dec	17.4	37.8
Jan	19.1	56.9
Feb	16.3	73.2
Mar	14.0	87.2
Apr	8.3	95.5
May	3.9	99.4
June	0.6	100.0

Harvesting potatoes in Maine

Dew Point

Dew point is the temperature to which a parcel of air must be cooled in order to become saturated—pressure and water vapor content remaining constant. At the dew-point temperature, invisible water vapor condenses into visible water droplets. Dew point is determined with a psychrometer and computed tables are consulted. It is said to be a conservative figure in that it does not vary unless moisture is added or subtracted or unless its pressure is changed. Dew point is important in classifying air masses. Maritime and tropical air masses usually have high dew points, and polar and continental air masses have low dew points.

Relative Humidity

Humidity is a measure of the water vapor content of the air. When expressed as a ratio of the amount that is in the air in relation to what the air could hold if fully saturated at that temperature, it is called relative humidity and is expressed as a percentage. Relative humidity is obtained most accurately by use of a psychrometer, which determines the present air temperature (dry bulb) and the temperature of evaporating water (wet bulb). Reference to computed tables furnishes a figure expressed as a percentage. The capacity of air to hold moisture depends on temperature, so relative humidity varies, decreasing with rising temperature and increasing with falling temperature. On a normal day the relative humidity will be highest in the morning when the temperature is lowest, and lowest in the afternoon when the temperature is highest. When comparing the humidity of one day with that of the next, figures should be taken at identical hours.

Temperature-Humidity Index

Temperature-Humidity Index (THI) provides a means of expressing the relative comfort factor of current atmospheric conditions. It is an arbitrary figure weighing both prevailing moisture and temperature conditions. The THI is determined by measuring current dry and wet bulb temperatures with a psychrometer and employing the following formula:

THI = 0.4 (dry bulb °F + wet bulb °F) + 15.

If the temperature is 90° and the wet bulb 70°, the THI is:

$$0.4 \ (90 + 70) \ \text{or} \ 64 + 15 = 79$$

THI figures below 70 are generally comfortable for all. From 70 to 75, some people become uncomfortable; from 76 to 79, many are uncomfortable; at 80 and above everyone is not only uncomfortable but miserable.

Atmospheric Pressure

Atmospheric pressure is difficult to measure precisely, since corrections must be applied to each reading of a mercurial barometer for altitude, 50° standard temperature, capillarity, and instrument error. Records of stations at some elevation above sea level are only roughly comparable.

Low Pressure. The lowest atmospheric pressures at the surface of the earth in New England have occurred in hurricane situations. Pressures slightly below 28.00"/949.2mb may have been attained in New England on September 21, 1938, and on September 11, 1954, but no barometer at an official station of the National Weather Service was in the path of the inner core of the center to measure it. The lowest officially accepted pressure reading in New England was 28.04"/949.5mb at Hartford at 4:17 P.M. on September 21, 1938, during the passage of the center of the New England Hurricane a short distance west.

In nonhurricane situations, the lowest pressure registered in New England was 28.17"/954.0mb at Caribou, Maine, on December 2, 1942. A comparable reading was recorded on March 7, 1932, when the barometer at Block Island, R.I., dropped to a minimum of 28.20"/955.0mb as a very deep coastal storm passed close by.

High Pressure. Two anticyclones stand out in the record books of the twentieth century in New England. Northern stations reached their highest pressures of record on January 31–February 1, 1920, when a Hudson Bay High of great magnitude brought a cold wave of extreme proportions and a very stormy period. Northfield, Vermont, peaked at 31.14"/1054.4mb just before midnight of the thirty-first, and Portland, Maine, reached 31.09"/1052.8mb early on the first. The latter figure is the highest ever recorded at a station at sea level in the United States. Southerly stations generally reached their highest pressures of record on Christmas Day in 1949. Both New York City and Boston recorded 30.06"/1052.8mb, while Caribou in northern Maine was close to the anticyclone's center with a reading of 31.13"/1054.2mb. Little wind and mostly fair weather attended the passage of this great high-pressure area.

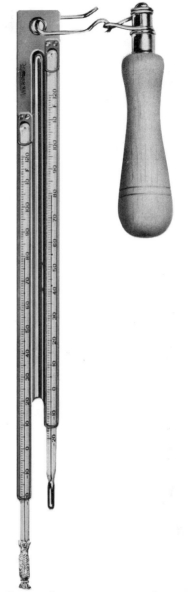

A sling psychrometer measures dew point and relative humidity.

Wind-Chill Index

The wind-chill concept, first developed in environmental studies for the military in polar regions, is an attempt to provide a measurement of the human body's relative cooling power, or rate of heat removal, under various combinations of wind speed and low temperature. After a number of experiments were performed, an empirical formula was developed to determine the length of time required for a measured quantity of water to give off the heat it contains and freeze. A wind-chill scale was established using comparisons between cooling rates at different temperatures and wind speeds. The lower limits of human physical endurance were determined by establishing the length of elapsed time before exposed portions of the human body turned white or actually froze at various wind speeds and subfreezing temperatures. Subjects were unclothed and in the shade for these tests.

In the wind-chill curve, cooling is expressed in kilograms per square meter per hour for various temperatures and wind speeds. The cooling rate is based upon a body with skin temperature given the neutral value 33°C (91.4°F). When the cooling rate is less than the rate of body heat production, excess heat is removed by evaporation, radiation, and conduction.

In the wind-chill table, the cooling power of the wind, for various combinations of actual air temperature and wind speed, are presented as the equivalent temperature when the wind is blowing at 3 mph. The wind-chill index is only an approximation because how one actually feels will also depend on other variables such as type of clothing worn, amount of exposed flesh, amount of radiation, and physical condition at that time.

Consult the table below for various temperature and wind combinations that give the equivalent temperature, here presented as the wind-chill index. For example, on Boston's coldest day in modern records when the outdoor temperature stood at −18°F, the wind-chill index would have been equivalent to −42°F with a 10-mph wind and to −65°F with a 20-mph wind blowing.

WIND CHILL

Equivalent Temperatures °F

WIND SPEED (MILES PER HOUR)

Calm	35	30	25	20	15	10	5	0	−5	−10	−15	−20	−25	−30	−35	−40	−45
5	33	27	21	16	12	7	1	−6	−11	−15	−20	−26	−31	−35	−41	−47	−54
10	21	16	9	2	−2	−9	−15	−22	−27	−31	−38	−45	−52	−58	−64	−70	−77
15	16	11	1	−6	−11	−18	−25	−33	−40	−45	−51	−60	−65	−70	−78	−85	−90
20	12	3	−4	−9	−17	−24	−32	−40	−46	−52	−60	−68	−76	−81	−88	−96	−103
25	7	0	−7	−15	−22	−29	−37	−45	−52	−58	−67	−75	−83	−89	−96	−104	−112
30	5	−2	−11	−18	−26	−33	−41	−49	−56	−63	−70	−78	−87	−94	−101	−109	−117
35	3	−4	−13	−20	−27	−35	−43	−52	−60	−67	−72	−83	−90	−98	−105	−113	−123
40	1	−4	−15	−22	−29	−36	−45	−54	−62	−69	−76	−87	−94	−101	−107	−116	−128
45	1	−6	−17	−24	−31	−38	−46	−54	−63	−70	−78	−87	−94	−101	−108	−118	−128
50	0	−7	−17	−24	−31	−38	−47	−56	−63	−70	−79	−88	−96	−103	−110	−120	−128

Equivalent Temperatures °C

WIND SPEED (MILES PER HOUR)

Calm	+2	0	−4	−8	−12	−16	−20	−24	−28	−32	−36	−40
5	+1	−1	−6	−10	−14	−19	−23	−27	−31	−35	−38	−44
10	−6	−7	−13	−18	−23	−28	−32	−36	−41	−47	−51	−57
15	−8	−10	−17	−23	−28	−34	−39	−43	−49	−54	−58	−65
20	−11	−13	−20	−25	−31	−37	−43	−48	−54	−60	−64	−71
25	−13	−15	−22	−28	−34	−41	−46	−52	−58	−64	−68	−76
30	−15	−17	−24	−30	−36	−42	−48	−54	−60	−66	−71	−78
35	−16	−18	−26	−31	−37	−44	−51	−56	−61	−68	−73	−81
40	−17	−19	−27	−32	−38	−45	−52	−57	−64	−70	−74	−82
45	−17	−19	−28	−33	−39	−46	−52	−58	−64	−70	−75	−83
50	−18	−19	−28	−33	−39	−46	−52	−58	−64	−71	−75	−84

Opposite: Radiosonde is used for radio sounding of the upper atmosphere. Temperature, humidity, and pressure are relayed to a ground station by radio transmitter.

Vertical Clouds

cumulus (cu)—detached clouds, generally dense and sharply outlined, developing as rising mounds, domes, towers, brilliant white in sunlight, often extending from relatively dark and nearly horizontal base, in low to middle levels. (From Latin *cumulus,* an accumulation, heap, pile.)

cumulonimbus (cb)—heavy dense clouds of considerable vertical extent (often to 40,000 feet or more), in the form of a mountain or huge tower, upper part usually smooth, sometimes fibrous, with top flattened to anvil shape or vast cirrus plume, composed of water droplets and, in upper portion, ice crystals; producer of lightning, hail, tornadoes, heavy rain, and high winds. (From *cumulus* and *nimbus.*)

Cloud Classification

The first general systems of classifying clouds were proposed by the French naturalist Lamarck in 1802 and by the English pharmacist Luke Howard in 1803. The latter employed a series of Latin names and compounds that proved popular in international usage and have been followed by most observers to the present. In 1891 an International Meteorological Conference endorsed the Howard system, as modified in 1887, in a publication by Ralph Abercromby of England and H. H. Hildebrandsson of Sweden. An *International Cloud Atlas* was published in 1896; revised editions appeared in 1910, 1932, and 1956. The traditional names and classifications have been retained, since they permitted an unskilled observer, from the appearance of the cloud alone, to transmit a useful description to the weather analyst.

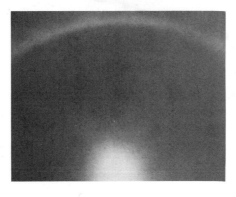

High Clouds

cirrus (ci)—detached wisps of clouds, hairlike (fibrous), formed of delicate filaments, patches, or narrow bands, predominantly composed, like other high clouds, of ice crystals. (From Latin *cirrus,* a lock of hair, a tuft of horse hair, a bird's tuft.)

cirrostratus (cs)—a transparent, whitish veil of fibrous or smooth appearance, covering part or all of the sky, producing halo phenomena. (From *cirrus* and *stratus*.)

cirrocumulus (cc)—thin, white, grainy, and rippled patches, sheets, or layers showing very slight vertical development in the form of turrets or shallow towers. (From *cirrus* and *cumulus*.)

Middle Clouds

altostratus (as)—a grayish or bluish cloud sheet or layer of striated, fibrous, or uniform appearance, covering part or all of the sky, composed of water droplets, ice crystals, raindrops, snowflakes; thin enough in parts to reveal sun at least vaguely, as through ground glass. (From Latin *altum,* height, upper air, and *stratus*.)

altocumulus (ac)—most often seen as an extensive sheet of regularly arranged cloudlets, white and gray, and somewhat rounded; sometimes seen as parallel rolls separated by lanes and, rarely, as a honeycomb of ragged holes, alternating with cloudlets, composed of water droplets, with ice crystals forming only at very low temperatures. (From *altum* and *cumulus*.)

Low Clouds

stratus (st)—a gray cloud layer with a rather uniform base, low lying, producing drizzle, ice prisms, or snow grains, often opaque enough to mask the sun, sometimes formed by gradual lifting of fog layer. (From Latin *stratus,* past participle of the verb *sternere,* to extend, to cover with a layer.)

nimbostratus (ns)—a dark, gray cloud layer, thick enough to blot out sun, continuous rain or snow without electrical activity of thunderstorm, occurs in low and middle levels. (From Latin *nimbus,* rainy cloud, and *stratus*.)

stratocumulus (sc)—gray and whitish layers of cloud with dark patches formed of rounded masses and rolls, nonfibrous, like altocumulus but lower, with larger elements, composed of water droplets except in extreme cold weather. (From *stratus* and *cumulus*.)

CHAPTER 6
Storm Warnings and Safety Rules

People who live in New England are familiar with the surprises that weather holds for them. Hurricanes, tornadoes, blizzards, and flash floods are ever-present possibilities, and in recent years, air pollution has become a major problem—even in rural areas. The following warnings and safety rules are taken from publications of the U.S. Department of Commerce, National Oceanic and Atmospheric Administration Public Affairs Office.

HURRICANES

WARNINGS

The National Hurricane Center at Miami has overall responsibility for supervision of the hurricane warning program in the Atlantic, Caribbean, and Gulf of Mexico. It issues forecasts for hurricane-affected areas. Responsibility subsequently passes to the Washington office when the storm moves north of Cape Hatteras (35°N) and to the Boston office when it moves north of Long Island (41°N).

Small-craft Warning. When a hurricane moves within a few hundred miles of the coast, advisories warn small-craft operators to take precautions and not to venture into the open ocean.

Gale Warning. When winds of 38–55 miles per hour (33–48 knots) are expected, a gale warning is added to the advisory message.

Storm Warning. When winds of 55–74 miles per hour (48–64 knots) are expected, a storm warning is added to the advisory message.

Gale and storm warnings indicate the coastal area to be affected by the warning, the time during which the warning will apply, and the expected intensity of the disturbance. When gale or storm warnings are part of a tropical cyclone advisory, they may change to a hurricane warning if the storm continues along the coast.

Hurricane Watch. If the hurricane continues its advance and threatens coastal and inland regions, a hurricane watch is added to the advisory, covering a specified area and duration. A hurricane watch means that hurricane conditions are a real possibility; it does not mean they are imminent. When a hurricane watch is issued, everyone in the area covered by the watch should listen for further advisories and be prepared to act quickly if hurricane warnings are issued.

Hurricane Warning. When hurricane conditions are expected within 24 hours, a hurricane warning is added to the advisory. Hurricane warnings identify coastal areas where winds of at least 74 miles per hour are expected to occur. A warning may also describe coastal areas where dangerously high water or exceptionally high waves are forecast, even though winds may be less than hurricane force.

When the hurricane warning is issued, all precautions should be taken immediately. Hurricane warnings are seldom issued more than 24 hours in advance. If the hurricane's path is unusual or erratic, the warnings may be issued only a few hours before the beginning of hurricane conditions. Precautionary actions should begin as soon as a hurricane warning is announced.

SAFETY RULES

Enter Each Hurricane Season Prepared. Every June through November, recheck your supply of boards, tools, batteries, nonperishable foods, and the other equipment you will need when a hurricane strikes your town.

When You Hear the First Tropical Cyclone Advisory, listen for future messages; this will prepare you for a hurricane emergency well in advance of the issuance of watches and warnings.

When Your Area Is Covered by a Hurricane Watch, continue normal activities, but stay tuned to radio or television for all National Weather Service advisories. Remember, a hurricane watch means possible danger within 24 hours; if the danger materializes, a hurricane warning will be issued. Meanwhile, keep alert. Ignore rumors.

When Your Area Receives a Hurricane Warning, Plan Your Time before the storm arrives and avoid the last-minute hurry which might leave you marooned, or unprepared.

Keep Calm until the emergency has ended.

Leave Low-Lying Areas that may be swept by high tides or storm waves.

Leave Mobile Homes for more substantial shelter. They are particularly vulnerable to overturning during strong winds. Damage can be minimized by securing mobile homes with heavy cables anchored in concrete footing.

Moor Your Boat Securely before the storm arrives, or evacuate it to a designated safe area. When your boat is moored, leave it, and don't return once the wind and waves are up.

Board Up Windows or protect them with storm shutters or tape. Danger to small windows is mainly from wind-driven debris. Larger windows may be broken by wind pressure.

Secure Outdoor Objects that might be blown away or uprooted. Garbage cans, garden tools, toys, signs, porch furniture, and a number of other harmless items become missiles of destruction in hurricane winds. Anchor them or store them inside before the storm strikes.

Store Drinking Water in clean bathtubs, jugs, bottles, and cooking utensils; your town's water supply may be contaminated by flooding or damaged by hurricane floods.

Opposite: A large tree felled by the September 1938 hurricane. *Above:* A swath of trees cut down by wind on a hillside

Check Your Battery-Powered Equipment. Your radio may be your only link with the world outside the hurricane, and emergency cooking facilities, lights, and flashlights will be essential if utilities are interrupted.

Keep Your Car Fueled. Service stations may be inoperable for several days after the storm strikes, due to flooding or interrupted electrical power.

Stay At Home, if it is sturdy and on high ground; if it is not, move to a designated shelter, and stay there until the storm is over.

Remain Indoors During the Hurricane. Travel is extremely dangerous when winds and tides are whipping through your area.

Monitor the Storm's Position through National Weather Service advisories.

Beware the Eye of the Hurricane. If the calm storm center passes directly overhead, there will be a lull in the wind lasting from a few minutes to half an hour or more. Stay in a safe place unless emergency repairs are absolutely necessary. But remember, at the other side of the eye, the winds rise very rapidly to hurricane force, and come from the opposite direction.

When the Hurricane Has Passed: Seek Necessary Medical Care At Red Cross disaster stations or hospitals.

Stay Out of Disaster Areas. Unless you are qualified to help, your presence might hamper first-aid and rescue work.

Drive Carefully along debris-filled streets. Roads may be undermined and may collapse under the weight of a car. Slides along cuts are also a hazard.

Avoid Loose or Dangling Wires, and report them immediately to your power company or the nearest law enforcement officer.

Report Broken Sewer or Water Mains to the water department.

Prevent Fires. Lowered water pressure may make fire fighting difficult.

Check Refrigerated Food for spoilage if power has been off during the storm.

Remember that hurricanes moving inland can cause severe flooding. Stay away from river banks and streams.

TORNADOES

Predicting the general areas of probable severe thunderstorm and tornado development is the function of the National Severe Storms Forecast Center in Kansas City, Missouri. Warnings and watches are distributed to all National Weather Service offices and released directly to press wires.

A severe thunderstorm watch or tornado watch bulletin issued by the center usually identifies an area about 140 miles wide by 240 miles long. Although the watch bulletin states approximately where and for how long the severe local storm threat will exist, it does not mean that severe local storms will not occur outside the watch area or time frame —the watch is only an indication of where and when the probabilities are highest.

Watches are not warnings. Until a severe thunderstorm or tornado warning is issued, persons in watch areas should maintain their normal routines, but watch for threatening weather and listen to the radio or television for further severe weather information.

A severe thunderstorm warning or tornado warning bulletin is issued by a local office of the National Weather Service when a severe thunderstorm or tornado has actually been sighted in the area or indicated by radar. Warnings describe the location of the severe thunderstorm or tornado at the time of detection, the area (usually the counties) that could be affected, and the time period (usually one hour) covered by the warning. The length of this area is equal to the distance the storm is expected to travel in one hour.

When a warning is received, persons close to the storm should take cover immediately, especially in the case of a tornado warning. Persons farther away from the storm should be prepared to take cover if threatening conditions are sighted.

All-clear bulletins are issued whenever the threat of severe thunderstorms or tornadoes has ended in the area previously warned in a tornado or a severe thunderstorm warning bulletin. When a warning is cancelled, but a watch continues in effect for the same area or a warning is in effect for an adjacent area, a "Severe Weather Bulletin" is issued; this qualified message is also issued when a portion, but not all, of a watch area is cancelled. This permits a continuous alert in the path of the storm, with the alert being cancelled as the severe weather moves through the watch area.

SAFETY RULES

A tornado *watch* means tornadoes are expected to develop. Keep a battery-operated radio or television set nearby, and listen for weather advisories—even if the sky is blue. A tornado *warning* means a tornado has actually been sighted or indicated by weather radar. Seek inside shelter (in a storm cellar or reinforced building) and stay away from windows. Curl up so that your head and eyes are protected. Keep a battery-operated radio or television nearby, and listen for further advisories.

In Office Buildings, go to an interior hallway on the lowest floor, or to the designated shelter area.

In Homes, the basement offers the greatest safety. Seek shelter under sturdy furniture if possible. In homes without basements, take cover in the center part of the house, on the lowest floor, in a small room such as a closet or bathroom, or under sturdy furniture. Keep some windows open, but stay away from them.

In Shopping Centers, go to a designated shelter area (not to your parked car).

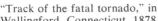

"Track of the fatal tornado," in Wallingford, Connecticut, 1878

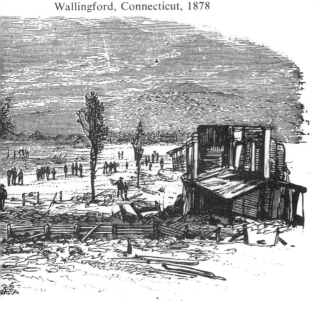

In Schools, follow advance plans to an interior hallway on the lowest floor. If the building is not of reinforced construction, go to a nearby one that is, or take cover outside on low, protected ground. Stay out of auditoriums, gymnasiums, and other structures with wide, free-span roofs.

In Open Country, move away from the tornado's path at right angles. If there is not time to escape, lie flat in the nearest ditch or ravine.

Mobile Homes are particularly vulnerable to overturning during strong winds and should be evacuated when strong winds are forecast. Damage can be minimized by securing trailers with cables anchored in concrete footing. Trailer parks should have a community storm shelter and a warden to monitor broadcasts throughout the severe storm emergency. If there is no shelter nearby, leave the trailer park and take cover on low, protected ground.

Tornadoes Are Only One of a Thunderstorm's Killers—Lightning Is the Worst Killer. Stay indoors and away from electrical appliances while the storm is overhead. If you are caught outside, stay away from and remain lower than high, conductive objects.

Thunderstorm Rains cause flash floods. Be careful where you take shelter.

WINTER STORMS

WARNINGS

There are warning systems for winter storms. The terms *watch* and *warning* are employed, as for other natural hazards, when combinations of cold, wind, and some type of precipitation are forecast.

Heavy snow is a frequently issued winter warning in New England. The term means that four inches or more are expected in a twelve-hour period, or six inches or more in a twenty-four-hour period. Blowing and drifting snow may increase the hazards. Blowing snow is defined as snow lifted from the surface by the wind and blown about to such a degree that horizontal visibility is greatly restricted. The term *drifting snow* is employed in forecasts to indicate that strong winds will blow falling or loose snow on the ground into significant drifts.

Blizzards are the most dramatic and perilous of all winter storms, characterized by low temperatures, strong winds, and large amounts of snow. Most of the snow accompanying a blizzard is in the form of fine, powdery particles that are whipped about in such quantities that visibility is sometimes reduced to only a few yards. True western blizzard conditions typical of the Great Plains seldom occur in New England, but eastern blizzard conditions can arise.

Blizzard warnings are issued when winds with speeds of at least 35 mph are accompanied by considerable falling or blowing snow and temperatures of 20°F or lower are expected to prevail for an extended period of time. A *severe blizzard* warning is issued when winds will exceed 45 mph, with a great density of falling or blowing snow, and a temperature of 10°F or lower.

Hazardous driving (travelers) warnings are by far the most frequently issued winter warnings in New England. These indicate that falling, blowing, or drifting snow, freezing rain, sleet, or strong winds will make driving difficult.

SAFETY RULES

Keep ahead of the winter storm by listening to the latest weather warnings and bulletins on radio and television.

Houses buried in snow after the storm of February, 1969, in West Peabody, Massachusetts

Check Battery Powered Equipment Before the Storm Arrives. A portable radio or television set may be your only contact with the world outside the winter storm. Also check emergency cooking facilities and flashlights.

Check Your Supply of Heating Fuel. Fuel carriers may not be able to move if a winter storm buries your area in snow.

Check Your Food and stock an extra supply. Your supplies should include food that requires no cooking or refrigeration in case of power failure.

Prevent Fire Hazards due to overheated coal or oil burning stoves, fireplaces, heaters, or furnaces.

Stay Indoors During Storms and cold snaps unless in peak physical condition. If you must go out, avoid overexertion.

Don't Kill Yourself Shoveling Snow. It is extremely hard work for anyone in less than prime physical condition, and can bring on a heart attack, a major cause of death during and after winter storms.

Rural Residents: Make Necessary Trips for Supplies Before the Storm Develops or Not At All; arrange for emergency heat supply in case of power failure; be sure camp stoves and lanterns are filled.

Dress to Fit the Season. If you spend much time outdoors, wear loose-fitting, lightweight, warm clothing in several layers; layers can be removed to prevent perspiring and subsequent chill. Outer garments should be tightly woven, water repellent, and hooded. The hood should protect much of your face and cover your mouth to ensure warm breathing and protect your lungs from the extremely cold air. Remember that entrapped, insulating air, warmed by body heat, is the best protection against cold. Layers of protective clothing are more effective and efficient than single layers of thick clothing; and mittens, snug at the wrists, are better protection than fingered gloves.

Automobile Preparations. Your automobile can be your best friend—or worst enemy—during winter storms, depending on your preparations. Get your car winterized before the storm season begins. Everything on the checklist shown below should be taken care of before winter storms strike your area.

—ignition system	—fuel system	—wiper blades
—battery	—lubrication	—defroster
—lights	—exhaust system tight	—snow tires installed
—tire tread	—heater	—chains
—cooling system	—brakes perfectly adjusted	—winter-grade oil

Keep water out of your fuel by maintaining a FULL tank of gasoline.

Be Equipped for the Worst. Carry a winter storm car kit especially if cross country travel is anticipated or if you live in the northern states.

Suggested Winter Storm Car Kit: blankets or sleeping bags, matches and candles, empty 3-pound coffee can with plastic cover, facial tissue, paper towels, extra clothing, high-calorie, nonperishable food, compass and road maps, knife, first aid kit, shovel, sack of sand, sand, flashlight or signal light, windshield scraper, booster cables, two tow chains, fire extinguisher, catalytic heater, axe.

WINTER AUTO TRAVEL SAFETY

Winter travel by automobile is serious business. Take your travel seriously.

If the storm exceeds or even tests your limitations, seek available refuge immediately.

A street in New Bedford, Massachusetts, after a snowstorm

Plan your travel and select primary and alternate routes.

Check latest weather information on your radio.

Try not to travel alone; two or three persons are preferable.

Travel in convoy with another vehicle, if possible.

Always fill gasoline tank before entering open country, even for a short distance.

Drive carefully, defensively.

IF A BLIZZARD CATCHES YOU IN YOUR CAR

Avoid Overexertion and Exposure. Exertion from attempting to push your car, shovel heavy drifts, and perform other difficult chores during the strong winds, blinding snow, and bitter cold of a blizzard may cause a heart attack—even for persons in apparently good physical condition.

Stay in Your Vehicle. Do not attempt to walk out of a blizzard. Disorientation comes quickly in blowing and drifting snow. Being lost in open country during a blizzard is almost certain death. You are more likely to be found, and more likely to be sheltered, in your car.

Don't Panic.

Keep Fresh Air in Your Car. Freezing wet snow and wind-driven snow can completely seal the passenger compartment.

Beware the Gentle Killers: Carbon Monoxide and Oxygen Starvation. Run the motor and heater sparingly, and only with the downwind window open for ventilation.

Exercise by clapping hands and moving arms and legs vigorously from time to time, and do not stay in one position for long.

Turn on Dome Light at Night, to make the vehicle visible to work crews.

Keep Watch. Do not permit all occupants of car to sleep at once.

FLASH FLOODS

WARNINGS

Flash flood waves, moving at incredible speeds, can roll boulders, tear out trees, destroy buildings and bridges, and scour out new channels. Killing walls of water can reach 10 to 20 feet. You won't always have a warning that these deadly, sudden floods are coming. But you can save yourself—your family—if you know what to expect and how to react.

On small streams, especially near the headwaters of river basins, water levels may rise quickly in heavy rainstorms, and flash floods can begin before the rain stops falling. There is little time between detection of flood crest. Swift action is essential to the protection of life and property.

NOAA's Weather Service has helped set up flash flood warning systems in about 100 communities. In these, a volunteer network of rainfall and river observing stations is established in the area, and a local flood warning representative is appointed to collect reports from the network. The representative is authorized to issue official flash flood warnings based on a series of graphs prepared by the Weather Service.

These graphs show the local flooding that will occur under different conditions of soil moisture and rainfall. On the basis of reported rainfall, the representative can prepare a flood forecast from these graphs, and spread a warning within minutes. Communities within range of a Weather Service radar have the additional protection of advance warning when flood-producing storms approach.

Successful operation of a flash flood warning system requires active community participation and planning, but very little financial outlay. Still, the communities with cooperative flash flood warning systems are only a small fraction of the thousands of communities which need them.

Flash flood warnings are the most urgent type of flood warning issued, and are transmitted to the public over radio, television, and by sirens and other signals.

TERMS USED IN FORECASTS AND WARNINGS

Flash Flood means the occurrence of a dangerous rise in water level of a stream or over a land area in a few hours or less caused by heavy rain, ice jam breakup, earthquake, or dam failure.

Flash Flood Watch means that heavy rains occurring or expected to occur may soon cause flash flooding in certain areas and citizens should be alert to the possibility of a flood emergency which will require immediate action.

Flash Flood Warning means that flash flooding is occurring or imminent on certain streams or designated areas and immediate precautions should be taken by those threatened.

SAFETY RULES

Before the Flood know the elevation of your property in relation to nearby streams and other waterways. Investigate the flood history of your area and how man-made changes may affect future flooding. Make advance plans of what you will do and where you will go in a flash flood emergency.

When a Flash Flood Watch Is Issued listen to area radio and television stations for possible Flash Flood Warnings and reports of flooding in progress from the National Weather Service and public safety agencies. Be prepared to move out of danger at a moment's notice. If you are on the road, watch for flooding at highway dips, bridges, and low areas due to heavy rain not observable to you, but which may be indicated by thunder and lightning.

When a Flash Flood Warning Is Issued for your area act quickly to save yourself. You may have only seconds:

1. Get out of areas subject to flooding. Avoid already flooded areas.
2. Do not attempt to cross a flowing stream on foot where water is above your knees.
3. If driving, know the depth of water in a dip before crossing. The road may not be intact under the water. If the vehicle stalls, abandon it immediately and seek higher ground—rapidly rising water may engulf the vehicle and its occupants and sweep them away.
4. Be especially cautious at night when it is harder to recognize flood dangers.
5. When you are out of immediate danger, tune in area radio or television stations for additional information as conditions change and new reports are received.

After the Flash Flood Watch or Warning Is Cancelled stay tuned to radio or television for follow-up information. Flash flooding may have ended, but general flooding may come later in headwater streams and major rivers.

Opposite: Flood waters left these railroad tracks suspended in the Vermont flood of 1927. *Above:* A bridge destroyed by flood waters

MARINE WEATHER

Weather warnings for boating areas in the United States and Puerto Rico are issued every six hours by the National Weather Service. Each forecast covers a specific coastal area, as, for example, "Eastport, Me., to Block Island, R.I." If strong winds or sea conditions hazardous to small-boat operations are expected, forecasts include a statement as to the type of warning issued and the areas where warnings are in effect.

Similar forecasts and warnings are issued for numerous inland lakes, dams, reservoirs, and river waterways throughout the country. Daily advices indicating expected stream flow, river gage heights, and flood warnings as required are also issued by the National Weather Service.

WARNING DISPLAY SIGNALS

SMALL CRAFT

Daytime. Red Pennant.

Nighttime. Red Light Over White Light.
Indicates: Forecast winds as high as 33 knots and sea conditions considered dangerous to small-craft operations.

GALE

Daytime. Two Red Pennants.

Nighttime. White Light over Red Light.
Indicates: Forecast winds in the range 34–47 knots.

STORM

Daytime. Square Red Flag With Black Square Centered.

Nighttime. Two Red Lights.
Indicates: Forecast winds 48 knots and above no matter how high the wind speed. If the winds are associated with a tropical cyclone (hurricane), storm warnings indicate forecast winds of 48–63 knots.

HURRICANE

Daytime. Two Square Red Flags With Black Square Centered.
Nighttime. White Light Between Two Red Lights.
Indicates: Forecast winds of 64 knots and above, displayed only in connection with a hurricane.

SAFE BOATING WEATHER RULES

BEFORE SETTING OUT

1. Check local weather and sea conditions.
2. Obtain the latest weather forecast for your area from radio broadcasts.

Heavy surf on the Atlantic coast

When warnings are in effect, don't go out unless you are confident your boat can be navigated safely under forecast conditions of wind and sea. Be cautious when you see warning displays at U.S. Coast Guard stations, yacht clubs, marinas, and at other coastal points.

WHILE AFLOAT

1. Keep a weather eye out for the approach of dark, threatening clouds, which may foretell a squall or thunderstorm; any steady increase in wind or sea; any increase in wind velocity opposite in direction to a strong tidal current. A dangerous rip tide condition may form steep waves capable of broaching a boat.
2. Heavy static on your AM radio may be an indication of nearby thunderstorm activity.
3. Check radio weather broadcasts for latest forecasts and warnings.
4. If a thunderstorm catches you afloat: —stay below deck if possible. —keep away from metal objects that are not grounded to the boat's protection system. —don't touch more than one grounded object at the same time (or you may become a shortcut for electrical surges through the protection system).

What about navigation? Do you have the NOAA National Ocean Survey charts and other publications covering your part of coastal or Great Lakes waters? Check your local office of the National Weather Service or National Ocean Survey and other essential aids to navigation.

The *Reliance* heels under a stiff wind in 1903.

HEAT WAVE SAFETY RULES

Slow Down. Your body can't do its best in high temperatures and humidities, and might do its worst.

Heed Your Body's Early Warnings That Heat Syndrome Is on the Way. Reduce your level of activities immediately and get to a cooler environment.

Dress for Summer. Lightweight, light-colored clothing reflects heat and sunlight, and helps your thermoregulatory system maintain normal body temperature.

Put Less Fuel on Your Inner Fires. Foods (like proteins) that increase metabolic heat production also increase water loss.

Don't Dry Out. Heat wave weather can wring you out before you know it. Drink plenty of water while the hot spell lasts.

Stay Salty. Unless you're on a salt-restricted diet, take an occasional salt tablet or some salt solution when you've worked up a sweat.

Avoid Thermal Shock. Acclimatize yourself gradually to warmer weather. Treat yourself extra gently for those first critical two or three hot days.

Vary Your Thermal Environment. Physical stress increases with exposure time in heat wave weather. Try to get out of the heat for at least a few hours each day. If you can't do this at home, drop in on a cool store, restaurant, or theater—anything to keep your exposure time down.

Don't Get Too Much Sun. Sunburn makes the job of heat dissipation that much more difficult.

Know the Heat Syndrome Symptoms and First Aid.

LIGHTNING
SAFETY RULES

Top: Lightning strikes downtown Boston. *Bottom:* A photograph of ball lightning; the upper ball of fire is about 42 feet across.

These safety rules may help to save your life when lightning threatens

1. Stay indoors, and don't venture outside, unless absolutely necessary.
2. Stay away from open doors and windows, fireplaces, radiators, stoves, metal pipes, sinks, and plug-in electrical appliances.
3. Don't use plug-in electrical equipment like hair dryers, electric tooth brushes, or electric razors during the storm.
4. Don't use the telephone during the storm—lightning may strike telephone lines outside.
5. Don't take laundry off the clothesline.
6. Don't work on fences, telephone or power lines, pipelines, or structural steel fabrication.
7. Don't use metal objects like fishing rods and golf clubs. Golfers wearing cleated shoes are particularly good lightning rods.
8. Don't handle flammable materials in open containers.
9. Stop tractor work, especially when the tractor is pulling metal equipment, and dismount. Tractors and other implements in metalic contact with the ground are often struck by lightning.
10. Get out of the water and off small boats.
11. Stay in your automobile if you are traveling. Automobiles offer excellent lightning protection.
12. Seek shelter in buildings. If no buildings are available, your best protection is a cave, ditch, canyon, or under head-high clumps of trees in open forest glades.
13. When there is no shelter, avoid the highest object in the area. If only isolated trees are nearby, your best protection is to crouch in the open, keeping twice as far away from isolated trees as the trees are high.
14. Avoid hill tops, open spaces, wire fences, metal clothes lines, exposed sheds, and any electrically conductive elevated objects.
15. When you feel the electrical charge—if your hair stands on end or your skin tingles—lightning may be about to strike you. Drop to the ground immediately.

Persons struck by lightning receive a severe electrical shock and may be burned, but they carry no electrical charge and can be handled safely. A person "killed" by lightning can often be revived by prompt mouth-to-mouth resuscitation, cardiac massage, and prolonged artificial respiration. In a group struck by lightning, the apparently dead should be treated first; those who show vital signs will probably recover spontaneously, although burns and other injuries may require treatment. Recovery from lightning strikes is usually complete except for possible impairment or loss of sight or hearing.

The National Meteorological Center near Washington, D.C., issues daily reports of weather conditions relating to air stagnation and transmits charts depicting the areas of stagnation across the United States, giving the height of the surface-based mixing layer and the mean transport of wind within the layer. A measure of the stagnation potential is the ventilation factor. In New England this is affected by the depth of the stagnant layer, the winds at the top of the layer, whether the air has any overwater trajectory, whether precipitation is occurring or will take place, and what type of pollutants are being produced. Furthermore, there is a seasonal variation in the pollution potential. Summer is the lowest pollutant season since little fuel oil for heating is being burned. Some of the worst stagnation conditions have occurred in the autumn (as in late November, 1966) when anticyclonic conditions often prevail for several consecutive days.

An Environmental Meteorological Support Unit is located at the National Weather Service Office at Logan International Airport in Boston to serve Massachusetts and Rhode Island. When the atmosphere is expected to become stagnant for a period of approximately thirty-six hours, an Air Stagnation Advisory is issued with particulars for regional and individual urban areas. Other sections of New England are served by National Weather Service offices at Portland (for Maine and New Hampshire), Albany (for Vermont), and New York City (for Connecticut).

Air stagnation advisories are issued to the Federal Environmental Protection Agency (EPA), local and state pollution control agencies, and the general public. The advisories are integrated into emergency alerting procedures and help to activate various stages of the pollution alert.

SYSTEMS FOR RATING THE REGIONS FOR CLEAN AIR

The classification system works like this. Each control region is graded by EPA as Priority I, Priority II, or Priority III, on the basis of the known or estimated levels of the six pollutants presently covered by national standards. Hence, the most heavily polluted regions are PRIORITY I; regions with less pollution are PRIORITY II; and those with pollution levels below or just above standard levels are PRIORITY III.

Moreover, a given control region may have different classifications for different pollutants. It could be classified as Priority I for sulfur oxides and Priority III for carbon monoxide. And some regions, where precise air quality data are lacking, may be classified according to population—for example, any region with an urban concentration exceeding 200,000 people will generally be classified as Priority I. If several regions within one state share the same classification for a given pollutant, the state may develop one plan for that pollutant with provisions applicable to all of those control regions.

Smoke from a paper mill fills the Maine air.

IV Weather Is Necessary to a

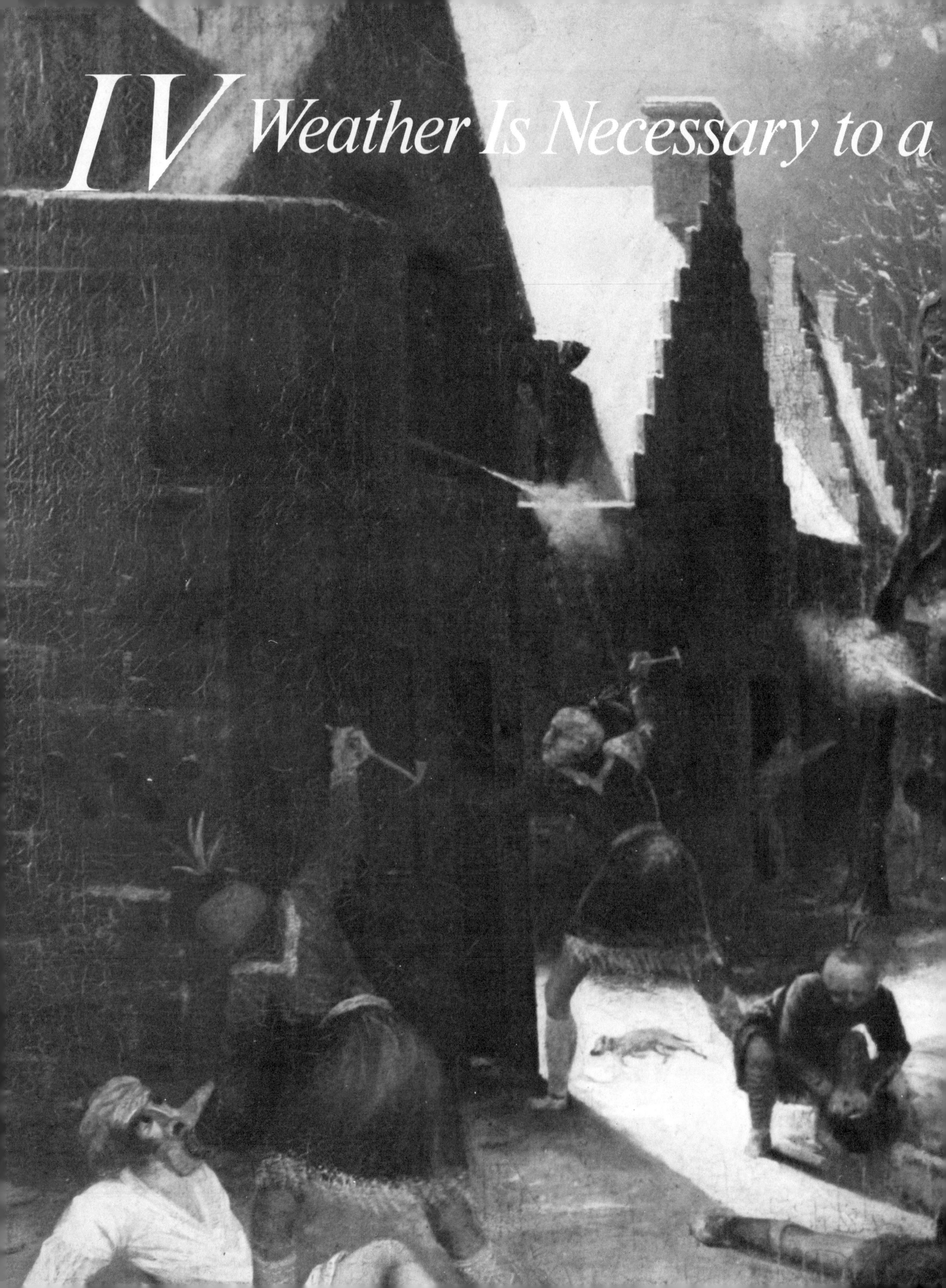

Narrative of Human Experience

CHAPTER 7
Early Weather Observers

Weather played a most influential role in the lives of the aboriginal population of New England, since theirs was a life spent in full exposure to all the varied elements of nature. Over the centuries the Indians had acquired a keen understanding of atmospheric behavior and utilized that knowledge in their struggle to survive under ever-changing weather conditions. Unfortunately for us, they had no means of preserving their understanding of these and other natural phenomena except by oral tradition. There is little reference to Indian weather lore in the writings of the first Europeans to visit the New World except for a few words in John Jocelyn's *Two Voyages,* a description of trips made in 1638 and 1663. Nor did the early colonial almanacs draw on Indian culture for their weather wisdom.

One must bear in mind that the age of science was just at its threshold at the time Plymouth Plantation and Massachusetts Bay Colony were establishing a foothold on the continent. Galileo was still alive, and Descartes and Pascal had not yet commenced their work in formulating the principles of the scientific method. By 1643, when Evangelista Torricelli enunciated the principle of atmospheric pressure and experimented with a barometer, settlers had moved into all the present New England states except Vermont. Among the learned, the main reliance for weather information rested on the body of classical pseudoscientific writing such as that produced by Aratus, Theophrastus, Aristotle, Virgil, Ovid, and Pliny. For the general populace, there was little to serve as weather guides. Since the English Puritans were opposed to making prognostications of the almanac variety, no New England almanac carried weather information for the first forty years of publication. Not until 1681 did an almanac contain weather forecasts and information similar to that published in England.

During the first century of settlement, several individuals did record some information about New England weather conditions. Gov. John Winthrop of Massachusetts Bay Colony, a graduate of Cambridge University, maintained a daily log of wind and weather conditions on the trip from England to America in 1630, and urged his son to do the same on his return to England several years later so that conditions in the two places could be compared. Winthrop's important journal, maintained to 1649, made note of many major storms and unusual weather happenings in the vicinity of Boston during that period and included a vivid description of the Great Colonial Hurricane in 1635. Combined with Gov. William Bradford's contemporary account of the storm at Plymouth, it gives us an adequate picture of the first big New England weather event.

Above: Gov. John Winthrop
Opposite: Benjamin Franklin

Samuel Sewall

Cotton Mather

After the passing of these two leaders with literary inclination and training, the reporting of meteorological phenomena ran thin for a number of years. The diary of mint tender John Hull of Boston contains a sketchy account of the character of New England winters from 1654 to 1678, and Rev. John Pike of Dover, New Hampshire, kept a diary from 1677 to 1700 that included a separate section of "Observable Seasons," listing the dates of snowstorms and a few other weather events.

The two great diaries depicting the details of Puritan social and intellectual life in Boston, by Judge Samuel Sewall (1674–77 and 1685–1729) and Cotton Mather (1681–1727), mention an occasional weather event, but they are by no means daily weather diaries. Some individuals did jot down daily weather notes on the pages of interleaved almanacs, but these brief entries are fragmentary and only a few such volumes have been preserved. Nothing of lasting value was composed in the seventeenth century that described the characteristics of the New England climate or assembled a body of useful weather indications or lore.

The first stirrings in New England toward a scientific outlook on the world of nature came in the early years of the eighteenth century. Thomas Robie (Harvard 1708) became a tutor and instructor in mathematics at his alma mater in 1714. In that year, at the urging of the secretary of the Royal Society of London, he commenced a series of weather observations on a daily basis, although Harvard at that time did not possess a barometer or thermometer. Indeed, neither instrument was obtainable in New England. Robie's series appears to have been continued through 1722; a summary of his observations was dispatched to the Royal Society, and brief excerpts were published in *The Philosophical Transactions of the Royal Society* in an effort to compare the weather in Old and New England on identical days.

Robie has been described by C. K. Shipton in *Sibley's Harvard Graduates* as "probably the first New Englander to whom science was a systematic body of knowledge and not just something curious." His scientific train of thought and innovative activities embroiled him with the traditionalists in the smallpox inoculation controversy that raged in Boston in the early 1720s. Soon afterward he retired from the academic battleground to the more peaceful practice of medicine in the village of Salem and was honored in 1725 with election to membership in the Royal Society, a fitting tribute to the man who was the embodiment of the new trend of scientific thinking in New England and the founder of a meteorological tradition at Harvard.

The reputation of Cotton Mather has been greatly refurbished in late years as a result of studies into the beginnings of scientific activity in colonial America. Mather's magnum opus in this field, *The Christian Philosopher* (1721), was an attempt to reconcile the principles of the new scientific outlook with the tenets of revealed religion. Some meteorological material appeared in this lengthy work, but Mather's principal contribution to the field lay in a series of letters on observations of natural science, his "Curiosa Americana," which he periodically dispatched to the Royal Society from 1712 to 1724. Many of these were published in digest form in the *Transactions;* his accounts of the Dark Day of 1716, the Great Snow of 1717, and the Tide and Flood of 1723 were particularly graphic and informative.

Mather was credited by a contemporary for making the first meteorological observations in New England with scientific instruments. Dr. William Douglass, who had emigrated from Bristol with the avowed purpose of practicing medicine and studying the meteorology of New England, stated in 1725 that there was neither barometer nor thermometer in Boston or at Harvard College. Yet in the next year Cotton Mather came into the possession of both types of instruments, most likely from England. Mather induced a "wealthy baker" and "ingenious tradesman," a Mr. Feveryear (Anglicized from Febrier), to undertake

110

a series of observations for him, and although the original manuscript record has been lost, we know that an abstract was transmitted to the Royal Society in 1727. Mather envisioned a series of weather-observation posts throughout the colony, but his death in 1728 put an end to the project.

Early science in New England took a major step forward in 1727 with the arrival of scientific apparatus at Harvard College. Through the generosity of a London merchant benefactor, Harvard was equipped with scientific laboratory equipment comparable to that possessed by leading European universities. Included in the shipment were a barometer and a thermometer. The custodian of the new laboratory was Isaac Greenwood, who became the first Hollis Professor of Mathematics and Experimental Philosophy. Greenwood promised to send the Royal Society "an Annual Account of ye State of ye Weather in these parts of ye World, especially at Cambridge." If he ever carried out the plan, the results have disappeared. Greenwood did compose an original format for taking weather observations on shipboard, from which he anticipated assembling a view of the climate of the world through the systematic collection and analysis of instrumental records from many diverse points. Greenwood's main contribution to American meteorology was his continuation of Robie's practice of training students to take a scientific view of the natural world and to include meteorological observations in their everyday activities. Among Harvard graduates who followed the tradition was Paul Dudley, who became chief justice of the colony. His weather observations were given notice in the *Transactions* in 1731.

Isaac Greenwood

The two dominant figures in colonial meteorology were of Boston origin but of quite different backgrounds and pursuits. Benjamin Franklin represented the unschooled original thinker and inventive genius so characteristic of many early Americans. His treatises on the nature of lightning and the behavior of coastal storms along the Atlantic seaboard were the only lasting contributions made by a colonial to theoretical meteorology. Franklin's contemporary, Prof. John Winthrop, a sixth-generation descendant of the founder and first governor of the Massachusetts Bay Colony, represented the university-trained mind who was able to impart his knowledge to a full generation of Harvard students. Winthrop's activities in the classroom and in the observatory comprised the major contribution by a colonial to practical meteorology. In January, 1739, he was installed as the second Hollis Professor of Mathematics and Natural Philosophy, succeeding his tutor, Isaac Greenwood, who was dismissed by the Harvard Overseers because of his inability to keep the cork in his bottle of wine. Winthrop was soon recognized as America's leading academic scientist and was honored by election to English and Scottish scholarly institutions. His main interests and original contributions to science were in the field of astronomy, but he did devote considerable time to meteorology. On December 11, 1742, he commenced a "Meteorologic Diary," which he continued for thirty-seven years until April 29, 1779, five days before his death. During this period he missed only about 300 days, either because of illness or absence from his post at Cambridge. He usually made his observations twice a day and included temperature, barometer, wind direction, and state of the sky. After the drought of 1749, he added rain gauge readings from a device of his own making. As a result of Winthrop's faithful attention to his instruments, we are now able to document the weather conditions attending important historical events before and during the War of Independence in New England.

Edward A. Holyoke

One of Winthrop's students, who was destined to follow a distinguished career in practical science, was Edward A. Holyoke, son of a Harvard president, who practiced medicine at Salem from June, 1749, to March, 1829—a period of almost eighty years. On his hundredth birthday in 1828, he arose, shaved, dressed himself, read his thermometer and barometer, and walked downtown to the Essex House where

Samuel Williams

his fellow townsmen gave a centennial banquet in his honor.

Since Professor Winthrop lived in the president's house, young Holyoke must have been introduced to the professor's weather watching at an early age. On January 1, 1754, Holyoke commenced his own "Meteorological Journal" at Salem with daily entries of temperature, wind, and state of the weather. He continued this series through 1785. Despite the disruptions of life caused by the war (he took a passive Loyalist stance, thinking independence inevitable but premature at that time), he continued his observations daily, and his was the only instrumental meteorological record in New England that is complete for the entire war period.

In 1786 Holyoke expanded his observations to four a day and included barometer readings. He employed a system of fifty-eight symbols to indicate the condition of the weather, in much the same manner that meteorologists now employ a set of international symbols. Fortunately, his manuscript record was edited and published in 1833 in book form, so information on weather conditions for this important span of New England history is available to scholars.

The Harvard tradition in meteorology was continued in the 1780s by Rev. Samuel Williams of Bradford, a former student of Winthrop who succeeded to his mentor's chair in 1780. Williams had carried on a series of meteorological observations at his home since 1772, and he soon instituted a new series at Harvard. In 1784 he received a set of meteorological instruments of the latest design from the Meteorological Society of the Palatinate at Mannheim, Germany, which was attempting to foster a system of weather observations in a number of countries. Some of the results were published annually in the *Ephemerides Societatis Meteorologicae Palatinae*.

At Harvard Williams seems to have aroused the enmity of his colleagues, partly for his propensity for wearing a scarlet coat (his confreres dressed in black), and partly for his indulgence in high living—his appetite for gourmet foods and fine Madeira. These activities also brought him into dire financial straits and he was accused of shenanigans in the handling of money from a colleague's estate. Williams departed Cambridge one step ahead of the law and settled in the independent Republic of Vermont, where many another man in difficulties sought sanctuary. Williams resumed his meteorological activities at Rutland the next year, so he must have taken his thermometer and barometer along in his hasty departure. In 1795 he composed a chapter on the climate of Vermont for his two-volume history of the Green Mountain region. This was the best climatological study of a particular state produced in eighteenth-century America.

The culmination of scientific activity in colonial New England came with the founding of the American Academy of Arts and Sciences at Boston in 1780. Although several New Englanders had published articles in the *Transactions of the American Philosophical Society* at Philadelphia in the 1770s, the suspected French connection of that institute raised political and cultural eyebrows in Boston circles, where Francophobia ran strong. John Adams was instrumental in securing a charter for the new institution from the General Court and in inviting prominent intellectual and political figures to participate in its activities. The general purpose of the academy was "to promote and encourage the knowledge of antiquities of America and the natural history of the country," and one of its particular concerns was "to promote and encourage meteorological observations."

The replacement of the Winthrop series of observations fell to Rev. Edward Wigglesworth ("Wiggie" to his students), who was then Professor of Divinity at Harvard. His records eventually ran through 1795, though only those from 1781 to 1783 were published in full in the first volume of the academy's *Memoirs* in 1785. Later Harvard series by President Webber (1790–1806) and by Prof. John Farrar (1807–1817) were published in abstract form. The academy's main

Diaries

A number of other famous New England diarists make frequent mention of the weather in their journals. Among the most useful in reconstructing the weather events of the seventeenth and eighteenth centuries are the following, arranged chronologically with the principal location and the years covered indicated.

John Winthrop, Boston, 1630–1649. *Winthrop's Journal.*

John Hull, Boston, 1654–1677. *Public Journal.*

Samuel Sewall, Boston, 1674–1729. *Diary of Samuel Sewall.*

John Pike, Dover, N.H., 1682–1700. *Journal of the Rev. John Pike.*

Joshua Hempstead, New London, Conn., 1711–1757. *Diary of Joshua Hempstead of New London, Conn.*

contribution to early American meteorology was the publication in full of Dr. Holyoke's daily observations at Salem, covering the period from 1786 to 1829.

One of Thomas Robie's students carried the scientific outlook to Yale College where, in the mid 1730s, the lack of laboratory equipment was similar to the Harvard situation a decade before. When Thomas Clap became president at New Haven in 1740, he instituted what was said to be "the earliest vigorous, continuing study of science" in the colonies. He possessed a thermometer, at least, during the Hard Winter of 1740–41, since he later made mention of some of his low readings that season. Also, a barometer was listed as needing repair in 1744. But there is no indication that a regular series of meteorological observations were carried on at Yale during the Clap regime, which lasted until 1766.

Clap's teaching must have instilled an interest in meteorology in young Ezra Stiles, class of 1746, for he frequently made mention of weather conditions in his diary and commenced his "Thermometric Register" in 1763 when Benjamin Franklin stopped by his home in Newport, Rhode Island, and delivered a thermometer he had procured for Stiles in England. (Franklin, among other duties as colonial agent for several colonies in London, seems to have served as procurer of meteorological instruments for several of his fellow colonists.) Soon after commencing his thermometer record at Newport, Stiles suggested that other locations such as Charleston, Williamsburg, Philadelphia, New York, and Boston exchange their observations so that conditions in different colonies could be compared.

In addition to the daily temperature and weather entries in his diary, Stiles included copies of news accounts and extracts from his wide-ranging correspondence about weather events taking place in other colonies. His published *Literary Diary* contains many references to weather conditions, such as the lengthy documentation of the Dark Day of May, 1780, and comparisons between the severity of outstanding winters. He certainly deserves the title of historian of meteorology in colonial America.

Stiles served pulpits at various locations (Newport, Dighton, and Portsmouth) before assuming the presidency of Yale in July, 1778, when he immediately commenced his meteorological observations and continued to make several per day until his death in 1795. He also entered many news notes about weather throughout the country that would otherwise have been lost to history. He was ably assisted in this by his daughter Elizabeth, who later married Rev. Abiel Holmes of Cambridge, himself an avid weather watcher. Their son, Oliver Wendell Holmes, continued the family interest in meteorology by celebrating some of New England's outstanding weather events in verse.

The pursuit of meteorology in colonial America was an individual activity. Even at the colleges it was the initiative of a single professor that produced a meteorological record and it was the responsibility of one person to continue it. Whatever exchange of information that took place was also accomplished by individuals. The institutionalizing of meteorology on a national basis would not come until the middle of the next century.

The Revolutionary War years played havoc with the orderly progress of intellectual life in America. In meteorology a number of barometers and thermometers fell victim to the ravages of armies that used college buildings for barracks and hospitals, to the detriment of all equipment housed there. Military service took many individuals away from home for many months at a time, resulting in lengthy breaks in their records or diaries, and in some cases putting an end to their weather observing. Even the procurement of a thermometer or barometer became difficult in the years during and after the war. It would be well into the next century before the science of meteorology would have as many well-trained adherents as existed in 1775.

Ezra Stiles

Ebenezer Parkman, Westborough, Mass., 1719–1782. *The Diary of Ebenezer Parkman.*

Thomas Smith, Falmouth (Portland), Maine, 1722–1787. *Journals of the Rev. Thomas Smith.*

Samuel Lane, Stratham, N.H., 1739–1803. *A Journal of the Years 1739–1803.*

Matthew Patten, Bedford, N.H., 1754–1788. *The Diary of Matthew Patten.*

Ezra Stiles, Newport, R.I., and New Haven, Conn., 1769–1795. *The Literary Diary of Ezra Stiles.*

William Bentley, Salem, 1784–1819. *Diary of William Bentley, D.D.*

Jeremiah Alling, Hamden, Conn., 1785–1810. *A Register of the Weather.*

For a full listing of diaries and mention of those having weather content, see:

William Matthews. *American Diaries: An annotated bibliography of American diaries prior to . . . 1861.* Berkeley, University of California Press, 1945.

CHAPTER 8
Colonial Almanacs

The almanac has always held an esteemed place in the eyes of the American reading public. In the days before the War of Independence, when books were scarce and magazines almost nonexistent, the almanac was considered a household necessity. This annual supplied the home with down-to-earth information, serving as a guide to everyday living as the ever-present family Bible did for the spiritual conduct of life. Among the helpful items the almanac provided were: a calendar for keeping track of the passage of days, weeks, and months; an ephemeris of the moon's phases, the sun's rising and setting, solar and lunar eclipses, and the position of the planets for astrological planning; tide tables for mariners; a forecast of the weather as an aid to farm and other outdoor activities; hints for the husbandman for better farming; time-honored remedies for the relief of aches and pains; recipes for a more wholesome and tasty diet; conversion tables for changing currency; road distances; historical chronologies; much verse—some humorous for amusement, some serious for inspiration; and many proverbs and aphorisms to serve as guides for better living. In short, the almanac was a treasure of educational, entertaining, and uplifting information packed into a small, inexpensive pamphlet.

First English Almanacs

A form of almanac appears to be as old as the study of astronomy. Not until the twelfth century, however, was a calendar tabulation resembling the present form established, and the word *almanack* first appeared in English from the pen of Roger Bacon in 1267. Manuscript almanacs in Latin for certain years of the twelfth century have been preserved, but none written in the English language are known until about 1431.

The first printed almanacs containing calendrical and astronomical information were published in Europe during the last years of the fifteenth century. Printed on a single sheet in the form of a broadside, they were easily affixed to a wall for quick reference. Separate publications were also issued under the title "Prognostications." The content of these had been condemned by ecclesiastical authorities about the time of the Reformation and were specifically banned in England by an act against "sorcery without benefit of clergy." But the public popularity of the prognostications caused a repeal of the act in the brief reign of Edward VI (1547–53).

By 1533 both sheet almanacs and sheet prognostications were being printed in English and the two types of publications were soon combined into one to make a double-sheet format. Weather forecasts first appeared in the prognostications about 1550 when Anthony Askham featured a weather outlook in his series of almanacs.

The weather predictions rapidly caught on with almanac readers, as the publication of *Ephemerides Meteorographicae* in 1571 demonstrated, but the growing use of forecasts in almanacs did not go un-

Witches, it was once believed, had the power to influence weather. This early print shows a couple conjuring up a shower of rain.

challenged. A critic of the almanac publishers denounced them in a pamphlet, *Four great Lyers,* probably published in 1585. Here the author, "W.P.," compared the weather forecasts of four of England's leading almanac compilers and showed how greatly they differed among themselves as to what the weather for a selected day was expected to be.

The nonconformist sects in England opposed these prognostications—a prejudice that was transferred to Puritan New England, but weather forecasts continued to be popular among a majority of Englishmen. In 1598 there appeared a publication entitled *Perpetual and natural prognostications of the change of the weather,* prepared by "J.F.," and weather lore was put in its classic form with the appearance in 1670 of *The Shepherd of Banbury's Rules.* Much material was lifted from this English publication by American almanac makers, and editions have even appeared in the present century.

Seventeenth-Century American Almanacs

In 1638 the first printing press in Britain's North American colonies arrived in Massachusetts Bay Colony. It had been the property of Rev. Joseph Glover, who died on the voyage out from England. When the former Mrs. Glover married Rev. Henry Dunster, the first president of Harvard College, the press was moved into the presidential house at Cambridge to become the progenitor of the renowned Harvard University Press. It was known in its first years as the Stephen Daye Press, after the name of its journeyman operator.

According to Gov. John Winthrop's *Journal,* the first publication to come off the press was the *Freeman's Oath* in 1638; one copy has survived and is now the prize Americana exhibit in the John Carter Brown Library at Providence, Rhode Island. Also on the authority of Winthrop, the second work from the press was an *Almanack Calculated for New England, by Mr. Pierce, Mariner,* issued in 1639. No copy is extant. Bibliographers list American almanacs in each succeeding year to the present, even though no copies survive for many of the early years.

The earliest existing copy of a New England almanac is one prepared by Samuel Danforth of Roxbury, Massachusetts, a Harvard tutor. An imperfect copy with a torn cover bearing the title (it is believed) *An Almanack for 1646* is now in the collections of the Henry E. Huntington Library. The Danforth series of almanacs continued through 1649 and in general appearance and format they were not unlike many of those produced for the next 150 years. Twelve of the sixteen pages were devoted to calendar and astronomical data; a page or two usually announced the solar and lunar eclipses expected during the year; and the remaining space was often filled with miscellany such as election dates and court calendars. What little verse appeared in the early almanacs of the seventeenth century carried a distinct Puritan tone.

Almanacs appeared each year from the Cambridge press with astronomical data compiled by various individuals. Of the forty-four separate almanacs issued before 1687, which were located by Charles L. Nichols in a 1912 survey, forty-one were prepared by twenty-six different graduates of Harvard College, ten of whom were serving as tutors in that institution at the time of publication.

Not until 1675 did the General Court grant permission for a second printing press in Massachusetts. This was originally owned in part by Cotton Mather and operated by John Foster, a graduate of Harvard in 1667. The press produced a series of almanacs from 1676 to 1681, and Foster is thought to have compiled the astronomical data as well as printing and publishing them.

Some of Foster's early almanacs differed in format from their earlier American counterparts by the addition of a blank page facing each monthly calendar page. These extra pages contained a column

The Man of Signs, from the Weatherwise almanacs. It was believed that the twelve parts of the human body were controlled by twelve corresponding signs of the heavens.

115

for the days of the month with times of sunset and sunrise, then a wide blank space for personal entries or for brief notes of the daily weather. A copy of the 1676 edition, now in the Watkinson Library of Trinity College, Hartford, contains almost daily weather entries in the pen of the unknown owner of the almanac.

The availability of this convenient recording form stimulated many New Englanders to take up weather watching as a hobby, and because of this we are better informed about New England weather events in the days before professional and academic weather observers came on the scene. But alas, the cost of the added pages was too high, and later Foster almanacs reverted to the standard sixteen-page format. This caused several inveterate weather observers to write their weather notes over the text on the appropriate date, often making both print and handwriting undecipherable; some found a solution by interleaving blank pages and stitching them into the binding.

Foster early recognized the public's interest in the weather. His first issue for 1675 carried an article dealing with "Prognosticks of unhealthy seasons" containing a series of paragraphs on "Signs of Rain . . . Wind . . . Storm . . . Hot Weather . . . Cold Weather . . . and Fair Weather." No other special meteorological information appeared until the 1680 issue, which included an article explaining how the position of the planets affects the weather: "The Nature and Operations of the seven planets with the Newes and characters given them by Astronomers." The most educational item in the entire series was an account of the Copernican system, and the most interesting report was an account of the comet, or "blazing star," that was visible in the Boston heavens from November 18, 1680, until February 10, 1681.

The next almanac series of scientific significance was begun in 1687 by John Tulley, a mariner from Saybrook, Connecticut, who deserves to be recognized as America's first weather forecaster. It was Tulley who first introduced the now-venerated practice of inserting forecast words and phrases among the calendrical and astronomical data of the almanacs. Charles Evans, an eminent American bibliophile, declared that Tulley "became noted—almost notorious for his skill in weather prediction."

Tulley's words of weather wisdom, however, did not meet with universal approval. One Christian Lodowick was incensed by Tulley's alleged usurpation of the role of the Almighty in deciding what the weather was to be and rushed into print with *The New-England Almanack for the year of our Lord Christ MDCXCV, and of the World 5644,* which contained the following blast against "Astrological Predictions":

> It has been matter of lamitation to diverse Pious minds, to see such dark Stuff Offered to the Publick, in this Land of Light, as has been done by Mr. (?) Tully in his Almanacks, the direct tendency whereof is, to withdraw Persons from a holy Reliance on God's will and Providence, and to precipitate the minds of such as are lovers of specious Novel ties, into a sinful of that Soul-bewitching Vanity of star Prophecy, commonly called Astrology, the foundation of which are mier Chimeras.

Lodowick also had a low regard for the science of meteorology:

> As for Meteorology, it is merely conjectural: How often is it Stormy in our part of N E while in another at the same time, they enjoy a Calm. Many times it rains upon one Town, and not upon another a few miles off. You may yourselves observe such weather conjectures to be fallible, by those influences of them, (for that day) I have given you in the Preceding Pages, according to the common rules of Meteorology. Perhaps the most Probable way of Predicting the Weather would be that of the famous Old Lord HOWARD: His method was to take such Almanacks as Tullies: and where they wrote, Foul, he wrote, Fair; where they wrote Good, he wrote Bad, and his contradictions, he found frequently truer than their Predictions.

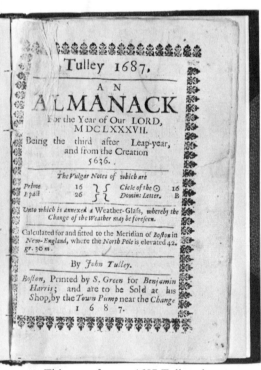

Title page from a 1687 Tulley almanac

The general public apparently did not sustain Lodowick's view, as his almanac made only one appearance, while Tulley's continued annually until the latter's death. Even so, Tulley seems to have been somewhat chastened by the criticism of Lodowick and others, and he began his 1696 edition by stating:

> As for the Weather in the Preceding Pages, I have endeavored to insert it according to the common Rules of *Meteorology* which I have often found to fail, as to hit right; for only the Wise and All-knowing God that Creator of the Heavens and the Earth, and the Sun and Moon and Stars, may and many times doth so order it, that all Signs shall fail, as well upon other accounts, as this about the Weather, and therefore as I have said heretofore, I expect Charitable censure concerning it.

In addition to weather forecasts, Tulley occasionally introduced additional weather material of an educational nature. In the first issue for 1687 there was an article on the back page entitled "Prognostica Georgica: Or the Country-mans Weather-Glass." This commenced with "Prognosticks of Tempests,"—a paragraph on winds, rains, and fair weather, all lifted from a translation of Virgil's famous poem on Roman agricultural ways.

Other meteorological articles by Tulley appeared in the following years:

1690 "Of the Rain-Bow" and "Of Thunder and Lightning"
1691 "PROGNOSTICKES or Passages of the Weather by the Sun, Moon, & Stars"
1692 "Astronomical Observations of the Weather & Winds from the Planets & their Aspects"
1693 "A Brief discourse of the Natural causes of Watry Meteors, as Snow, Hail, Rain, &c."
1696 "Concerning Astrology & Meteorology"
1700 "Natural Prognosticks for the judgment of the Weather"

Quite apart from his other accomplishments, Tulley's descriptive weather terms are of interest. We quote from the first and last editions:

> *1687* Wind . . . snow and dark weather and cold . . . blustering weather . . . moist . . . moon in hot and dry sign . . . thunder about this time, with rain and wind clearing the air . . . denotes thunder and tempests about this time . . . moon in wet sign . . . moon in dry sign . . . dark windy . . . Swithin . . . Dog Days . . . cool morning & frost . . . cloudy, cold . . . cold weather expected . . . winterlike weather . . . often inclining to snow, or weather cold and cloudy.

> *1702* Cold enough . . . Snow upon Snow Norwesters Keen Twil freeze by the Fire side Pity the poor . . . Too many stay at home [Sunday] . . . fair in some places Cold in all . . . over Shoes and Boots . . . little business to be done for the Weather . . . Some large Rivers frozen over . . . Hard Weather . . . Cloudy if not Stormy . . . Pritty fair . . . Winter not done yet . . . much time lost . . . too thin an appearance [Sunday] . . . Raw Easterly winds . . . Windy! Windy! Sometimes a Southerly turn . . . too soon yet to leave off winter clothes . . . weary Traveling . . . many Colds got by Gardening too soon . . . dripping weather at times . . . weather (and People) very changeable . . . Perhaps Fair, if it Rain, let it Rain . . . Much may be Done . . . Mixed weather . . . Don't Ride too hard . . . Weather various . . . Faint Weather . . . Thunders but not everywhere . . . Very Faint traveling . . . sometimes Fair, sometimes Foul . . . now and then thunder . . . He will be well if the English Harvest be found all without a blast . . . Cold, it will be well if a frost keep off . . . Good Weather if people can but be content . . . more Steady Weather, but yet never Settled . . . Time to think of Winter . . . Some Snow before the Month out [Oct. 23] . . . Are your Winter Stores all laid in? [Oct. 28] . . . Norwesters will be blustering about this time . . . Bad Beating on the Coast . . . Snow, and Rain, and Hail . . . Weather often changing . . . Times so uncertain, no body can foresee [Dec. 26].

Samuel Clough, describing himself on the title page as "A Lover of Mathematics," produced a series of *New England Almanacks* for the years 1700 to 1708. Nothing of unusual meteorological interest appeared in these except for his introductory complaint about the necessity of including weather forecasts in his volumes. He wrote:

> Reader, as to the Weather I desire a very favourable construction; it is against my mind to put any such thing in, but considering the People who have been used to it in the Almanacks of late, I have set it down to gratify those who desire it. I would not have any so ruled by it as to expect just such weather always on the day it is set, tho' it is possible it may so happen; for the very rules that the foretelling of the weather is grounded upon are not to be trusted to or depended upon; for certain it is that the times & seasons are in the Hands of God alone, and He changes them as He Pleaseth. Indeed, this we may know certainly;
>
> > *That if the air be fair and clear*
> > *The ways will then more clean appear*
> > *But if it chance to Snow or Rain*
> > *Then they will dirty be again.*

Faithful to his readers' wishes, Clough continued to include weather forecasts in his series of nine almanacs, but his heart was not in it and his words were rather dull and uninspiring.

Two series of distinctive almanacs were commenced in the year 1709 by Harvard associates, both of whom were to become well versed in weather observing and would go on to distinguished academic careers. While serving as a tutor in preparation for his later presidency of the college, Rev. Edward Holyoke produced an *Ephemeris of the Coelestial Motions for 1709;* and Thomas Robie, who was engaged in making weather observations at the college, as already noted, also brought out an almanac with an identical title and continued his annual series through 1720.

Edward Holyoke's almanac served to introduce New Englanders to what scientific men abroad were thinking and reading. The issue for 1713 carried the following note: "Here I thought it not improper to insert An Account of the Trade Winds, from the learned Capt. Halley." This occupied a full page in the back of his almanac.

Another note in a humorous vein appeared in the 1715 issue, suggesting a regal influence on the weather in opposition to the prevailing conception of divine control:

> N[ew] King GEORGE was Proclaimed at Boston in New-England upon Wednesday, September, 22. 1714 with great Joy; which was very much increased and our Illuminations inlightened, by the Plentiful, Refreshing Rain with which God was Pleased to Bless the Night following, after a long, distressing Drought.
> > *Imbrex nodum deorant regalia lucis:*
> > > *Rex populum, tanquam gramma tensa, viget!*
> > *Night's Showers crown the Pomp of Night & Day:*
> > > *King George, as Rain on Mown grass, Come away!*

Ames Almanacs

The most popular series of almanacs in the years preceding the War of Independence was edited by the two Nathaniel Ameses, father and son, over a fifty-year period from 1726 to 1775. It was through the Ameses' able editing of a miscellany of material that the almanac became a household reference in New England. Each of the annual issues was entitled *An Astronomical Diary, or an Almanack for 1726 . . . 1775.* In the original issue Ames elder signed himself as "Student in Physic and Astronomy," though this designation was soon dropped as his repu-

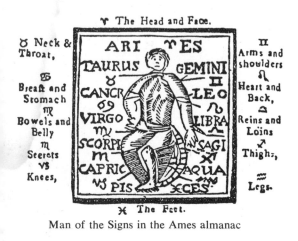

Man of the Signs in the Ames almanac

tation grew. The senior Ames was born at Bridgewater, Massachusetts, in 1708, but during the latter half of his life was associated with the town of Dedham. He was a physician by trade and after 1750 became a tavern keeper at the appropriately named Sign of the Sun, which became a famous way station noted for conversation, light and serious, and for conviviality. When he died in 1764, his son, Nathaniel Jr., a Harvard graduate, continued the series until the exigencies of the war caused a cessation of the publication after the issue for 1775 had been printed. By that time the Ames almanacs were selling at an estimated rate of 50,000 a year; before and after this date, spurious editions appeared with the Ames name attached; and the last pirated edition seems to have been for 1795.

As with most other contemporary almanacs, the main scientific emphasis of the Ames editions was on astronomy, with meteorology playing a rather minor role except for the forecast words. All issues did contain a "Judgment of the Weather," as the forecasts were called on the title page. The weather words appearing in the 1726 edition were expressive: "More snow than lillies . . . white clouds & fair weather . . . warm unwholesome air . . . white spreading clouds . . . hot thunder . . . turbulent air . . . cloudy & stormy with R. and Snow & Strange Weather . . . various kinds of weather." In the following year the second issue contained some unusual variations: "The year begins with various weather . . . unsettled Air with some W[eather] . . . Cloudy like R[ain] & Dirty W[eather] . . . Dropping moist wea . . . uncertain weather . . . piddling cloudy . . . watery clouds . . . hot with thun-clouds . . . cloudy cold or falling weather . . . suspicious weather."

Here and there throughout the fifty annual editions was scattered much lighthearted verse. On occasion some had a meteorological connotation:

1745   *Now Virgins will own*
       'Tis hard lying alone,
          Such Weather as this.
1747   *Many Things are frozen*
       All things are cold, the young ladies excepted.
1770   *So cold that all Business, even Cuckold making, ceases nowadays, but the Tongue of Slander is always limber.*
1771   *Enjoy the good Weather when you can catch it for it is as variable as Mrs. ——— Temper this Month.*
1772   *Old stile says 'tis Winter yet, which we may now believe, seeing the planets like the great ones here below, can't agree whether we shall continue under the grievance of Winter or enjoy the season's birthright, blooming spring.*
1774   *Pleasant giving Weather, but I esteem taking Weather most.*
       Showery and unsettled Weather without as Mrs. Coquetilla within.
       Puffing, belching fxxxxg Weather.
1775   *Fine weather for New England about the barracks, but stormy, tempestuous, and boisterous when those Irish hero's are much in it, or it in them.*
       Fine weather for fighting, and for lawyers who for one year's famine will have seven of plenty.
       Muggy air among tipplers, and thick smoky air among politicians, and it may end in storm.
       South winds then some quickening showers somewhere at least of Xantippe's kind, then serene air sometime except among those that charg'd too deep for the King's health, and too many sentimental toasts.

The Ames almanacs contained no articles on the principles of weather prognostication as earlier publications had included, and there were only two items commenting on the type of forecasts appearing in contemporary almanacs. In 1759 Ames wrote:

Kind Reader. I here present you with my Thirty-fourth ALMANACK published. Although a *Perhaps,* with Justice, might always be added to what I say of the Weather; yet I have collected the best Rules that

Title page from an Ames almanac of 1726

IV. APRIL hath 30 Days. 1775.

And when he falls amid the field of fame,
He leaves behind, a great and lasting name,
His Sire, his country still with joy surround,
His corse, and read their glory in his wound.
Both young and old shall sing his dirge of woe,
And his long fun'ral all the town pursue :
His tomb shall be rever'd ; his children thine
Through ev'ry age, a long extended line.

First Quart. 7 Day, 7 After. | Last Quarter 22 Day 3 After.
Full Moon 15 Day, 5 After. | New Moon 29 Day 3 Aftern.

Pages from an Ames almanac of 1775

V. MAY hath 31 Days. 1775.

Who never from the field of battle flies,
But for his children and his country dies,
Ne'er shall his glory fade, or cease his fame
Tho' laid in dust, immortal is his name.
But if the fable hand of death he shun,
Returning victor, with his glory won.

First Quart. 7 Day, 2 aftern. | Last Quart. 21 Day, 9 Aftern.
Full Moon, 15 Day, 4 Morn | New Moon, 29 Day 4 Morn.

[AMES, 1775.] B

Pages from an Ames almanac of 1775

Experience has taught me in that Affair, from the Aspects and Configurations of the Planets: I am therefore constantly obliged to trace the *rambling Moon,* and *wandering Planets,* in all their intricate Paths, which costs me much Labour and hard study.

After two seasons of distressing droughts, Ames in 1763 expressed his philosophy of prognosticating:

READER.

What I have said concerning the Continuance of the Drought and Scarcity this Year, in the Title Page Verse, is a Conclusion drawn from Premises that are not universally certain, therefore the Conclusion, viz. that this Year 1763 will be a dry and scarce Year is not certain.—He who has fore-ordained whatsoever comes to pass, knows, and he only knows with absolute Certainty, what will come to pass: The Book of Fate is hid from all created Beings:—Creatures know future Events only by Way of Argumentation and Deduction: and indeed in some Instances there is such a Connection between the Premises and Conclusion that the Event is known with great Certainty; but in general we know nothing of the Connection of Things, we cannot see the Links of that great Chain which binds with certainty all the Events of the wide extended Universe: Indeed the Devil does not know so much of future Events as many expect an Almanack Maker should foretell, although it must be owned that they are willing to allow him the Help of the Devil for his Information.

The last of the Ames almanacs was issued for 1775—a year that saw at least eighteen separate almanacs published in New England alone and a total of at least fifty-three in the continental British North American colonies. They were by all odds the best sellers of the day.

Weatherwise Almanacs

The name of Abraham Weatherwise, occasionally employed by early British almanac makers, probably appeared for the first time in America in 1739 in a publication of Christopher Sower, a German writer from Philadelphia. Later almanacs edited by "Abraham Weatherwise, Gent." were published in Philadelphia in 1759 and shortly thereafter in other American cities.

Up to the end of the century, at least 102 almanacs appeared with a form of the pseudonym Weatherwise attached to its title page. Abraham, or merely A., was the most popular first name. When Robert B. Thomas founded his *Farmer's Almanack* at Boston in 1793, Abe Weatherwise showed up as a member of the staff, and in this position he has put in an annual appearance in the publication, which is now known as *The Old Farmer's Almanack* and is, in 1976, in its 184th year.

A parody of the nonsense implicit in the Weatherwise method of weather forecasting was included in *The Massachusetts Calendar or Almanac for the year of our Lord 1772,* published by the respected Isaiah Thomas at his press—then located in Boston. Under the heading "Jonathan Weatherwise's Prognostics" appeared the article "Signs of an Approaching Cold Winter." The leading sentences of each paragraph give the gist of what followed:

That if the last three days of October are cold, the next three months will be too.

If proportion to the blackness of it [a goosebone], so will the severity of the season be.

Bears leaving the woods and coming down upon us.

Unless they [quails and partridges] appear in very large flocks, it will be of no more consequence than if there were none at all.

If any gray squirrels put their tail in their mouths when tumbling out of a tree, it is a sign of a hard winter.

WONDERFUL DARK DAY, MAY 19, 1780.

During almost four centuries of settlement by Europeans in New England, weather conditions have generally been conducive to the physical and economic well-being of the inhabitants. On occasion, however, the elements have combined to produce mighty storms that have devastated portions of the land and taken a toll of human lives. The following list of outstanding weather events demonstrates the extremities to which the New England atmosphere has been stirred in the past. It may serve also as a warning of what could happen again in the future.

CHAPTER 9
New England's Outstanding Weather Events

THE COLONIAL PERIOD

Great Colonial Hurricane of August, 1635

"No storm more dismal"; occurred on August 25–26; probable track from Narragansett Bay northeast between Plymouth and Boston; vividly described by Governors Bradford and Winthrop; "thousands of trees torn up by the roots"; 14-foot storm tide "drowned 8 Indians flying from their wigwams"; shipwrecks and loss of life.

Second Great Colonial Hurricane of September, 1675

"Dreadful storm of wind and rain at east"; path again across southeast; slightly inferior to 1635 in severity; extensive damage at New London, Stonington, and Boston; occurred on September 7–8; "much loss of corn and hay—multitude of trees blown down."

Hurricane and Flood of August, 1683

Severe tropical storm crossed the southeast coast after striking Virginia; extensive damage reported at New London and Narragansett Bay; "great storme that blasted all the trees"; caused second great flood of summer on Connecticut River, reached 26-foot stage at Wethersfield.

Hard Winter of 1697–98, Severest of Seventeenth Century

"The terriblest winter for continuance of frost and snow, and extremity of cold, that ever was known"; 31 snowstorms from November 20 to April 9; Charlestown, Mass., ferry frozen for six weeks; 42-inch snow depth reported at Cambridge; reputation for severity survived for many years.

Great Snow of 1717

New England's most famous legendary snowstorm; consisted of four storms, two major and two minor, from February 27 to March 7; snow depth upwards of three feet in Boston area, five feet in New Hampshire and Maine; many animals perished, houses collapsed, travel hampered; sheep buried under drifts for 28 days dug out alive; Cotton Mather wrote historic account for Royal Society of London.

Great Tide at Boston in 1723

"Tide and storm of uncommon circumstances" on March 7 described by Mather and others; strong northeaster arrived at time of spring tide; drove water 20 inches higher than known before, sweeping wharves, inundating many streets, flooding cellars; also described by young Benjamin Franklin in humorous article in his brother's *New England Courant*.

Hard Winter of 1740–41

Considered more severe by old-timers than 1697–98, with more snow and longer freeze-up; three severe winter periods in November, early January, and February-March; Boston Harbor frozen 30 days, Charlestown ferry 10 weeks; snow 36 inches deep in central Connecticut; Connecticut River at Deerfield, Mass., frozen over and snow near Ashburnham 30 inches deep on April 10.

Winter of the Deep Snows in 1747–48

Thirty snowstorms from December 25 to April piled up unprecedented snow cover; 5.5 feet deep at Portland, Maine, 4 to 5 feet deep at Cambridge, Mass.; travel exceedingly difficult; snow melted into unfrozen ground with no serious flooding.

Colonial Droughts in 1749 and 1761–62

Spring drought in 1749, from April to early July, caused crop losses, field fires, and human distress; relief came on July 6, good crops were harvested; in 1761 summer drought damaged crops; no full relief until mid August; drought returned in 1762; fields and villages burned, public fasts held; final relief on August 18; crops light, hay cost four times normal price.

Hard Winter of 1780, Severest of Eighteenth Century

Series of heavy December snowstorms followed by thawless January, the coldest month in history; all highways blocked for many weeks except Great Road from Boston to Hartford; all harbors frozen for four to six weeks; snow in southern Connecticut 42 inches on level ground; military forces immobilized, ships frozen in, troops snowbound; citizens suffered great hardship.

Famous Dark Day on May 19, 1780

Darkness at noon descended on much of New England as smoke from western forest fires filtered sun's rays; maximum darkness moved southeastward during day from Vermont to Cape Cod; landscape and objects took on yellowish-green hue; great consternation among populace, some believed doomsday at hand.

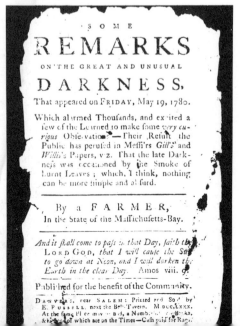

SOME

REMARKS

ON THE GREAT AND UNUSUAL

DARKNESS,

That appeared on FRIDAY, May 19, 1780.

Which alarmed Thousands, and excited a few of the Learned to make some very curious Observations—Their Result the Public has perused in Meffi'rs Gill's and Willis's Papers, viz. That the late Darkness was occasioned by the Smoke of burnt Leaves; which, I think, nothing can be more simple and abfurd.

By a FARMER,
In the State of the Maffachufetts-Bay.

And it shall come to pass in that Day, faith the LORD GOD, that I will cause the Sun to go down at Noon, and I will darken the Earth in the clear Day. Amos viii. 9.

Published for the benefit of the Community.

DANVERS, near SALEM: Printed and Sold by E. RUSSELL, next the Bell-Tavern. M DCC LXXX. At the fame Place may be had, a Number of Books, &c. for many of which are on the Times—Cash paid for Rags.

Triple Big Snows in Early December, 1786

Greatest snowfall since 1717; Hamden, Conn., near New Haven, had 20 inches on December 4–5, 9 inches on December 7–8, and 8 inches with sleet on December 9–10, total 37 inches; Kingston, Mass., near Plymouth, had 48 inches on ground, Boston nearly four feet; great tide accompanied third storm, destroying wharves and shipping; record early cold wave followed, −12° at Hartford on the twelfth.

NINETEENTH CENTURY

Cold Friday, January 19, 1810

After a warm day, cold northwest blast struck, lowering temperature overnight from 42° to −13° at Portsmouth, N.H.; extreme wind chill over all New England; family tragedy at Sanbornton, N.H., when gale collapsed farmhouse causing three small children to perish in cold; many frostbitten.

Great September Gale of 1815

Extreme hurricane on September 23, 1815, made landfall near Saybrook, Conn., bisected New England northward; great destruction along coast from New London east; downtown Providence flooded; massive forest blowdowns in eastern Massachusetts, New Hampshire, and Maine; several casualties, great property and crop losses; Oliver Wendell Holmes later wrote descriptive poem.

For the CENTINEL.

Thermometrical and other Observations, made at Waltham, ten miles west of Boston, in the months of July, 1815 and 1816.

Day of mon.	Th at sunrise		at 2 or 3 P.M.		at 9 P.M.		mean heat		exc's of 1815	Remarks on weather, 1816.	Winds.
	1815	1816	1815	1816	1815	1816	1815	1816			
1	66	46	91½	73½	77	57	79	58	21	Clear.	E.
2	66	48	91½	86½	73	66	76	66	10	Clear.	SW.
3	58	51	90	80	64	66	70	65	5	Fair. Clear. Windy.	SW.
4	53	55	78	75½	59	60	63	63	0	Clear.	SW.
5	51	58	87½	82	66	67	68	69	.	Clear.	SW.
6	57	64	85	73	63	58	68	65	3	Fair. Very windy.	SW. to NW.
7	53	59	87½	73	72	60	70	61	9	Clear. Windy.	W. NW.
8	63	44½	73	72	73	55	70	57	13	Clear. Frost in places.	N. NW.
9	74	44	90	68½	76	53	79	55	24	Clear. Windy. Frost do	N. NW.
10	67	47	91½	85½	78	68	73	64	14	Clear.	SW.
11	72	49	91	86	75½	69	79	65	14	Fair. Hazy.	SW.
12	64	59	90½	77½	75½	57	76	61	15	Foggy. Fair.	SW. E.
13	71	55	96	74	79	56	82	61	21	Cloudy. Fair P.M.	E.
14	73	55	85	79	69	60	75	64	11	Cloudy. Fair.	E. NE.
15	61	56	71	88	68	72	66	72	.	Clear.	SW.
16	65	64	79	90	70½	74	71	76	.	Slight rain. Clear P.M.	SSW.
17	68	68	86	87½	68	58	74	71	3	Cloudy. Fair. Very windy.	SW. to NW.
18	60	50	85	77	63	58	69	61	8	Clear. Windy.	W. NW.
19	55	48	90	88	68	70	71	68	3	Clear. Drought severe.	SW.
20	61	59	94½	91	78	70	77	73	4	Clear. Brisk wind. Heavy	SW.
21	70	63	94	83	77½	64	80	70	10	Clear. thunder shower.	NE.
22	69	54	94	8½	74	63½	81	66	15	Cloudy.	E.
23	76	62	95	81	74	63	81	68	13	Cloudy. Fair P.M.	SE E.
24	63	61	93	84	78½	69	78	71	7	Clear. Fair. Cloudy.	W. NW.
25	78	57	99	76	70	62½	82	65	17	Rainy morn. Clear P.M.	NW.
26	60	51½	72	80	65	61	66	64	2	Clear.	W SW.
27	62	56½	85	80	67	62½	71	66	.	Shower. Chly. Sl't rain.	NNE. E.
28	60	62	87½	67	73	59	73	62	11	Very rainy day.	NE.
29	70	57½	92	68	80	56½	80	60	20	Cloudy. Clear P.M.	NE.
30	65	47	89	74	73	56	75	59	16	Clear.	NE. E.
31	64	54	92	75	80	57½	80	63	18	Cloudy. Fair P.M.	E.

Mean heat for July 1815, 75° nearly. Do. for July 1816, 66½°.—Greatest heat, 1815, 25th day, 99°. Do. 1816, 20th day, 91°.—Least heat, 1815, 5th day, 51°. Do. 1816, 9th day, 44°.

REMARKS.—From the above comparison it will be seen, that the month of July, like the rest of the season, has been unusually cool, particularly the nights. For the convenience of such as do not keep a journal, it was judged proper to give a statement of the same month for two years. It may however be observed, that the month of July last season was as remarkable for its continued heat, as the past has been for its general coolness. They may therefore be considered as the extremes of heat and cold, (for that month) for the last 25 years. Vegetation is uncommonly backward, and much warm weather will be necessary to bring to maturity the fruits of the earth.   Waltham, Aug. 1, 1816.

*A mean of 70 degrees is considered good weather for vegetation.

Cold Summer of 1816

Snow and cold in early June, cold nights in July and August, drought all summer, killing frost in September, all combined to cause failure of crops in north; short rations in winter and spring for man and beast; stimulated "Ohio Fever" for western migration the following summer.

Twin Winds of September, 1821

The Windy Week of early September, 1821, commenced with Redfield's Hurricane; smashed ashore near Stamford, Conn., late on September 3; continued northward through Berkshire region; great structural damage and forest devastation; the Great New Hampshire Whirlwind followed on September 9, moving from the Connecticut Valley across Lake Sunapee, over Mount Kearsarge, and down into the Merrimack Valley near Boscawen; several killed, property damaged.

New England's Bitterest Daylight, December 16, 1835

Arctic outbreak on December 15–16 sent thermometers below −20° in the north; cold hit the south about dawn, Boston temperature dropped from −1° to −10° in evening of the sixteenth with NW gale blowing all day; Providence from −4° to −12°; Nantucket from +5° to −6° during daylight hours; New York City had its most destructive fire that night.

Great Rainstorm, January Thaw, Ice Breakup, and Flood in 1839

Severe storm center moved over Pennsylvania and New York on January 26–27; put New England in warm sector, temperature rising from zero to 50s; rain, snow melt, and ice jams caused all rivers to flood; extensive damage, many casualties.

RUINS OF ROMAN CATHOLIC CHURCH

Triple Storms in December, 1839

Three northeasters battered New England coast and buried interior in deep snow on December 15, 22–23, 27–28; Gloucester Harbor a disaster area on the fifteenth with 50 vessels wrecked, many lives lost; gales on December 28 very severe at Boston, Cape Cod and the islands; deep snow in interior raised cover to 36 inches; losses over $1 million; descriptive pamphlet "Awful Calamities" published in several editions.

Memorable October Gale of 1841

Severe, fast-moving hurricane brushed Cape Cod and the islands on night of October 3–4; enormous shipping losses; 19 vessels stranded on Nantucket; 57 men from Truro perished along with many others from nearby fishing ports.

Lighthouse Storm in April, 1851

Severe northeaster with whole gales lashed coast on April 15–16; spring tide rose to unprecedented height in Boston, 4 feet over Long Wharf, streets flooded up to Custom House, Boston Neck inundated, cutting city from mainland; much structural damage; new Lighthouse at Minot Ledge near Scituate, 114 feet high, toppled by tremendous waves, both keepers drowned.

Severe Winter Week in January, 1857

Northeaster dropped foot of snow under zero conditions on January 18–19, then two more cold outbreaks followed; Cold Friday II on January 23 with −20° maximums in north, as low as −55° reported on January 24; Boston area below zero all day January 23; Nantucket as low as −11°; January mean at Cambridge 15.7°; coldest month since January, 1780.

Saxby's Gale and Great Northeast Flood in October, 1869

Severe hurricane hit Down East Maine and Bay of Fundy on October 3–4, great damage at Eastport; combined with deep, eastward-moving trough to deluge all New England with 6 inches and more precipitation; greatest six-state flood of nineteenth century resulted; many drowned, enormous property losses.

Wallingford Tornado in Connecticut, August, 1878

Powerful tornado made short track through residential area of north side of Wallingford, near New Haven, on August 9; church destroyed along with surrounding colony of Irish immigrants; 34 killed; 100 injured; $200,000 damage.

Yellow Day on September 6, 1881

Smoke from forest fires in Michigan filtered sun's rays creating a semidarkness; lighting required during day; eerie atmosphere with yellowish tinge to all objects; upper-air pall moved eastward during day; very hot, still day, 90° and above.

Blizzard of '88, Greatest Storm of Modern Period

Coastal storm stalled near Block Island on March 12 with extreme cold air mass to west; enormous quantities of snow fell for three days in Connecticut, Massachusetts, Vermont, and southern New Hampshire; 50 inches measured at Middletown, Conn., 46 inches at New Haven and Albany, N.Y., 36 inches in Vermont and New Hampshire; mostly rain or slush at Boston and Cape Cod; huge drifts, all communications and commerce disrupted for three days to a week.

Vineyard Sound Waterspout in August, 1896

New England's most famous waterspout formed near 1:00 P.M. on August 19 off Cottage City (now Oak Bluffs) on Martha's Vineyard, 5.5 miles offshore; height 3,600 feet, diameter of tube at water 720 feet; formed three times, greatest duration 18 minutes; seen by hundreds of vacationers and well photographed.

Portland Storm in November, 1898

Severe northeast snowstorm on November 26–27 developed low barometric pressure of 28.90″/978.7mb and winds of 70 mph over Cape Cod and islands; deep snow fell to west of track, New London had 27 inches; S.S. *Portland* sailed into teeth of gale, sank off Cape Cod with no survivors from list of 191; many other sea tragedies raised death toll to estimated 400.

Great Atlantic Coast Blizzard in February, 1899

Severe cold wave on February 8–11 ended in great blizzard on February 12–14; over 24 inches on Cape Ann and elsewhere; 16 inches fell at Boston with temperature below 10° during heavy snow period, raised snow depth to all-time record of 23 inches; whole gales lashed the coast.

TWENTIETH CENTURY

Christmas Night Storm 1909

Coastal storm developed great energy off SE coast; lowest pressure 28.84″/976.6mb; highest wind 72 mph at Hull, 45 mph at Boston; great tide in Boston Harbor surged to within one inch of Lighthouse Storm tide; heavy snow fell inland; many shipping losses.

Hottest Fourth of July, in 1911

Thermometers reached all-time maximums in four states on July 4, 1911, in midst of north's most prolonged, intense heat wave: Vernon, Vt., 105°; Nashua, N.H., 106°; Bridgton, Maine, 105°; Lawrence, Mass., 106°; Boston and Albany had 104°.

Winter of 1917–18, Severest of Twentieth Century

Coldest December and coldest January in the record books during the only full winter of our participation in World War I; severe cold wave arrived Christmas afternoon and continued until January 4; another period of persistent cold extended from January 18 to February 3; January temperatures averaged 7–9 degrees below normal; no overnight thaws until February 12; snowfall about normal, but cold preserved snow cover through late February in south; soldiers suffered in flimsy barracks, civilians felt acute fuel shortage.

Great Snow and Sleet Storm in February, 1920

Boston's most paralyzing winter storm occurred on February 5–7; 12 inches of snow fell, then 3.7 inches of ice pellets (sleet), the mixture with previous snows making a total of 19.8 inches on ground; all froze into icy mass, some remained until late March; serious disruption of vehicular traffic all February.

Severe Ice Storm in November, 1921

Central New England underwent its worst modern icing experience on November 26–29, 1921; the Worcester area was most seriously affected with three-inch accumulations on wires and trees; electrical outages, transportation at standstill, business suspended; enormous damage to forests.

Vermont Flood in November, 1927

Tropical storm over eastern New England poured moist, Atlantic air over interior mountains on November 3–4; greatest amounts in Green Mountains: Somerset 8.77 inches in 24 hours, 9.35 inches total; all streams in Vermont, New Hampshire, western Massachusetts and Connecticut in high flood; 84 perished, damage $28 million in Vermont alone.

New England's Coldest Temperature: −50° in 1933

Lowest temperature of −50° recorded by Weather Service at Bloomfield on upper Connecticut River in Northeast Kingdom of Vermont on December 30, 1933; several other Vermont stations below −40°; other state minimums: −44° at Pittsburg, N.H., and −41° at Woodland, Maine.

Coldest Month of Modern Record in Southern New England: February, 1934

Most stations in the south had their record coldest month in February, 1934, and many set records for all-time minimums: Boston −18°, Providence −17°, and New Haven −15° on February 9; state minimums were Connecticut −26°, Rhode Island −22°, and Massachusetts −27°; a cold wave at end of month insured that February, 1934, was the coldest month since January, 1857.

All–New England Flood in March, 1936

Two heavy rainstorms, on March 9–11 and 18–19, falling on deep snow cover raised most streams and rivers in six-state area to record stages; Connecticut River at Hartford peaked at all-time high of 37.6 feet on March 21, city inundated; enormous property damage, over $100 million.

New England Hurricane on September 21, 1938

Made landfall near Milford, Conn., moved northward west of New Haven and Hartford, up Connecticut Valley, then NW diagonally across Vermont; lowest barometric pressure 28.04″/949.5mb at Hartford; Block Island sustained 82-mph wind for five minutes, Blue Hill gusts to 186 mph; extreme coastal destruction; downtown Providence record high inundation; widespread forest blowdown; excessive rains on saturated soil sent rivers into high flood; more than 600 killed; damage estimated at $306 million.

Valentine's Day Storm in February, 1940

Heavy snowfall of 14 inches accompanied by gale-force NE winds peaking at 58 mph created gigantic drifts; traffic blocked, many hundreds stranded overnight in downtown Boston after attending ice show featuring Sonja Henie, public transportation ceased operating.

The Snowiest Winter in Southern New England, 1947–48

December, 1947, was cold (2.2–4.2 degrees below normal) and snowfall average of 23.2 inches was 290% of normal; the Big Snow on December 26–27 was main feature; January temperatures averaged 5.6 degrees below normal, snowfall was 246% of normal; no major storms but snow reached record depths; February also cold and snowy (116% of normal); total snowfall of 70.2 inches (205% of normal) for the three months actually exceeded the 64.4 inches (119% of normal) in the north. Boston set an all-time seasonal snowfall record with 89.2 inches, Providence with 75.6 inches.

Great Easterly Gale in November, 1950

Deep storm center over Pennsylvania and New York caused strong southeast and east flow over all New England on November 25–26, Thanksgiving weekend; gusts at Hartford 100 mph; Concord, N.H., 110 mph; Putnam, Conn., 92 mph; sustained winds at Burlington, Vt., 72 mph; Concord, N.H., 72 mph; Hartford 70 mph; extensive structural damage especially in western sections.

Worcester County Tornado on June 9, 1953

Most powerful and deadly tornado in New England history cut a diagonal southeastward through Worcester County, Mass.; Holden and NE Worcester suffered greatest losses; 94 killed, 1,288 injured; damage $52.1 million.

Hurricane Season of 1954

Three major hurricanes struck or affected New England: Carol on August 31 bisected region from Saybrook, Conn., to Quebec, downtown Providence flooded, 50 killed, $438 million damage; Edna on September 11 crossed Cape Cod and the islands, 40 killed, $40.5 million damage; Hazel in New York State brushed western New England, 1 killed, $350,000 damage.

Floods from Hurricanes Connie and Diane in August, 1955

Hurricane Connie on August 12–13 produced heavy rains, then Diane on August 18–19 dropped up to 19 inches more; all rivers in Connecticut, Rhode Island, and Massachusetts in high flood; Connecticut suffered most damage; 82 killed, $800 million damage.

The Great Northeast Snowstorm in February, 1958

Classic snowstorm swept entire region on February 16–17; 20 inches fell over wide area; Norfolk, Conn., 19.8 inches; Blue Hill, Mass., 22.2 inches; Cavendish, Vt., 24.3 inches; Lebanon, N.H., 32.5 inches; blizzard conditions prevailed on the seventeenth with temperature below 10°; gale-force NE winds and blowing snow; 15-foot drifts in Vermont, roads closed.

Severe Northeast Drought from 1961 to 1966

Abnormally dry conditions first appeared in September, 1961; severe in summer of 1962, but winter rains came; serious concern about reservoirs arose in October, 1963, one of the warmest and driest Octobers; after wet winter, drought returned; by September, 1964, many reservoirs at lowest levels known; rainfall in 1965 generally 50% normal; not until September and October, 1966, did rains permanently alleviate the long drought.

Year-End Down East Blizzard of 1962

Wild, blizzard conditions prevailed over Maine on December 29–31; snow and a severe wind chill swept remainder of New England; new state record for a single storm set when 46 inches of snow fell at Ripogenus Dam; 24-hour record set at Orono with 40 inches; temperatures ranged from zero to −15°; wind gusts reached 60 mph at many places; the cold air penetrated to Nantucket and Martha's Vineyard where −3° was registered.

Big Snowstorm of February, 1969

Snow fell at Boston for 100 hours with only a 20-minute break from February 24 to 28 to a depth of 26.3 inches, a single-storm record; Blue Hill nearby had 38.7 inches; Portsmouth's 33.8 inches and Portland's 26.9 inches were also single-storm records; 77 inches at Pinkham Notch, N.H., and 56 inches at Long Falls Dam in Maine set state records; February, 1969, was the snowiest month of record, at Pinkham Notch 130 inches, Portland 61.2 inches, Blue Hill 65.4 inches, and Boston 41.3 inches.

Winter of Record Cold, 1969–70

January, 1970, was the coldest month in over 100 years of records in Vermont and New Hampshire; Burlington's all-time coldest month (average 3.6°) and coldest two consecutive months, January–February (average 10.3°); Concord, N.H., also had coldest month, very dry January with only light snows, no absolute minimums set, but persistent below-zero readings established new marks.

The Biggest Snow in Northern New England, 1970–71

Seasonal snowfalls of 100 inches or more measured in all New England states except Rhode Island; seasonal totals far exceeded previous records; First Connecticut Lake, N.H., 261 inches; Long Falls Dam, Maine, 204 inches; Waitsfield, Vt., 198 inches; Washington, Mass., 138 inches; Norfolk, Conn., 139 inches; Conway, N.H., a representative valley location in the ski country, had 146 inches.

Hot Saturday of August 2, 1975

Thermometers hit all-time maximums on August 2, 1975, in eastern and southern New England when a torrid air mass from the Great Plains was borne into the region by a northwest wind; maximums were 107° at Chester and New Bedford in Massachusetts (New England records) and 104° at Providence, Rhode Island (a new state record); heat was unprecedented in eastern Maine near sea level: Jonesboro 104° and Bar Harbor 101°.

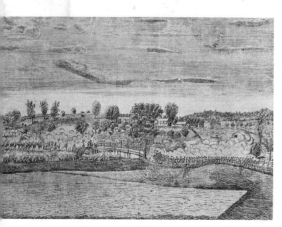

Top: British troops fire on the rebels in Lexington. *Bottom:* The engagement at North Bridge in Concord

CHAPTER 10
The Weather of Independence

War, to the despair of generals and privates alike, is subject to all the vagaries of weather. The land battles of the American War of Independence were fought over a vast terrain stretching from the frozen Saint Lawrence River in the north, to the hot and humid lowlands of Georgia in the south, and westward to the often-flooded banks of the Mississippi River. As might be expected, a variety of climatic conditions visited this territory during the six and a half years of active warfare, and the prevailing weather occasionally had a direct bearing on the outcome of a battle. What follows is a description of the weather at the time of New England's Revolutionary engagements, with an assessment of its effect upon each battle.

Lexington and Concord

The exact nature of weather conditions on April 19, 1775, the day of the military engagements at Lexington and Concord, was long a matter of curiosity among historians. The subject was discussed at several meetings of the Massachusetts Historical Society in the nineteenth century, but no positive evidence was introduced. Several diarists were quoted as attesting that the weather was cool, contrary to the long-standing tradition that the day had been warm for the season and that early fruit trees were in blossom.

At least three monographs on the military aspects of the Lexington and Concord action were produced by scholars in the Boston area in anticipation of the 150th anniversary celebration, but these shed little factual light on the weather conditions of the day. Apparently, none of the authors extended his research into the readily available files of the Harvard University Archives, where the meteorological records of Prof. John Winthrop have been carefully preserved and contain thermometer, barometer, and rain-gauge readings for almost every day from 1742 until Winthrop's death in 1779.

These records indicate that a cold front passed through eastern Massachusetts about noon on April 18, bringing an end to the showery conditions, a shift of wind to the west, a rising barometer, and a rather rapid postfrontal clearing. Visibility was good late in the evening when the signal lamps were hung in the steeple of Old North Church and seen by Colonel Conant at Charlestown across the river. Paul Revere later recalled that the moon was rising and that it was very pleasant at his takeoff hour of eleven o'clock. The *Almanack for 1775* by Nathaniel Ames scheduled the moon, now four days past full, to rise at 10:48 P.M.

The weather station location at Harvard College was close to the line of advance and withdrawal of the British regulars. Winthrop's records relate that his thermometer at 6:00 A.M. on April 19 read 46°F, his barometer 29.56 inches and rising, that there was a light wind from the west and a very fair sky overhead—in all, a cool, fresh, spring morning. His observation was made soon after the skirmish had taken place at Lexington Green during the hour after daylight. Sunrise came at 5:19 A.M., according to the Ames *Almanack*.

Winthrop, as was his custom, took a second observation at 1:00 P.M., after the embattled farmers had made their morning stand at Concord Bridge and while the king's troops were in the process of their painful withdrawal through Lexington and Arlington on the road back to Charlestown. At this time the wind had picked up to moderate from the west, still bringing cool, dry air across the area. The thermometer rose only to 52° and the sky was "fair with clouds"—probably fair-weather cumulus floating peacefully across the troubled scene below. He concluded his observations with the notation: "Battle of Concord will put a stop to observing."

Conditions in the general area were confirmed by the contemporary meteorological observations of Dr. Edward A. Holyoke at Salem, some twenty-five miles northeast of Concord. The passage of the storm system on April 18 was noted with "moist air and rain" in the morning, followed by "fair with some wind" in the afternoon and evening. Holyoke's morning thermometer reading on the nineteenth was 51°, but this was in a sheltered door entry. His remarks for the day were "serene, dry air, pleasant, cool."

For a local view of the weather on the famous day, the diary of Rev. Jonas Clarke of Lexington noted: "April 18. a fine rain. April 19. clear, windy." Other weather watchers in eastern New England made diary entries indicating that fine conditions prevailed generally on the nineteenth. Dr. John Jeffries of Boston recorded the day as "clear & fair, fresh wind at W." Rev. William Marrett of Burlington called it a "fair, windy & cold" day. Paul Litchfield at Scituate described conditions as "somewhat blustery and cool." To the south at Newport, Rhode Island, Elizabeth Stiles registered a temperature of 53° at 11:00 A.M. with the wind west and the sky fair. To the north at Dover, New Hampshire, Rev. Jeremy Belknap had "fair, windy, cool, and west wind" for his entry.

All meteorological evidence indicates that the day of Lexington and Concord had a normally crisp morning and an afternoon somewhat on the cool side, skies fair, wind movement fresh—in all, an ideal day for outdoor activity.

Bunker Hill

The American initiative in fortifying the crown of Breed's Hill across the Charles River from Boston precipitated the action known as the Battle of Bunker Hill, the bloodiest engagement of the entire war in proportion to the relative numbers involved. Construction of the small redoubt was carried out in about four hours, between midnight and dawn on the morning of June 17, 1775.

Two British warships in the estuary between Boston and Charlestown were keeping watch on the enemy, as well as on current weather conditions. H.M.S. *Lively,* whose lookout first sighted the rebel entrenchments, recorded "moderate and fair weather" at 0400 in her log. H.M.S. *Glasgow* nearby recorded "fresh breezes & clear" that morning. Unfortunately, the ensuing action caused the omission of any further weather entries during the day on any of the British ships supporting the amphibious attack.

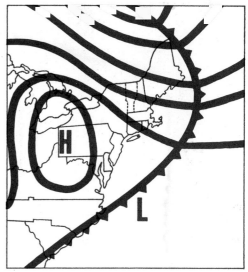

A surmise of weather conditions at Lexington and Concord, April 19, 1775

John Trumbull's painting shows the mortally wounded rebel leader Joseph Warren at Bunker Hill.

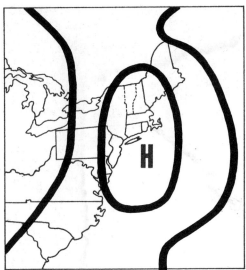

A surmise of weather conditions at Bunker Hill, June 17, 1775

Dr. Edward Holyoke at Salem, some thirteen miles northeast of Bunker Hill, was the nearest meteorologist to the scene. He recorded a morning temperature of 64°, presumably taken at 8:00 A.M. Professor Winthrop, now located at Andover some twenty miles north and inland, read 61° on his thermometer that morning. Wind was light from the west shifting to southwest during the day. Holyoke marked the day as "serene, dry air, hot." Both observers had afternoon temperatures of 80°, though the exact times of the readings were not specified. Probably the maximum at the battle scene that afternoon was a bit higher, possibly as high as 85°.

Recently, a historian of the engagement, Richard M. Ketchum, has described the atmospheric effects within the fortification where the principal action took place: "The sun was blinding white, high in a clear sky. Inside the redoubt on Breed's Hill the dust hung like a motionless curtain, and men inhaled it with every breath they drew; sweat ran down their faces, little rivulets streaking the dirt and stubble of beard."

The last rains in the Boston area had fallen on June 14, according to our meteorological observers. Though no barometer readings were taken at this period by the two nearby watchers, a weather map reconstruction for the morning of the seventeenth would probably have shown the center of a high-pressure area over eastern New England and southward along the Atlantic seaboard. A cold front with showers had moved through on the fourteenth and was now well out over the Atlantic Ocean. A northwesterly flow of polar air from Canada followed —the afternoon reading at Salem on the fifteenth, which would approximate the maximum for the day, was only 67°. Winds were west on the sixteenth with the afternoon reading at 72°—the weather very fair on both the sixteenth and seventeenth as stable air conditions dominated the area.

Sometime during the afternoon of June 17, when the battle was raging, the winds backed farther into the southwest and by next morning to south, indicating the passing eastward of the ridge line of the high-pressure area and a gradual falling off of barometric pressure. The southerly flow overnight brought a tropical airstream into the region with increasing heat as shown by the afternoon readings at Salem of 91° on the eighteenth and 92.5° on the nineteenth. Dr. Holyoke listed June 18 as "very hot," and Benjamin Craft at nearby Manchester noted it as a "very hot day" after his lamented failure to make any entry concerning the weather on the all-important previous day. The only contemporary diarist whose weather impression of the seventeenth has been uncovered, Paul Litchfield at Scituate on the open Atlantic to the southeast, thought the famous day "something warm."

As in the case of many other summertime battles fought long ago, the tradition gradually grew that it took place on "a very hot day." Rev. William Gordon, who published a valuable three-volume history of the war as early as 1788, added an item to his account of Bunker Hill— "and the day exceeding hot." This was long the assumption about the day of Lexington and Concord, too, until corrected recently by contemporary meteorological data recorded near the site of the military action. The same impression about the battle for Charlestown was reflected by the biographer of Capt. Stephen Olney writing in 1838: "The Battle of Bunker's Hill, it will be recollected, was fought on one of the hottest days ever known in the country."

To set the record straight, the engagement now known as the Battle of Bunker Hill was fought on the afternoon of June 17, 1775, under rather optimum conditions for a mid-June day—the ground was dry, the sky clear, the temperature warm but not excessively so, and the air still relatively dry, though growing more humid hourly. If the action had taken place a day or two later, conditions would have been much warmer, more humid, and physically more uncomfortable for the participants.

Guns from Ticonderoga

The rebels' capture of Ticonderoga on Lake Champlain in May, 1775, yielded an array of heavy artillery—cannon, howitzers, and mortars, of which the Continentals had precious few. The prize had to remain there through the summer, however, until the first snowfalls provided a frozen surface on which the guns could be sledded to the seacoast, some 260 miles distant, where they were desperately needed. Col. Henry Knox was dispatched by General Washington to accomplish this arduous task and arrived at Ticonderoga on December 5.

Weather conditions during the first phase of the trip did not favor the operation. No continuous meteorological records are available at a location closer than Concord, Massachusetts, where Prof. John Winthrop had set up his thermometer after fleeing Cambridge at the outset of hostilities with other patriots from the Harvard faculty. Even so, his records suggest the general type of air mass overlying the upper Hudson Valley and western Massachusetts and approximate the general prevailing temperatures, but they are not valid for the amount of precipitation or for sky condition.

Guns captured by the rebels were hauled from Fort Ticonderoga to Boston by sledge.

Winthrop's record indicated that mild weather prevailed until December 20, when wintry conditions descended on New England and held the region in its grip for the next ten days. Temperatures at Concord dropped into the single figures on several nights and did not rise above freezing in daytime until December 31. During this solid freeze the Knox party made good progress southward along the west bank of the Hudson River, reaching Albany by New Year's Day. A severe northeast snowstorm on Christmas Eve raised the snow depth in the area to "nearly two feet," greatly facilitating the passage of the cumbersome sleds.

A thaw and rainstorm set in on the night of December 30–31 causing a delay and difficulties in crossing the Hudson River to the east bank. This lasted until January 10, when another spell of almost continuously freezing weather solidified the roads and accelerated the progress of Knox's train. The unusual caravan turned east at Claverack, New York, crossed the Berkshires along present Route 23, and descended the long slope into the Connecticut Valley amid good snow conditions. On reaching the floor of the valley at Springfield, however, the snow surface wore thin as a result of another thaw.

Detailed information as to surface conditions east of Springfield are not available, as the diarist of the expedition returned home to New York after reaching Springfield, but meteorological records indicate very cold weather between January 18 and 21, with light snowfalls. It is not known whether the military cargo remained on sleds or was transferred to heavy wagons at Springfield, but at any rate the surface proved satisfactory and the seventy remaining miles to Framingham were accomplished by January 25. After a forty-day trek from Ticonderoga, Knox's "noble train of artillery" was at George Washington's disposal.

Siege and Evacuation of Boston

Boston Harbor became the focus of military activity during the winter of 1775–76. The king's troops were confined to the irregular peninsula on which the city stood, while the Americans took up positions on the principal roadways leading into the countryside.

Weather conditions during the season of 1775–76 ran quite close to the expected. Temperatures averaged below normal, but not greatly so. There were several spells of near-zero conditions when thick ice formed on the rivers and estuaries surrounding the city, and in February the inner bay froze over for about ten days. Snowfall, however, was less than normal. After the season's biggest storm on the day before Christmas, there were no major snowfalls. Varying amounts of snow were reported on the ground during January, but during February it virtually disappeared.

The nearest thermometer record was maintained by Dr. Edward A. Holyoke at Salem, located on the north shore of Massachusetts Bay about fourteen miles from Boston. His thermometer, though placed in a protected position in an entryway, was observed at minimums of 3.5° in December, 3° in January, and 7° in February. These were not the absolute lows, since he did not have a self-registering instrument. Capt. William Bamford of the British Fortieth Regiment of Foot described conditions on January 27: "Very severe frost last night, excessive cold day, freezes hard . . . The ink freezes in the pen, as I write by the fireside . . . A good deal of snow on the ground."

During February, with little or no snow cover, the frost penetrated deep into the soil. Col. Jeduthan Baldwin gave an idea of the trenching difficulties entailed by the cold on Lechmere's Point: "19th—the ground has frosen 22 inches Deep as hard as a rock, & in one night it frose in the trenches 8 inches deep, so that we pryed up cakes of frosen Earth 9 feet long and 3 feet broad."

Daniel McCurtin observed on February 22 that there were "very high frosts, but little or no snow." The last week of February brought on another thaw.

Although the ice was gone from the rivers and the ground bare of snow, winter was not quite finished. March came in like a lion. The first day was described as "excessive cold" with a northwest gale sending the thermometer down to 13°, and cold continued through the third, when the wind shifted to a southerly quarter with thawing conditions. The early morning of the fifth was "warm, pleasant"—conditions known as a "weather breeder" at this season of the year in New England.

General Washington had planned to take advantage of the wintry weather and frozen surface of the waterways to mount an attack on Boston, but the late February thaw prevented his carrying out this daring and probably ill-conceived operation. He decided on an entirely different plan—to mount the guns from Ticonderoga on Dorchester Heights, an elevation on a promontory extending out into the bay immediately south of Boston, from which American gunners on the heights could harass the defenses of the city and menace the ships in the harbor.

Wind and weather conditions favored the installation of the guns on the night of March 4–5. Haze reduced visibility and a temperature inversion muffled the transmission of sound. The British suspected that something was afoot on the heights, but they did not realize the full scale of their predicament until dawn, when the guns and protective embankments became clearly visible. British General Howe decided on immediate action. Orders were issued for his troops to prepare for a landing on the Dorchester peninsula early on the sixth.

During the evening hours of the fifth there arose "a hurrycane, or terrible storm," in the words of Timothy Newell. Other Americans in the vicinity described the impact of the unexpected storm. Gen. William Heath recalled: "About midnight the wind blew almost a hurricane from the south. Many windows were forced in, sheds and fences blown down and some vessels blown on shore." John Rowe experienced the same: "A very severe storm; it blew down my rail fences, both sides and the front of the house." Samuel Webb related that "the heavy gale from S.E. last night blew two of the transports [British] on the shore of the harbour at Boston." It was "a very stormy night very hard gale indeed—southerly," according to Dr. Samuel Adams. Capt. Samuel Richards observed: "As night approached an uncommonly severe South East rain storm came on with very high winds." Rev. William Gordon thought it "such a storm as scarce any one remembered to have heard."

A woodcut shows Washington taking command of the army at Cambridge.

Both of the regular weather observers in the vicinity, Prof. John Winthrop at Concord and Dr. Edward Holyoke at Salem, noted the strong wind flow from a southerly quadrant attending various phases of the storm. Winds had shifted from southwest through south to southeast, indicating the approach of a deep trough of low pressure from the west. The center of the vigorous cyclonic disturbance must have passed to the north of Boston, probably moving from the Ohio Valley across central New York and northern New England on a northeast track parallel to the Saint Lawrence Valley. Dr. Holyoke's register for March 6 read: "S.E. Very high Wind. Stormy. Rain." His thermometer mounted to a morning reading of 53°.

Boston Harbor, opening to the east-southeast, is especially susceptible to winds from that quarter, since they kick up a heavy surf on the western side and make Dorchester Point a dangerous lee shore. H.M.S. *Centurion,* anchored in the bay, logged "fresh gales and squally weather" early on the morning of the sixth.

The impact of the unanticipated storm disrupted the initial stages of the planned assault. The transports could not disembark their troops, and the flatboats that were to be employed as landing craft were unable to leave the docks at Boston. General Howe next day blamed the fiasco on "the badness of the weather."

The extra hours of grace gave the Americans time to strengthen their defenses, and now they knew where and how the British intended to attack. Mindful of the bloody experience on Bunker Hill in a similar situation, Howe showed no inclination to attempt the assault again when the storm had subsided. Instead he turned to another plan he had been considering. In view of the frustrations of the past year—his supply difficulties, the open opposition of much of the local population, and the lack of worthwhile military objectives in the hinterland—he decided to evacuate Boston and find a better place to fight the war.

The British troops were to have boarded ship on March 14. Lt. John Barker related that the wind proved unfavorable for three days until the seventeenth when "we quitted Boston with a fair wind and sailed down to King Road below Castle William." Dr. Holyoke at Salem noted the seventeenth as "fair pleasant warm." His thermometer stood at 39° in the morning and at 53° in the evening—the wind was brisk at west, ideal conditions for sailing down the bay to the fleet rendezvous.

The seventeenth of March has ever since been celebrated as a regional holiday, Evacuation Day, to commemorate the victory of New Englanders and their fellow Americans over the British.

General Howe evacuating the British troops from Boston

Montreal and Quebec

The American invasion of Canada in the early months of hostilities represented the most ambitious offensive undertaking of the entire war. A handful of untrained and ill-equipped men, operating hundreds of miles from their bases, sought to reduce British power in the Saint Lawrence Valley in hostile country and under weather conditions known to be unfavorable.

Col. Benedict Arnold, leading a force from a starting point on the Kennebec River in Maine, found the going hard and the weather adverse when he was deep in the Maine woods on the forty-six-day trek to a point on the Saint Lawrence opposite Quebec. He was beset first by a three-day storm in late October, 1775, accompanied by gale winds of sufficient force to level trees and by drenching rains that raised small streams to torrents and flooded low ground at the principal portage. There followed a hard snowstorm, adding to the hardships of the dwindling number of undernourished and ill-clad members of the expedition.

The other arm of the attack, led by Gen. Richard Montgomery, advanced down the Champlain-Richelieu waterway toward Montreal and encountered the same storm systems. During the fifty-five-day siege of Saint John, Montgomery's camp was located on low ground, which became a mire under the incessant autumnal rains. Saint John finally capitulated in early November and Montreal fell several days later, but the delay had seen the season turn from autumn to winter. Not until December 5 were Montgomery's and Arnold's forces joined and in position before Quebec.

Montgomery planned to attack the Lower Town on a dark and stormy night, "in the first norwester," when bitter cold and blowing snow would offer some chance of surprise. "It was a hard chance, but the only one; and even that hung upon the favor of the weathercock," as Justin H. Smith, one historian of the expedition, has written. All was ready for the assault by Christmas Day, but the desired weather conditions did not commence until the afternoon of December 30. Capt. Thomas Ainslie, who kept a weather diary within Quebec throughout the winter although he did not have a thermometer or barometer, wrote of conditions on the night of December 30–31: "It snow'd all the night, it was very dark, the wind strong at N.E." The critical visibility was not as low as Montgomery wanted, and it proved too difficult to haul artillery along the icy path that led to the town. Surprise was impossible, and the small attacking force, after forcing their way into the streets, was shattered by well-placed defensive fire. On New Year's Eve a mighty snowstorm literally buried those Americans who were still alive.

A winter siege followed. The handful of Americans camped outside the citadel in whatever shelter they could contrive, exposed to all the fury of a harsh Canadian winter. There were six snowstorms in January, 1776, and the weather grew excessively cold toward the end. The major storm of the winter developed on February 9–10: "A heavy wind at N.E. with thick snow—before the morning the storm increased to a perfect hurricane, it was impossible to face the weather but for a minute," Sgt. Caleb Haskell declared. He had never seen such a mighty storm in his native New England. The snow drifted so deep against the fortifications that one could walk through the gun embrasures into the citadel.

After an early March thaw, a second winter descended and not until April 10 did the weather grow mild: "Wind westerly soft weather, —the streets are full of water, the snow under it is porous and rotten— if one steps out of the path he sinks to the knee," wrote Captain Ainslie. Three inches of snow fell on May Day and a hard freeze followed that night.

The siege was finally lifted upon the sighting of a large relief fleet from England that arrived on May 6. The besiegers, now reduced to about 250 tattered men, retreated pell-mell upriver, leaving the entire valley in British hands. Crown Point on the New York shore of upper Lake Champlain became the American outpost in the summer of 1776 as it had been at the start of the campaign the previous autumn.

Valcour Island

The battle off Valcour Island in Lake Champlain between two tiny flotillas of small armed ships on October 11–12 was the highlight of the 1776 campaign in the north. Its outcome determined the control of Lake Champlain in that year and played an important role in tipping the scales of battle in 1777.

This most important inland naval conflict of the war was fought between two army generals: Brig. Gen. Benedict Arnold and Sir Guy Carleton. During the summer of 1776 the Americans assembled fifteen small vessels—schooners, sloops, and gunboats—at the southern end of the lake. Meanwhile, Carleton built several vessels at Saint John and carried others over in sections from the Saint Lawrence to be re-

The American attack on Quebec was fatally hampered by a violent storm.

assembled on the Richelieu. The British outgunned the Americans by a total of fifty-three to thirty-two and had larger vessels and trained crews.

Arnold's ships, sailing northward in mid September, took up a defensive position behind Valcour Island, which lies on the New York side of the lake between Port Kent and Plattsburgh. It was early October before Carleton was ready to sail and seek the enemy. His flotilla, favored by a strong northerly wind, passed by Valcour Island completely before the rear lookout spied the American line off the starboard beam to the northwest. The British had to beat against the wind for several hours in order to maneuver close enough to open fire on the American ships. "The wind was so unfavorable that for a considerable time nothing could be brought into action," declared the British commander, and not until noontime did firing commence. The Americans sustained serious losses in ships and men that afternoon from the heavier British cannon; but still favored by the weather gauge that enabled them to maneuver upwind from the British, they held their position until nightfall.

During the ensuing darkness, which was accompanied by fog and mist, the Americans got under way and headed south, closely hugging the shore. The British commander later blamed "the extreme obscurity of the night" for preventing his watch from spotting the Americans. The wind, however, now shifted to the south so progress in the face of the head wind was painfully slow for Arnold's battered ships. At dawn the British sighted the withdrawing vessels to the south and set out in pursuit.

Again the wind shifted in the vicinity of the British, this time to the northeast, so they were favored in the first phase of the pursuit by a following wind. Apparently a wind shift line, possibly a weak cold front following the south wind and overcast night, moved southward, propelling the British forward while the Americans were still struggling against a head wind. This gave the British the advantage of the weather gauge for some crucial minutes, enabling them to close swiftly on Arnold's remaining ships. By 11:00 A.M. they were near enough to open another withering fire. One American ship struck its colors, the others were beached and abandoned, and Arnold landed the *Congress* in Button Bay on the Vermont shore near Vergennes, set the ship afire, and escaped on foot by a roundabout route to Crown Point.

The season was now well advanced. When snow appeared on the peaks of the Adirondack and Green mountains, Carleton decided to withdraw to Saint John and await the coming of another summer and reinforcements before resuming the campaign. Historians have credited Arnold's small ships on the waters of Lake Champlain with giving the Americans a full year of grace to prepare for the day when the British would be able to mount a full-scale campaign for control of the lake and the upper Hudson Valley. So it might be said that the presence of the small, ill-fated flotilla made possible the victory at Saratoga in 1777.

Enter Burgoyne

Maj. Gen. John Burgoyne returned to Canada in May, 1777, after wagering that he "would be back home victorious from America, by Christmas Day 1777." In fact, he would spend that day in Boston with spirits entirely unlike those of a victorious general: he had been defeated in the wilds of interior America as a result of a faulty strategy, compounded by adverse terrain, unfavorable weather, and a resolute foe.

The usual lateness of the winter breakup prevented Burgoyne's forces from taking the field and engaging the Americans in the Champlain Valley until July 1. Fort Ticonderoga was abandoned by the Americans, leaving Lake Champlain entirely in British hands.

Major General John Burgoyne, by Sir Joshua Reynolds

Hubbardton

Burgoyne's troops set off in pursuit of the Americans, who were re-treating through the forests of western Vermont. As described by Christopher Ward, a military historian, "The day, July 6th, became hotter and hotter as it wore on. Over that road, shut in on both sides by dense forest walls, there were no cooling breezes, and the men sweltered in the overpowering heat." There was no thermometer nearby to report the exact figure, but one may surmise that the temperature on a hot summer's day would be in the high 80s or low 90s. Next morning in a predawn march, the British came on a sizable American rear guard preparing breakfast, and the Battle of Hubbardton ensued. Another hot day was dawning. Before midmorning the fighting ended in a complete British victory, and the thermometer again mounted toward the 90s.

Bennington

Now well behind schedule, Burgoyne sent a foraging expedition into Vermont to secure horses and wheeled vehicles to expedite the south-ward progress of the main body. To the west of Bennington—almost astride the present New York–Vermont border, these German merce-naries and Indian auxiliaries came into contact with an American militia force under Gen. John Stark.

The intervention of a rainstorm worked to the advantage of the Americans by delaying the start of the conflict by twenty-four hours and allowing time for additional militia on the road to join the main force at Bennington and swell their ranks. In addition, the overnight deluges made difficult the Germans' preparation of earthwork defenses; the hard rain washed down dirt walls, filled trenches with water, and made the troops miserable in their exposed position on a hillside. Muddy roads and high water also delayed a column of German reinforcements that had been urgently dispatched from the British base on the Hudson River when word reached Burgoyne of the size of the American force assembling at Bennington. In the words of their commander, Lieutenant Colonel Breyman: "The crossing of the Battenkill consumed considerable time, for the men had to wade through the water. The great number of hills, the bottomless roads, and a severe and continuous rain, made the march so tedious that I could scarcely make one-half of an English mile an hour." As a result of the slow progress of this column, the Americans were able to deal with the two enemy forces separately: they surrounded and captured the original column and halted and put to rout the second. The coming of darkness put an end to the fighting. "Had day lasted an hour longer," declared Stark, "we would have taken the whole body of them."

Burgoyne had learned a bitter lesson. As he later wrote, "The New Hampshire Grants [Vermont] . . . a country unpeopled and almost un-known in the last war, now abounds with the most active and rebellious race on the continent, and hangs like a gathering storm upon my left." It would be another stroke from this "storm country" that finally sealed the British fate two months later. Meanwhile, the Battle of Oriskany in central New York, fought during a heavy thunderstorm, had blunted the western prong of Burgoyne's advance, leaving his main army un-supported in the narrow confines of the Hudson Valley. And the Ameri-cans were closing in on him.

Prisoners captured by rebels at Bennington

Bemis Heights and Saratoga

The final phase of the Northern Campaign was played out on the west bank of the Hudson River between Bemis Heights and Schuylerville, about seventeen miles west of the Vermont border. It was now early autumn, the time of year when nights commence to grow uncomfortably cool, the first frosts whiten the morning grass and fields, and the foliage takes on a golden hue under brilliant sunshine by day. It was Indian summer, that interval between the seasons of heat and cold.

Autumn weather maps in the Northeast are often dominated by anticyclonic controls. With clear nighttime skies, radiation of heat to outer space occurs. This results in fog, sometimes mistakenly called mist. Poor morning visibility was the meteorological factor most prominent in the military action prior to the surrender at Saratoga. Several engagements were either delayed or aborted by the presence of fog enshrouding valley bottoms and lower hillsides. As one soldier commented, "We turned out every morning an hour before daybreak to enjoy the morning air, which was composed partly of hoar-frost and partly of a mist so dense that you could in very truth grasp it with your outstretched hands. Nor did it disappear before nine o'clock."

The first of the decisive series of engagements took place almost at the autumnal equinox on September 19, 1777. A fog covered the battlefield during the early morning hours, delaying action until after ten o'clock, and a hot battle raged most of the day, with the British unable to achieve a breakthrough of the American left to open the road to Albany. The next morning was described by one soldier as "very dark and foggy," and another declared that "the day dawned thick and misty. The fog obscured everything at a distance of 20 yards." Visibility did not improve until the fog lifted between ten and eleven o'clock, and then "the sun shone very warm," but the morning fog had caused Burgoyne to delay launching his planned attack. His previous day's losses had been substantial and he now decided to await news of favorable developments from the British forces supposedly operating in the lower Hudson Valley.

The Battle of Freeman's Farm

The next fighting did not occur until 2:30 in the afternoon of October 7, when Burgoyne again sought to test the American left. Weather conditions were not an influential factor in this action, but because of the late start darkness was descending on the battlefield just when the rebels were on the verge of breaking into the British interior defenses, and the fighting sputtered to a halt.

The final phase of the campaign commenced on October 8 when Burgoyne, despairing of relief from the south, decided to retreat northward into Canada. With no meteorologist on his staff to advise him, he chose the least propitious time to set out. The retreat commenced about nine in the evening after a very warm day, but next morning it began to rain. General Riedesel wrote of the scene: "The progress was slow beyond belief, not more than a mile an hour. It was a dolorous march. Rain was falling heavily. The road, bad enough before, was a bog. The tired men could hardly drag their feet out of the mud. The wagons stuck fast and were unable to go on. The tents and baggage were left behind."

In pursuit of the retreating British and Germans, the rebels also moved at a very slow pace. On the morning of the eleventh an American column, thinking they were following a rear guard, almost marched into the main British position, which was hidden in the fog. It was a near disaster for the Americans. If a general engagement had developed under these adverse conditions, the outcome might have permitted the British to withdraw unmolested.

Burgoyne's defensive position remained strong, but the American right was strengthened daily by the arrival of small groups of New Englanders. Finally on October 12, eleven hundred New Hampshire militiamen crossed the Hudson River north of Burgoyne and cut his last escape route. Terms were asked on the thirteenth and the capitulation took place on the seventeenth.

A factor in Burgoyne's decision to surrender may have been the advanced state of the season, since frosty nights and cold mornings already gave a hint of what was to come. The first snow fell on October

Burgoyne (left) surrenders to Gates at Saratoga.

135

21, and a hard freeze followed. On the twenty-eighth there was "alternately hail, rain and snow." These harbingers of the northern winter occurred while the captured army was moving southeastward toward the seacoast and a winter's confinement in the relative comfort of urban Boston—during the same season that the Continental Army under Washington was enduring the rigors of Valley Forge.

The Sea Battle off Newport

After the evacuation of Boston in March, 1776, there was no strong British presence in New England until the capture of Newport, Rhode Island, in December of that year. Although the Americans subsequently threw a cordon across the central part of the island, they were unable to move against the enemy's main defenses because of the mobile fire power of British warships in the vicinity. Not until the arrival of a strong French fleet under Comte d'Estaing in July, 1778, was parity of naval forces achieved in American waters. After an unsuccessful attempt to enter New York Bay and get at the main British fleet under Admiral Howe, d'Estaing routed the smaller naval forces stationed before Newport and sailed past the British land forces to consult with the American commander, Maj. Gen. John Sullivan, on joint operations.

The British fleet in New York immediately sailed eastward and took up position off Newport on August 9. They held the weather gauge in the form of a favoring southwest wind, which normally prevails at this time of year. D'Estaing was effectively bottled up in the bay under these wind conditions, but between seven and eight on the morning of the tenth, a squall occurred when a cold front moved through the area. The wind shifted abruptly to the north and the prevailing thick weather cleared quickly. Professor Winthrop's barometer at Cambridge indicated rapidly rising pressure that morning as a polar air mass from Canada spread over southern New England, and the southwesterly wind was replaced by a northerly flow.

The French now held the weather gauge and were quick to seize the opportunity. They cut cables and sailed out of the mouth of the harbor with "the wind moderate at N.E." to challenge the British fleet, which was approximately equal in strength but held a disadvantageous wind position. British Admiral Howe retired south-southwestward toward the open sea during the afternoon, hoping to "profit by the sea breeze, should it set in," or by "manoeuvering to gain the weather gauge." The wind, however, with mounting atmospheric pressure to the northward and falling pressure to the southward, continued from the northeast, enabling the French to close to about five to six miles by sundown. Next day, August 11, "the wind hung eastward, blowing fresh." At noon, conditions were logged as "thick hazy weather with moderate ENE breeze."

Admiral d'Estaing, encouraged by his progress and scenting a victory, described the developments of the afternoon:

> The wind having freshened, we were gaining on them sensibly. An hour-and-a-half after noon, there seemed no more doubt; we believed that we would certainly overtake them. The maneuvers of Lord Howe, who continued to flee before the wind, but losing distance, showed that he no longer flattered himself of escaping combat. The wind and sea increased. Our advance guard, in five hours and three-quarters, had reached the English rear guard; in luffing up they were engaged. The weather, which for four hours had been growing worse, and cloudy, was now blowing a gale. At six o'clock, I was compelled to take in all sail except the fore stay-sail and mizzen try-sail.

The enemy, of course, was undergoing the same weather experience, and as Thomas O'Beirne, who was aboard a British vessel, described the scene: "The wind at this time blew so fresh, that our ships were under close reefed topsails; and the sea ran so high, that Lord Howe could not return aboard his own ship."

These were the first hard puffs of a dangerous hurricane that was racing northeastward that afternoon in the Atlantic Ocean only a short distance offshore. By 6:00 P.M. on the eleventh, H.M.S. *Phoenix* was reporting "a fresh Gale with hard Rain." By 8:00 P.M., with the wind howling out of the east-northeast, H.M.S. *Roebuck* "Hove to under Close Reef." During the night H.M.S. *Renown* experienced first "hard gales" and then "strong gales," with "squally conditions" as the full fury of the advancing hurricane moved into the area where the two fleets lay in close proximity.

It was a memorable night for Admiral d'Estaing on the *Languedoc:* "At half past three in the morning—pardon me, sir, this excess of detail and precision, the man who has had both arms and both legs cut off, all at the same time, cannot in his sad narrative omit an instant—the bowsprit broke, then the foremast, then the main-top, then the mizzen mast; finally main-mast fell. Our rudder broke next. This last misfortune was the greatest of all. We were now only a floating mass with nothing to steady us, and nothing to guide us."

The hurricane raged all day on the twelfth as thick hazy weather with drizzling rain reduced visibility and heavy gales continued out of the northeast. Early on August 13 the wind commenced to back from northeast through north as the center of the hurricane came abreast of the latitude of Rhode Island. Wind direction reached northwest by nine in the morning, west-northwest by two in the afternoon, and west-southwest by nine in the evening, according to the log of H.M.S. *Renown.* Fresh gales raged until noon of the thirteenth, then the fury of the winds gradually started to subside.

On the fourteenth the hurricane had departed, though seas continued to run high. At dawn Thomas O'Beirne noted, "There were only fresh breezes and the sky was clear—a most welcome dawn after 60 hours of storm." But both fleets were crippled and scattered. After making emergency repairs, the ships headed for their bases: the British to New York Bay and the French to Newport and eventually to Boston where there were adequate shipyard facilities.

The August hurricane of 1778 must be rated just a notch below the greatest New England hurricanes. The center must have passed within fifty miles eastward of the impending battle scene and it swept all the coastline with strong northeasterly gales from New York to Maine, making a shambles of the tents in the American campground before Newport. On Martha's Vineyard the hurricane winds battered the corn crop to such an extent that the harvest was greatly reduced and famine threatened the inhabitants the following winter.

The opportunity for a decisive naval action between the principal fleets of the two nations in American waters—as was to occur three years later off Chesapeake Bay, had vanished under the wild winds of an August hurricane. Without the aid of the French navy, Sullivan was forced to give up his position on Rhode Island, and the most important strategic naval base in New England remained in British hands.

Masts of the *Languedoc* (right) were sheared off by hurricane winds, August 12, 1778.

TABLES

Snow crystal photographs taken by Wilson ("Snowflake") Bentley

EXTREMES OF SNOWFALL—STATES (INCHES & CENTIMETERS)

		GREATEST IN 24 HOURS	GREATEST IN ONE STORM	GREATEST IN ONE MONTH	GREATEST IN ONE SEASON
Connecticut	in	28.0 New Haven 3/12/1888	50.0 Middletown 3/11–14/1888	73.6 Norfolk 3/1956	177.4 Norfolk 1955–56
	cm	71	127	187	451
Maine		35.0 Middle Dam 11/23/1943	56.0 Long Falls Dam 2/24–28/1969	88.3 Long Falls Dam 2/1969	238.5 Long Falls Dam 1968–69
		89	142	224	606
Massachusetts		28.2 Blue Hill Obsy. 2/24–25/1969	47.0 Peru 3/2–5/1947	78.0 Monroe 2/1893	162.0 Monroe 1892–93
		72	119	198	412
New Hampshire*		56.0 Randolph 11/22–23/1943	77.0 Pinkham Notch 2/24–28/1969	130.0 Pinkham Notch 2/1969	323.0 Pinkham Notch 1968–69
		142	196	330	820
Rhode Island		34.0 Foster 2/8–9/1945	34.0 Foster 2/8–9/1945	62.0 Foster 3/1956	122.6 Foster 1947–48
		86	86	157	311
Vermont		33.0 St. Johnsbury 2/25/1969	50.0 Readsboro 3/2–6/1947	75.0 Waitsfield 12/1969	197.5 Waitsfield 1970–71
		84	127	191	502

* Mt. Washington not included.

EXTREMES OF COLD (FAHRENHEIT & CELSIUS) FROST DATES

STATION & PERIOD		ABSOLUTE MINIMUM	COLDEST MONTH	COLDEST TWO CONSECUTIVE MONTHS	COLDEST WINTER DEC.–FEB.	EARLIEST DATE 32°F 0°C	0°F −18°C	LATEST DATE 0°F −18°C	32°F 0°C
Connecticut									
Bridgeport 1905–	°F	−20 2/9/34	15.6 2/34	23.2 1–2/34	24.0 1969–70		not compiled		
	°C	−29	−9.1	−4.9	−4.4				
Hartford 1905–		−26 1/22/61	16.5 2/34	19.2 12/17–1/18	21.2 1917–18	9/21/62	12/7/64	3/19/67	5/13/62
		−32	−8.6	−7.1	−6.0				
New Haven 1871–		−15 2/9/34	17.4 2/34	21.6 12/17–1/18	23.3 1917–18	9/30/1888	12/9/02	3/13/1885	5/30/1884
		−26	−8.1	−5.8	−4.8				
Maine									
Caribou 1939–		−41 2/1/55	3.8 1/61	7.3 1–2/72	8.0 1958–59	9/5/63	11/21/59	4/2/64	6/12/50
		−41	−15.7	−13.7	−13.3				
Eastport 1874–		−23 12/30/33*	11.5 1/20	14.7 1–2/40	16.5 1904–05	9/22/04	11/30/1875	3/29/23	6/19/1875
		−31	−11.4	−9.6	−8.6				
Portland 1871–		−39 2/16/43	12.2 1/71	15.7 1–2/04	17.2 1917–18	9/14/63	12/3/40	2/26/60	5/31/61
		−39	−11.0	−9.1	−8.2				
Massachusetts									
Boston 1871–		−18 2/9/34	17.5 2/34	21.2 1–2/70	23.9 1917–18	10/5/1883	11/30/1875	3/6/1872	5/3/1882
		−28	−8.1	−6.0	−4.5				
Nantucket 1887–		−6 2/5/18	22.6 2/34	25.9 1–2/18	27.3 1917–18	10/6/65	12/9/02	2/27/00	5/17/57
		−21	−5.2	−3.4	−2.6				
Pittsfield 1939–		−25 2/15/43*	13.2 1/70	16.7 1–2/48	18.3 1947–48		not compiled		
		−32	−10.4	−8.5	−7.6				
Worcester 1893–		−24 2/16/43	14.4 2/34	19.5 12/17–1/18	21.3 1917–18	9/19/43	12/4/40	3/29/23	5/31/38
		−31	−9.8	−6.9	−5.9				
New Hampshire									
Concord 1871–		−37 2/16/43	11.0 1/20	14.3 1–2/04	15.5 1917–18		not compiled		
		−38	−11.7	−9.8	−9.2				
Hanover 1835–		−40 2/16/43	6.8 1/1888	9.9 1–2/1875	13.2 1872–73		not compiled		
		−40	−14.0	−12.3	−10.4				
Mt. Washington 1934–		−47 1/29/34	−5.3 2/34	0.5 1–2/48	2.1 1947–48		not compiled		
		−44	−20.7	−17.5	−16.6				
Rhode Island									
Block Island 1881–		−10 2/9/34	20.3 2/34	25.0 1–2/18	25.5 1917–18		not compiled		
		−23	−6.5	−3.9	−3.6				
Providence 1905–		−17 2/9/34	17.4 2/34	21.8 12/17–1/18	23.2 1917–18	10/4/45	12/8/06	1/26/28	5/12/07
		−27	−8.1	−5.7	−4.9				
Vermont									
Burlington 1884–		−30 1/15/57	3.6 1/70	10.3 1–2/70	12.1 1917–18	9/13/46	11/25/38	3/29/23	5/31/61
		−34	−15.8	−12.1	−11.1				
New York									
Albany 1820–		−28 1/19/71	9.7 1/70	14.4 1–2/1875	17.3 1867–68	9/14/63	11/26/38	3/29/23	5/27/70
		−33	−12.4	−9.8	−8.2				
New York City 1869–		−15 2/9/34	19.9 2/34	23.4 12/17–1/18	25.7 1917–18	10/15/1876	12/18/19	2/24/1873	5/6/1891
		−26	−6.7	−4.8	−3.5				

* Also in earlier years.

Year references are to twentieth century unless otherwise indicated.

EXTREMES OF SNOWFALL—CITIES (INCHES)

	GREATEST IN 24 HOURS	GREATEST IN ONE STORM	GREATEST IN ONE MONTH	GREATEST IN ONE SEASON	GREATEST DEPTH ON GROUND
Connecticut					
Bridgeport 1921–	16.7 2/9–10/69	17.7 2/9–10/69	47.0 2/34	71.3 1933–34	17.7 2/10/69
Hartford 1904–	19.0 2/28–3/1/49	19.2 2/28–3/1/49	45.3 12/45	82.8 1966–67	32.8 2/5/48
New Haven 1873–	28.0 3/12/88	44.7 3/11–14/88	46.3 2/34	76.0 1915–16	40.0 3/14/88
Maine					
Caribou 1939–	18.2 2/11–12/52	23.3 12/29–31/62	49.4 12/54	181.1 1954–55	51.0 2/11/68*
Eastport 1885–	18.5 4/9–10/46	18.5 4/9–10/46*	53.7 1/52	187.5 1906–07	42.0 3/14/23
Portland 1881–	23.3 1/23–24/35	26.9 2/24–28/69	61.2 2/69	141.5 1970–71	55.0 1/17/23
Massachusetts					
Blue Hill 1886–	28.2 2/24–25/69	38.7 2/24–28/69	65.4 2/69	136.0 1947–48	41.9 1/25/48
Boston 1872–	19.4 2/16–17/58	26.3 2/24–28/69	41.3 2/69	89.2 1947–48	23.0 2/14/99
Nantucket 1886–	20.1 2/27–28/52	31.3 3/3–5/60	40.2 3/60	82.0 1903–04	23.0 2/28/52
Pittsfield 1940–69	17.0 12/24–25/66	23.0 12/25–28/69	51.7 12/69	121.9 1955–56	40.2 3/20/56
Worcester 1901–	24.0 2/14–15/62	24.1 2/14–15/62	45.2 2/62	104.3 1960–61	42.0 2/5/61
New Hampshire					
Concord 1871–	19.0 1/6–7/44	27.5 3/11–13/88	59.0 2/93	122.0 1873–74	37.0 2/13/23
Rhode Island					
Providence 1904–	18.3 2/4/61	18.3 2/4/61	31.9 1/48	75.6 1947–48	30.0 2/5/61
Vermont					
Burlington 1906–	24.2 1/13–14/34	29.8 12/25–28/69	56.7 12/70	145.4 1970–71	33.0 12/28/69*
New York					
Albany 1885–	30.4 3/12/88	46.7 3/11–14/88	57.5 12/69	112.5 1970–71	46.0 3/14/88
New York City 1869–	26.4 12/26–27/47	26.4 12/26–27/47	30.5 3/96	63.2 1947–48	26.4 12/27/47

* Also in previous years.

Anders Celsius

EXTREMES OF HEAT (FAHRENHEIT & *CELSIUS*)

STATION & PERIOD		ABSOLUTE MAXIMUM	WARMEST MONTH	WARMEST TWO CONSECUTIVE MONTHS	WARMEST SUMMER JUNE–AUG.	EARLIEST DATE 90°F 32°C	EARLIEST DATE 100°F 38°C	LATEST DATE 100°F 38°C	LATEST DATE 90°F 32°C
Connecticut									
Bridgeport 1923–	°F	103 7/22/57	77.4 7/55	76.8 7–8/55	73.8 1973	not compiled			
	°C	39	25.2	24.9	23.2				
Hartford 1905–		102 7/3/66	77.0 7/55	75.7 7–8/73	74.4 1973	4/7/29	6/26/52	9/2/53	10/17/08
		39	25.0	24.3	23.6				
New Haven 1871–		101 7/22/26	75.4 7/55	75.1 7–8/55	72.3 1949	4/27/15	7/21/30	9/7/1881	9/26/1881
		38	24.1	23.9	22.4				
Maine									
Caribou 1939–		96 6/29/44	69.7 7/70	67.9 7–8/70	66.0 1973	5/29/60			9/7/45
		36	20.9	19.9	18.9				
Eastport 1872–		93 8/27/49	64.7 7/52	64.2 7–8/49	62.4 1949	5/31/37			9/16/39
		34	18.2	17.9	16.9				
Portland 1872–		103 7/4/11 & 8/2/75	72.4 8/37	71.5 7–8/37	68.9 1937	5/16/51	8/26/48*	8/27/48	9/18/55
		39	22.4	21.9	20.5				
Massachusetts									
Boston 1871–		104 7/4/11	77.5 7/52	75.9 7–8/55	74.1 1949	4/27/62	6/6/25	9/7/1881	10/12/54
		40	25.3	24.4	23.4				
Nantucket 1887–		100 8/2/75	71.8 8/37	70.6 7–8/44	68.7 1949	6/21/23			8/28/48
		38	22.1	21.4	20.4				
Worcester 1901–		102 7/4/11	74.3 7/52	73.0 7–8/49	71.9 1949	5/7/30	7/4/11	7/4/11	9/26/30
		39	23.5	22.8	22.2				
New Hampshire									
Concord 1871–		102 7/5/11	74.1 7/55	72.7 7–8/55	70.1 1949	not compiled			
		39	23.4	22.6	21.2				
Hanover 1931–		99 7/18/53	73.0 7/55	71.8 7–8/55	70.1 1949	not compiled			
		37	22.8	22.1	21.2				
Mt. Washington 1934–		72 8/2/75	53.8 8/37	52.6 7–8/37	50.2 1937				
		22	12.1	11.4	10.1				
Rhode Island									
Block Island 1881–		95 8/27/48	73.8 7/52	72.5 7–8/52	70.3 1949	not compiled			
		35	23.2	22.5	21.3				
Providence 1905–		104 8/2/75	78.2 7/52	75.8 7–8/49	74.5 1949	3/29/45	6/26/52	8/28/48	10/10/49
		40	25.7	24.3	23.6				
Vermont									
Burlington 1884–		101 8/11/44	75.4 7/21	72.9 7–8/47	72.2 1949	5/9/1889	7/3/11	8/11/44	9/16/39
		38	24.1	22.7	22.3				
New York									
Albany 1820–		104 7/4/11	79.7 7/1868	77.9 7–8/1872	76.4 1872	4/20/41	6/9/33	9/3/53	10/6/00
		40	26.5	25.5	24.7				
New York City 1869–		106 7/9/36	80.9 7/55	79.5 7–8/55	77.3 1966	4/18/1896	6/26/52	9/7/1881	10/10/39
		41	27.2	26.4	25.2				

MEAN WIND SPEED—MONTHS (MILES PER HOUR)

	JAN.	FEB.	MAR.	APR.	MAY	JUN.	JUL.	AUG.	SEPT.	OCT.	NOV.	DEC.	YEAR
Connecticut													
Bridgeport	13.1	13.8	13.6	13.0	11.8	10.5	9.9	10.0	11.1	11.9	12.9	13.0	12.0
Bradley International Airport	9.7	10.0	10.4	10.7	9.6	8.5	7.8	7.7	7.7	8.2	8.9	9.1	9.0
New Haven	8.3	8.5	8.8	8.4	7.4	6.6	6.3	6.4	7.0	7.4	8.1	8.3	7.6
Maine													
Caribou	12.4	12.0	12.9	11.7	11.4	10.4	9.8	9.3	10.4	10.9	11.1	11.5	11.2
Eastport	13.5	13.3	12.6	11.4	9.7	8.4	7.5	7.4	8.6	10.7	12.3	12.7	10.7
Portland	9.2	9.6	10.0	10.0	9.2	8.2	7.7	7.5	7.8	8.5	8.8	9.0	8.8
Massachusetts													
Blue Hill Observatory	17.4	17.3	17.4	16.6	14.7	13.8	13.0	12.6	13.5	15.2	16.4	16.8	15.4
Boston	14.4	14.4	14.1	13.5	12.3	11.4	10.9	10.9	11.5	12.3	13.2	14.0	12.7
Nantucket	14.7	15.2	15.2	14.6	13.0	12.0	11.0	10.9	11.8	12.9	13.4	14.1	13.2
Worcester	12.7	12.3	11.8	11.5	10.7	9.3	8.7	8.6	9.0	9.8	10.6	11.4	10.5
New Hampshire													
Concord	7.4	8.0	8.2	7.9	7.1	6.3	5.6	5.3	5.4	5.9	6.6	7.0	6.7
Mt. Washington	44.3	44.8	41.7	36.6	30.3	27.5	24.9	25.2	28.6	33.4	38.5	44.1	35.1
Rhode Island													
Providence	11.7	12.0	12.4	12.5	11.2	10.1	9.6	9.6	9.7	9.8	10.7	11.2	10.9
Vermont													
Burlington	9.6	9.4	9.2	9.3	8.8	8.2	7.8	7.4	8.0	8.6	9.5	9.7	8.8
New York													
Albany	9.8	10.3	10.5	10.4	9.0	8.1	7.3	6.9	7.3	7.9	8.9	9.1	8.8
New York City	10.9	10.9	11.1	10.5	8.9	8.1	7.7	7.7	8.2	9.0	10.0	10.4	9.5

WIND SPEED: MPH, KNOTS, AND METERS PER SECOND

mph	knots	m/s	mph	knots	m/s
1	0.9	0.4	56	48.6	25.0
2	1.7	0.9	57	49.5	25.5
3	2.6	1.3	58	50.4	25.9
4	3.5	1.8	59	51.2	26.4
5	4.3	2.2	60	52.1	26.8
6	5.2	2.7	61	53.0	27.3
7	6.1	3.1	62	53.8	27.7
8	6.9	3.6	63	54.7	28.2
9	7.8	4.0	64	55.6	28.6
10	8.7	4.5	65	56.4	29.1
11	9.6	4.9	66	57.3	29.5
12	10.4	5.4	67	58.2	30.0
13	11.3	5.8	68	59.1	30.4
14	12.2	6.3	69	59.9	30.8
15	13.0	6.7	70	60.8	31.3
16	13.9	7.2	71	61.7	31.7
17	14.8	7.6	72	62.5	32.2
18	15.6	8.0	73	63.4	32.6
19	16.5	8.5	74	64.3	33.1
20	17.4	8.9	75	65.1	33.5
21	18.2	9.4	76	66.0	34.0
22	19.1	9.8	77	66.9	34.4
23	20.0	10.3	78	67.7	34.9
24	20.8	10.7	79	68.6	35.3
25	21.7	11.2	80	69.5	35.8
26	22.6	11.6	81	70.3	36.2
27	23.4	12.1	82	71.2	36.7
28	24.3	12.5	83	72.1	37.1
29	25.2	13.0	84	72.9	37.6
30	26.1	13.4	85	73.8	38.0
31	26.9	13.9	86	74.7	38.4
32	27.8	14.3	87	75.5	38.9
33	28.7	14.8	88	76.4	39.3
34	29.5	15.2	89	77.3	39.8
35	30.4	15.6	90	78.2	40.2
36	31.3	16.1	91	79.0	40.7
37	32.1	16.5	92	79.9	41.1
38	33.0	17.0	93	80.8	41.6
39	33.9	17.4	94	81.6	42.0
40	34.7	17.9	95	82.5	42.5
41	35.6	18.3	96	83.4	42.9
42	36.5	18.8	97	84.2	43.4
43	37.3	19.2	98	85.1	43.8
44	38.2	19.7	99	86.0	44.3
45	39.1	20.1	100	86.8	44.7
46	39.9	20.6	110	95.5	49.2
47	40.8	21.0	120	104.2	53.6
48	41.7	21.5	130	112.9	58.1
49	42.6	21.9	140	121.6	62.6
50	43.4	22.4	150	130.3	67.1
51	44.3	22.8	160	138.9	71.5
52	45.2	23.2	170	147.6	76.0
53	46.0	23.7	180	156.3	80.5
54	46.9	24.1	190	165.0	84.9
55	47.8	24.6	200	173.7	89.4

EXTREMES OF ATMOSPHERIC PRESSURE (INCHES & MILLIBARS)

STATION & PERIOD	MAXIMUM in	mb	DATE	MINIMUM in	mb	DATE
Connecticut						
Hartford 1905	31.06	1051.8	2/1/1920	28.04	949.5	9/21/1938
New Haven 1873	31.04	1051.1	12/25/1949*	28.11	951.9	9/21/1938
Maine						
Caribou 1938	31.13	1054.2	1/21/1949	28.17	954.0	12/2/1942
Eastport 1873	31.04	1051.1	2/1/1920	28.24	956.3	12/16/1916
Portland 1871	31.09	1052.8	2/1/1920	28.40	961.7	12/2/1942
Massachusetts						
Boston 1871	31.06	1051.8	12/25/1949	28.45	963.4	3/7/1932
Nantucket 1887	31.02	1050.5	12/25/1949	28.18	954.3	9/11/1954
New Hampshire						
Concord 1903	31.09	1052.8	12/25/1949	28.45	963.4	12/2/1942
Rhode Island						
Block Island 1881	31.00	1049.8	12/25/1949	28.20	955.0	3/7/1932
Providence 1905	31.04	1051.1	12/25/1949	28.38	961.1	3/7/1932
Vermont						
Burlington 1907	31.12	1053.8	1/31/1920	28.28	957.7	1/3/1913
Northfield 1887–1943	31.14	1054.5	1/31/1920	28.35	960.0	1/3/1913
New York						
Albany 1874	31.10	1053.2	1/31/1920	28.46	963.8	1/3/1913
New York City 1869	31.06	1051.8	12/25/1949	28.38	961.1	3/1/1914

* Also in earlier years.

PRECIPITATION: CONVERSION OF INCHES TO MILLIMETERS

Inches	Millimeters	Inches	Millimeters	Inches	Millimeters	Inches	Millimeters
0.10	2.54	2.00	50.80	3.90	99.06	13.00	330.20
0.20	5.08	2.10	53.34	4.00	101.60	14.00	355.60
0.30	7.62	2.20	55.88	4.10	104.14	15.00	381.00
0.40	10.16	2.30	58.42	4.20	106.68	16.00	406.40
0.50	12.70	2.40	60.96	4.30	109.22	17.00	431.80
0.60	15.24	2.50	63.50	4.40	111.76	18.00	457.20
0.70	17.78	2.60	66.04	4.50	114.30	19.00	482.60
0.80	20.32	2.70	68.58	4.60	116.84	20.00	508.00
0.90	22.86	2.80	71.12	4.70	119.38	25.00	635.00
1.00	25.40	2.90	73.66	4.80	121.92	30.00	762.00
1.10	27.94	3.00	76.20	4.90	124.46	40.00	1016.00
1.20	30.48	3.10	78.74	5.00	127.00	50.00	1270.00
1.30	33.02	3.20	81.28	6.00	152.40	60.00	1524.00
1.40	35.56	3.30	83.82	7.00	177.80	70.00	1778.00
1.50	38.10	3.40	86.36	8.00	203.20	80.00	2032.00
1.60	40.64	3.50	88.90	9.00	228.60	90.00	2286.00
1.70	43.18	3.60	91.44	10.00	254.00	100.00	2540.00
1.80	45.72	3.70	93.98	11.00	279.40		
1.90	48.26	3.80	96.52	12.00	304.80		

EXTREMES OF PRECIPITATION (INCHES & *MILLIMETERS*)

STATION & PERIOD		GREATEST IN 24 HOURS	GREATEST MONTH	LEAST MONTH	GREATEST YEAR	LEAST YEAR
Connecticut						
Bridgeport 1894–	in	6.89 6/18–19/1972	18.77 7/1897	.07 6/1949	73.93 1972	23.03 1964
	mm	175	477	2	1878	585
Hartford 1900–		12.12 8/18–19/1955	21.87 8/1955	.18 10/1924	64.55 1972	29.45 1965
		308	556	5	1640	748
New Haven 1873–		8.73 8/8–9/1874	17.08 7/1899	.12 6/1949	60.26 1888	27.68 1965
		222	434	3	1531	703
Maine						
Caribou 1939–		6.23 9/11–12/1954	8.45 5/1958	.12 1/1944	51.11 1954	27.92 1966
		158	215	3	1298	709
Eastport 1873–		5.48 5/17/1881	13.22 5/1881	.13 5/1911	64.53 1883	21.24 1924
		139	336	3	1639	540
Portland 1872–		7.71 10/6–7/1962	12.29 1/1935	.09 10/1924	59.69 1920	25.27 1941
		196	312	2	1516	642
Massachusetts						
Boston 1871–		8.40 8/18–19/1955	17.05 8/1955	T 3/1915	65.63 1878	23.71 1965
		213	433	T	1667	602
Nantucket 1887–		6.53 5/24–25/1967	12.92 8/1946	.01 6/1947	60.39 1958	25.31 1965
		166	328	1	1534	643
Worcester 1893–		7.54 10/12–13/1895	18.68 8/1955	.04 3/1915	71.69 1972	27.92 1941
		192	475	1	1821	709
New Hampshire						
Concord 1853–		5.97 9/16–17/1932	10.97 9/1888	T 3/1915	54.33 1888	24.17 1965
		152	279	T	1380	614
Mt. Washington 1932–		10.38 2/10–11/1970	25.56 2/1969	.75 10/1947	130.14 1969	53.30 1941
		264	649	19	3306	1354
Rhode Island						
Block Island 1881–		6.22 7/12–13/1910	11.51 9/1961	T 6/1957	63.15 1884	24.08 1965
		158	292	T	1604	612
Providence 1905–		6.63 10/5–6/1962	12.24 8/1946	.04 6/1949	65.06 1972	25.44 1965
		168	311	1	1653	646
Vermont						
Burlington 1884–		4.49 11/3–4/1927	11.54 8/1955	.15 10/1924	46.28 1973	22.62 1914
		114	293	4	1176	575
New York						
Albany 1826–		4.75 10/8–9/1903	13.48 10/1869	.08 1/1860	56.78 1871	21.55 1964
		121	342	2	1442	547
New York City 1869–		11.17 10/8–9/1903	16.85 9/1882	.02 6/1949	67.03 1972	26.09 1965
		284	428	1	1703	663

T—Trace, or less than .01 in (0.025 mm)

PREPARED!
For this changeable winter weather.

TEMPERATURE: CONVERSION OF FAHRENHEIT TO CELSIUS

°F	°C	°F	°C	°F	°C	°F	°C	°F	°C
130	54.44	79	26.11	46	7.78	13	−10.56	−20	−28.89
120	48.89	78	25.56	45	7.22	12	−11.11	−21	−29.44
110	43.33	77	25.00	44	6.67	11	−11.67	−22	−30.00
109	42.78	76	24.44	43	6.11	10	−12.22	−23	−30.56
108	42.22	75	23.89	42	5.56	9	−12.78	−24	−31.11
107	41.67	74	23.33	41	5.00	8	−13.33	−25	−31.67
106	41.11	73	22.78	40	4.44	7	−13.89	−26	−32.22
105	40.56	72	22.22	39	3.89	6	−14.44	−27	−32.78
104	40.00	71	21.67	38	3.33	5	−15.00	−28	−33.33
103	39.44	70	21.11	37	2.78	4	−15.56	−29	−33.89
102	38.89	69	20.56	36	2.22	3	−16.11	−30	−34.44
101	38.33	68	20.00	35	1.67	2	−16.67	−31	−35.00
100	37.78	67	19.44	34	1.11	1	−17.22	−32	−35.56
99	37.22	66	18.89	33	0.56	0	−17.78	−33	−36.11
98	36.67	65	18.33	32	0.00	−1	−18.33	−34	−36.67
97	36.11	64	17.78	31	−0.56	−2	−18.89	−35	−37.22
96	35.56	63	17.22	30	−1.11	−3	−19.44	−36	−37.78
95	35.00	62	16.67	29	−1.67	−4	−20.00	−37	−38.33
94	34.44	61	16.11	28	−2.22	−5	−20.56	−38	−38.89
93	33.89	60	15.56	27	−2.78	−6	−21.11	−39	−39.44
92	33.33	59	15.00	26	−3.33	−7	−21.67	−40	−40.00
91	32.78	58	14.44	25	−3.89	−8	−22.22	−41	−40.56
90	32.22	57	13.89	24	−4.44	−9	−22.78	−42	−41.11
89	31.67	56	13.33	23	−5.00	−10	−23.33	−43	−41.67
88	31.11	55	12.78	22	−5.56	−11	−23.89	−44	−42.22
87	30.56	54	12.22	21	−6.11	−12	−24.44	−45	−42.78
86	30.00	53	11.67	20	−6.67	−13	−25.00	−46	−43.33
85	29.44	52	11.11	19	−7.22	−14	−25.56	−47	−43.89
84	28.89	51	10.56	18	−7.78	−15	−26.11	−48	−44.44
83	28.33	50	10.00	17	−8.33	−16	−26.67	−49	−45.00
82	27.78	49	9.44	16	−8.89	−17	−27.22	−50	−45.56
81	27.22	48	8.89	15	−9.44	−18	−27.78		
80	26.67	47	8.33	14	−10.00	−19	−28.33		

CLIMATOLOGICAL NORMALS: MEAN
MONTHLY TEMPERATURE (FAHRENHEIT)

STATION	JAN.	FEB.	MAR.	APR.	MAY	JUNE	JULY	AUG.	SEPT.	OCT.	NOV.	DEC.	AVERAGE
Connecticut													
Bridgeport	30.2	30.9	37.9	48.4	58.3	67.9	73.8	72.7	66.5	56.8	46.0	33.8	51.9
Falls Village	23.8	25.8	34.4	46.4	57.0	65.8	70.2	68.2	61.2	50.8	39.8	27.1	47.5
Hartford (Brainard Field)	26.4	28.4	36.8	48.2	58.4	67.7	72.7	70.6	63.3	53.3	42.2	29.7	49.8
Middletown	27.5	29.2	36.9	48.4	58.4	67.6	72.6	70.4	63.2	53.9	43.3	31.1	50.2
New Haven (Airport)	28.9	30.2	37.4	47.8	57.2	66.8	72.3	70.9	64.5	54.7	44.0	32.2	50.6
Norfolk	20.4	21.3	30.1	43.1	54.1	63.0	67.6	65.6	58.6	48.1	36.9	24.1	44.4
Norwalk	28.3	29.8	37.5	48.5	58.0	67.3	72.4	70.8	64.1	54.0	43.3	31.3	50.4
Storrs	25.3	26.8	34.5	45.9	56.0	65.1	69.9	68.0	61.2	52.1	41.2	28.6	47.9
Westbrook	28.0	29.5	36.5	46.6	55.8	64.8	70.0	68.8	62.5	53.0	42.7	30.8	49.1
Windsor Locks	24.8	26.8	35.6	47.7	58.3	67.8	72.7	70.4	62.8	52.6	41.3	28.2	49.1
(Bradley International Airport)													
Maine													
Bar Harbor	23.7	24.4	32.8	42.7	52.7	61.0	66.4	65.5	58.7	50.2	40.3	27.8	45.5
Caribou	10.7	12.9	23.6	36.7	49.7	59.6	64.9	62.3	54.1	43.8	31.4	16.1	39.8
Eastport	22.6	23.5	31.2	40.2	48.9	56.4	61.8	61.9	56.8	48.9	39.6	27.1	43.2
Gardiner	19.4	21.0	30.8	42.3	53.4	62.8	68.3	66.4	58.6	48.8	37.8	23.9	44.5
Greenville	12.5	14.4	24.7	37.1	49.5	59.6	64.4	62.2	54.3	44.4	32.4	17.9	39.5
Houlton	13.9	16.1	26.9	39.0	51.8	61.4	67.1	64.4	56.1	45.9	33.8	19.0	41.3
Lewiston	20.4	22.3	31.6	43.1	54.5	64.4	70.0	68.2	60.3	50.3	38.4	25.2	45.7
Madison	17.2	19.1	29.5	41.6	53.2	62.7	67.9	66.0	58.3	47.9	36.2	21.8	43.5
Old Town	15.6	16.9	27.6	39.8	51.1	60.8	66.8	64.8	56.2	45.8	35.0	20.5	41.8
Portland	21.5	22.9	31.8	42.7	52.7	62.2	68.0	66.4	58.7	49.1	38.6	25.7	45.0
(International Airport)													
Presque Isle	12.6	14.7	25.3	38.2	51.1	61.0	66.1	63.6	55.7	45.2	32.7	17.5	40.3
Ripogenus Dam	12.2	13.2	24.2	37.3	49.8	60.5	65.8	63.9	56.1	45.5	33.1	17.7	39.9
Rockland	23.3	24.2	32.5	42.6	52.2	61.2	66.9	65.7	58.7	49.5	39.5	27.1	45.3
Rumford	18.6	20.5	30.3	41.9	53.5	63.2	68.2	66.0	58.2	48.2	36.4	22.9	44.0
Waterville	19.3	21.3	31.5	43.6	55.0	64.3	69.6	67.8	59.7	49.6	38.0	23.8	45.3
Massachusetts													
Adams	21.0	22.2	31.6	44.4	54.7	64.4	69.0	66.6	59.4	49.2	38.2	25.3	45.5
Amherst	23.6	25.7	35.1	47.0	57.5	66.8	71.5	69.3	62.0	52.2	40.8	27.6	48.3
Blue Hill Obsy., Milton	26.2	27.5	35.2	46.3	56.6	65.5	71.1	69.4	62.4	53.2	42.3	29.7	48.8
Boston (Logan Airport)	29.2	30.4	38.1	48.6	58.6	68.0	73.3	71.3	64.5	55.4	45.2	33.0	51.3
Fitchburg	24.7	25.9	34.9	46.7	57.5	67.0	72.3	70.1	62.6	52.6	41.2	28.4	48.7
Framingham	26.0	27.4	36.7	48.1	58.6	67.8	73.1	70.9	63.4	53.2	42.5	29.7	49.8
Hoosac Tunnel	20.3	22.1	31.4	43.8	54.5	64.0	68.4	65.9	59.1	49.4	37.6	24.5	45.1
Lowell	26.4	28.2	36.7	48.2	59.0	68.4	73.7	71.3	63.8	53.8	42.4	29.9	50.2
Nantucket Airport	31.8	31.6	36.9	44.3	52.8	61.5	68.0	67.7	62.5	54.5	45.9	35.7	49.4
New Bedford	31.4	32.2	38.9	48.2	57.6	66.7	72.7	71.5	65.2	56.6	46.4	34.8	51.9
Plymouth	29.8	30.7	37.6	47.1	56.9	66.5	72.2	70.5	63.6	54.6	44.8	33.0	50.6
Rockport	27.8	28.7	35.6	45.1	54.6	64.0	69.7	68.3	61.5	52.6	42.8	31.6	48.5
Springfield	27.1	29.1	37.8	49.8	59.9	68.7	73.6	71.7	64.4	54.8	43.4	30.4	50.9
Stockbridge	22.1	23.8	32.6	44.8	55.0	63.3	67.6	65.4	58.7	49.4	38.9	26.2	45.7
Worcester	23.6	25.1	33.3	45.3	55.8	65.1	70.1	68.1	61.0	51.6	39.9	27.2	47.1
Airport													
New Hampshire													
Bethlehem	15.8	17.9	27.9	40.8	52.8	62.2	66.5	64.3	57.0	46.9	34.4	19.9	42.2
Concord	20.6	22.6	32.3	44.2	55.1	64.7	69.7	67.2	59.5	49.3	38.0	24.8	45.6
Durham	22.8	24.8	33.5	44.4	54.6	64.0	69.2	67.0	59.8	50.0	39.2	26.6	46.3
First Connecticut Lake	9.6	10.7	21.1	35.2	47.8	59.0	61.6	60.2	53.0	43.1	31.0	15.5	37.3
Franklin	20.5	22.4	32.2	44.4	55.6	65.5	70.3	68.0	60.4	49.8	38.0	24.5	46.0
Hanover	18.1	20.7	31.0	43.6	54.9	64.6	69.1	67.0	59.4	48.8	36.7	22.8	44.7
Keene	22.0	24.4	33.6	45.8	56.6	65.8	70.2	68.0	60.8	50.5	39.0	25.9	46.9
Lakeport	20.4	22.0	31.7	44.0	55.7	65.4	70.3	68.2	60.4	50.1	38.3	25.0	46.0
Manchester	22.2	23.9	33.1	44.8	55.6	65.0	70.0	67.3	59.9	49.9	39.2	26.6	46.5
Mount Washington	5.7	5.0	11.8	22.7	34.4	44.7	48.8	47.0	41.2	31.5	20.6	8.9	26.9
Nashua	22.8	24.4	33.6	45.1	55.5	65.0	70.1	67.7	60.1	50.2	39.2	26.6	46.7
Pinkham Notch	16.0	17.2	26.2	37.9	49.8	59.1	63.3	61.3	54.4	45.2	33.1	19.5	40.3
Rhode Island													
Block Island	31.4	31.3	36.9	45.3	53.8	63.1	69.5	69.2	63.8	55.3	46.0	35.2	50.1
Kingston	28.3	29.4	36.3	46.1	55.2	64.4	69.9	68.6	62.0	52.7	42.7	31.2	48.9
Providence (Warwick)	28.4	29.4	36.9	47.3	56.9	66.4	72.1	70.4	63.4	53.7	43.3	31.5	50.0
T.F. Green State Airport													
Vermont													
Burlington	16.8	18.6	29.1	43.0	54.8	65.2	69.8	67.4	59.3	48.8	37.0	22.6	44.4
Cavendish	17.9	20.1	30.0	42.8	54.8	63.7	67.8	65.4	57.9	47.6	35.9	22.3	43.9
Chelsea	14.7	16.5	27.2	40.6	51.7	61.7	66.2	63.7	56.4	46.2	34.7	19.7	41.6
Cornwall	19.2	21.5	31.7	45.3	56.5	66.1	70.7	68.4	61.0	50.6	38.6	24.2	46.2
Dorset	19.8	21.9	31.0	43.5	53.8	63.0	66.9	64.7	58.1	48.6	37.5	24.2	44.4
Newport	13.8	16.0	26.8	40.3	52.7	62.7	67.0	64.7	57.1	46.9	34.3	19.2	41.8
Rutland	20.6	22.9	32.5	45.2	56.0	65.3	69.3	67.0	60.1	50.4	39.2	25.6	46.2
St. Johnsbury	16.9	19.5	30.0	43.0	55.1	64.9	69.1	66.8	59.3	48.8	36.6	21.7	44.3
Woodstock	17.0	18.7	29.5	42.7	54.1	63.6	68.1	65.7	58.3	47.4	36.3	21.8	43.6

CLIMATOLOGICAL NORMALS: MEAN
MONTHLY PRECIPITATION (INCHES)

STATION	JAN.	FEB.	MAR.	APR.	MAY	JUNE	JULY	AUG.	SEPT.	OCT.	NOV.	DEC.	AVERAGE
Connecticut													
Bridgeport	2.71	2.71	3.49	3.39	3.57	2.56	3.44	3.80	2.88	2.79	3.83	3.44	38.61
Falls Village	2.70	2.43	2.97	3.75	3.63	4.08	3.85	3.74	3.55	3.03	4.03	3.41	41.17
Hartford (Brainard Field)	3.08	2.99	3.60	3.52	3.41	3.15	3.71	3.51	3.01	2.84	4.20	3.92	40.94
Middletown	3.36	3.35	4.18	4.14	4.07	3.36	3.78	3.95	3.95	3.42	5.05	4.04	47.01
New Haven (Airport)	3.21	3.09	3.97	3.72	3.67	2.73	3.13	3.82	3.10	3.05	4.25	4.07	41.81
Norfolk	3.78	3.71	4.44	4.28	4.06	4.43	4.08	4.21	4.13	3.76	5.05	4.70	50.63
Norwalk	3.03	2.99	4.24	3.94	4.18	3.18	4.02	4.30	3.57	3.40	4.42	4.03	45.30
Storrs	2.96	2.78	3.64	3.71	3.90	3.20	3.81	4.16	3.30	3.17	4.46	3.83	42.92
Westbrook	3.44	3.22	4.10	4.02	3.98	2.79	3.33	4.22	3.24	3.16	4.84	4.25	44.59
West Hartford	2.94	3.07	3.93	3.82	3.85	3.80	3.73	3.98	3.69	3.37	4.68	4.02	44.88
Windsor Locks	3.28	3.17	3.82	3.75	3.50	3.53	3.41	3.94	3.55	3.03	4.33	4.06	43.37
(Bradley International Airport)													
Maine													
Bar Harbor	4.24	4.16	3.90	3.65	4.26	2.90	2.88	2.99	3.75	4.27	6.21	5.18	48.39
Caribou	2.04	2.11	2.20	2.42	2.96	3.41	3.98	3.78	3.49	3.31	3.50	2.62	35.82
Eastport	3.56	3.51	3.00	3.18	3.36	2.98	2.94	2.91	3.16	3.39	5.09	4.06	41.14
Gardiner	3.18	3.44	3.37	3.66	3.57	3.19	3.30	2.87	2.98	3.74	5.43	4.03	42.76
Greenville	2.78	3.04	3.09	3.20	3.49	3.86	4.02	3.78	3.49	3.81	4.78	3.70	43.04
Houlton	2.48	2.50	2.41	2.54	2.88	2.95	3.35	3.34	3.05	3.28	3.96	3.39	36.13
Lewiston	3.48	3.71	3.66	3.52	3.35	3.23	3.06	2.98	3.06	3.50	5.40	4.25	43.20
Old Town	3.13	3.28	3.02	3.05	3.39	3.13	2.90	3.01	3.34	3.57	4.93	3.95	40.70
Portland	3.38	3.52	3.60	3.34	3.33	3.10	2.61	2.60	3.09	3.31	4.86	4.06	40.80
(International Airport)													
Presque Isle	2.16	2.13	2.13	2.26	2.93	3.29	3.89	3.59	3.38	3.27	3.47	2.59	35.09
Ripogenus Dam	2.41	2.55	2.42	2.80	3.16	3.70	4.14	3.83	3.19	3.75	4.04	2.97	38.96
Rockland	4.15	4.15	4.02	3.86	3.66	2.99	3.17	2.88	3.54	3.83	5.83	4.70	46.78
Waterville	2.65	2.79	2.75	3.04	3.24	3.04	3.12	3.19	3.04	3.53	4.85	3.61	38.85
Massachusetts													
Adams	2.66	2.41	3.02	4.03	4.10	4.01	4.52	3.26	3.84	3.07	4.29	3.33	42.54
Amherst	2.76	2.68	3.37	3.40	3.56	3.85	3.87	3.67	3.36	2.82	3.82	3.48	40.64
Blue Hill Obsy., Milton	4.12	3.97	4.51	3.64	3.62	3.15	2.95	3.83	3.65	3.62	5.06	4.70	46.82
Boston (Logan Airport)	3.69	3.54	4.01	3.49	3.47	3.19	2.74	3.46	3.16	3.02	4.51	4.24	42.52
Fitchburg	3.58	3.32	3.91	3.69	3.69	3.77	3.30	3.05	3.38	3.29	4.65	3.96	43.59
Framingham	3.59	3.41	3.96	3.59	3.33	3.32	3.31	3.53	3.42	2.94	4.66	4.22	43.28
Hoosac Tunnel	3.25	3.10	3.62	4.03	4.27	3.86	4.10	3.36	3.81	3.28	4.49	3.95	45.12
Hyannis	3.65	3.65	3.82	3.88	3.68	2.67	2.57	4.29	3.28	3.38	4.67	4.05	43.59
Lowell	3.45	3.15	3.77	3.39	3.34	3.04	3.15	3.21	3.10	3.09	4.65	3.91	41.25
Nantucket Airport	4.02	3.93	4.17	3.64	3.41	2.32	2.87	3.89	3.34	3.26	4.34	4.16	43.35
New Bedford	3.55	3.53	3.87	3.41	3.24	2.22	2.01	4.04	2.76	2.81	4.25	4.08	39.77
Plymouth	3.65	3.62	3.94	3.60	3.60	2.66	2.76	4.34	3.28	3.55	4.87	4.34	44.24
Rockport	4.15	3.90	3.90	3.38	3.58	2.89	2.73	3.13	3.17	3.12	4.72	4.55	43.22
Springfield	2.90	2.79	3.55	3.71	3.74	3.74	3.63	3.99	3.54	2.94	4.13	3.91	42.57
Stockbridge	2.88	2.67	3.13	3.75	3.63	3.92	4.41	3.42	3.78	2.90	3.95	3.55	41.99
Worcester Airport	3.35	3.18	3.85	3.83	3.97	3.60	3.62	4.19	3.52	3.54	4.68	3.93	45.24
New Hampshire													
Bethlehem	1.76	1.80	2.06	2.75	3.52	4.16	3.93	4.18	3.43	3.04	3.32	2.65	38.60
Concord	2.67	2.45	2.77	2.92	3.02	3.35	3.14	2.89	3.06	2.68	3.96	3.26	36.17
Durham	3.32	3.13	3.53	3.33	3.48	3.04	3.33	3.17	3.16	3.30	4.89	3.87	41.55
Franklin	2.86	2.97	3.03	3.18	3.73	3.50	3.39	3.03	3.22	3.07	4.38	3.62	39.98
Hanover	2.54	2.40	2.62	2.89	3.42	2.93	3.71	3.02	3.05	2.76	3.51	2.91	35.76
Keene	2.84	2.63	3.02	3.22	3.64	3.83	3.59	3.16	3.40	2.71	3.88	3.26	39.18
Lakeport	2.84	2.76	3.15	3.12	3.64	3.64	3.41	3.04	3.57	3.17	4.51	3.49	40.40
Manchester	3.04	2.79	3.15	3.30	3.52	3.23	3.48	3.20	3.10	2.81	4.40	3.63	39.65
Mount Washington	5.12	6.51	5.60	5.46	5.84	6.50	6.77	7.19	6.36	6.12	7.67	7.03	76.17
Nashua	3.23	3.04	3.41	3.35	3.51	3.30	3.35	3.10	3.18	3.24	4.58	3.75	41.04
Pinkham Notch	4.01	4.37	4.56	4.24	4.67	4.77	4.58	4.40	4.44	4.92	6.83	4.95	56.74
Rhode Island													
Block Island	3.41	3.32	3.88	3.51	3.25	2.20	2.74	3.86	3.00	2.88	4.35	4.11	40.51
Greenville	3.36	3.37	4.04	3.87	3.86	3.24	3.46	4.08	3.83	3.70	5.46	4.30	46.57
Kingston	3.66	3.37	4.23	3.76	3.75	2.61	2.92	4.20	3.46	3.28	4.85	4.16	44.26
Providence (Warwick)	3.52	3.45	3.99	3.72	3.49	2.65	2.85	3.90	3.26	3.27	4.52	4.13	42.75
T.F. Green State Airport													
Vermont													
Burlington	1.74	1.68	1.93	2.62	3.01	3.46	3.54	3.72	3.05	2.74	2.86	2.19	32.54
Cavendish	2.96	3.05	3.40	3.52	3.76	3.68	3.64	3.12	3.24	3.27	4.07	3.48	41.19
Chelsea	2.31	2.21	2.45	2.88	3.46	3.38	3.81	3.22	3.29	2.98	3.39	2.73	36.11
Dorset	3.00	2.78	3.30	4.05	4.24	4.25	4.43	3.79	3.72	3.60	4.21	3.43	44.80
Newport	2.29	2.40	2.34	2.99	3.07	3.80	3.77	3.91	3.38	3.14	3.36	2.79	37.24
Rutland	2.09	1.91	2.19	2.71	3.42	3.53	3.78	3.24	3.33	2.64	3.08	2.35	34.27
St. Johnsbury	2.19	2.23	2.31	2.77	3.17	3.70	3.60	3.25	2.99	3.05	3.27	2.80	35.33
Woodstock	2.81	2.59	3.02	3.16	3.68	3.33	3.52	3.16	3.20	2.97	3.79	3.32	38.55

PUBLIC WEATHER INFORMATION SOURCES

VHF-FM RADIO: GENERAL AND MARINE WEATHER

CONTINUOUS WEATHER BROADCASTS BY THE NATIONAL WEATHER SERVICE

The National Oceanic and Atmospheric Administration (NOAA) of the Department of Commerce has VHF-FM broadcasts that provide continuous weather information to receivers over an area of about 40 miles radius. Special information is provided for the general public, motorists, campers, sportsmen, and boatsmen on inland and offshore waters. The emphasis is on public safety. When dangerous weather threatens, routine transmissions are interrupted and an emergency warning is broadcast.

NOAA VHF-FM radio weather broadcasts are transmitted in plain voice on frequencies of either 162.55 KHz or 162.40 KHz from National Weather Service offices, 24 hours a day. Content of broadcasts is somewhat curtailed between 11:00 P.M. and 5:00 A.M. The taped messages are repeated every four to six minutes and routinely revised every three to six hours. They are amended as needed to match changing weather.

The broadcasts can usually be received at distances of 20 to 40 miles from the transmitting antenna site, depending on terrain and quality of receiver employed. Where transmitting antennas are on high ground, the range is somewhat greater, reaching 60 miles or more. Reception may vary in strength of signal during 24 hours.

The frequencies 162.55 and 162.40 MHz require narrow band FM receivers of 5 kilohertz deviation. In selecting a suitable receiver, special attention should be paid to the manufacturer's rating of the receiver's sensitivity. Generally speaking, a receiver with a sensitivity of 1 microvolt or less should pick up a broadcast at a distance of about 40 to 50 miles depending upon antenna height and terrain. Many low-cost AM-FM receivers are on the market with a special weather band that meets the above requirements.

As an added refinement, the transmitters can turn on specially designed radio receivers by means of a tone signal. This is transmitted at 1050 Hertz for three to five seconds before announcements of hazardous weather conditions. The tone signal alerts schools, hospitals, churches, and other places of assembly, public utilities units, emergency forces, and news media to be ready for critically important weather messages.

CITY	CALL	FRE-QUENCY
Boston, Mass.	KHB–35	162.40
Burlington, Vt.	KIG–60	162.40
Ellsworth, Maine	KEC–93	162.40
Hyannis, Mass.	KEC–73	162.55
New London, Conn.	KHB–47	162.40
New York, N.Y.	KWO–35	162.55
Portland, Maine	KDO–95	162.55

The contents of the broadcasts vary but in general contain the following information:

1. Description of the weather patterns affecting the eastern United States and coastal waters.
2. Regional and state forecasts with outlook for the third day.
3. Marine forecasts and warnings for coastal waters. Fishermen's forecast for Georges Bank and Nantucket Shoals.
4. Weather observations for selected National Weather Service and Coast Guard stations.
5. Radar summaries and reports.
6. Local weather observations and forecasts.
7. Special bulletins and summaries concerning severe weather.
8. Notices of local interest to mariners.

TELEVISION: AVIATION WEATHER

The National Weather Service and the Federal Aviation Administration cooperate in producing Aviation Weather over the facilities of the Public Broadcasting Service. Both national and regional weather situations and forecasts are discussed. The program is intended to inform pilots about the prospects for weekend flying weather, though much matter of general interest to the public is included. The programs are presented on Thursday and Friday evenings, usually at 7:00 and 11:30. Times may vary according to localities. The following are the PBS stations carrying the program in New England:

Connecticut

Bridgeport	WEDW	49
Hartford	WEDH	24
Norwich	WEDN	53

Maine

Augusta	WCBB	10
Calais	WMED	13
Orono	WMEB	12
Presque Isle	WMEM	10

Massachusetts

Boston	WGBX	44
Springfield	WGBY	57

New Hampshire

Berlin	WEDB	40
Durham	WENH	11
Hanover	WHED	15
Keene	WEKW	52
Littleton	WLED	49

Vermont

Burlington	WETK	33
Rutland	WVER	28
St. Johnsbury	WVTB	20
Windsor	WVTA	41

AMATEUR RADIO: GENERAL WEATHER

NEW ENGLAND WEATHER NET (AMATEUR RADIOPHONE): MIDDLE BAND

An amateur radio network, consisting of a membership of about 50 stations, gathers weather reports from 5:45 A.M. to 6:30 A.M., Monday to Saturday, in voice broadcasts on 3905 KHz. Net control station gives a summary of those participating that day at 6:30 A.M., which lasts for five to six minutes. Most of the stations are located in or about New England.

144

LONG-WAVE RADIO: AVIATION WEATHER

Air Navigation Stations in New England and the Northeast

Burlington, Vt.	BTV	323	44°28′ 73°09′	Continuous broadcast
Boston, Mass.	BOS	382	42°23′23″N 70°59′10″W	Continuous broadcast
Westfield, Mass.	BAF	230	42°15′42″N 72°41′49″W	15 min. past hour
Bangor, Maine	BGR	239	44°50′35″N 68°50′55″W	15 min. past hour
Millinocket, Maine	MLT	344	45°38′51″N 68°38′30″W	Continuous broadcast
Newark, N.J.	EWR	379	40°40′53″N 74°11′30″W	Continuous broadcast

Content:

Brief synopsis, flight precautions, and route forecasts; then airport weather: sky condition, ceiling, visibility, obstructions to vision, temperature, dew point, wind direction and speed, altimeter setting.

Airports in Boston broadcast:

Boston, Caribou, Portland, Bangor, Concord, Manchester, Hyannis, Nantucket, New Bedford, Providence, Windsor Locks (Bradley International Airport), LaGuardia, Poughkeepsie, Albany, Syracuse, Burlington, Montpelier.

Airports in Newark broadcast:

Teterboro, Islip, Newark, LaGuardia, White Plains, Cleveland, Pittsburgh, Philadelphia, Syracuse, Boston, Buffalo, Rochester, Watertown, Elmira, Bradford, Williamsport, Wilkes-Barre–Scranton, Philipsburg, Harrisburg, Atlantic City, Washington, Burlington, Albany, Erie.

(From 11:00 P.M. to 5:00 A.M. airport weather is omitted.)

TELEPHONE: LOCAL WEATHER AND FORECASTS

(NWS means broadcast originated either live or on tape from an office of the National Weather Service)

STATE AND CITY	NUMBER	TYPE OF MESSAGE
Connecticut		
Bridgeport	(203) 378-2344	NWS, 24 hours daily
	(203) 384-2711	Recorded, 24 hours daily
Hartford	(203) 623-3888	Recorded, 24 hours daily
New Haven	(203) 722-0410	Recorded, 24 hours daily
Maine		
Caribou	(207) 496-8931	NWS
Portland	(207) 775-7781	Recorded, marine and general, 24 hours
	(207) 773-0352	NWS, 8:00 A.M.–5:00 P.M., Mon.–Fri.
	(207) 775-3131	Ext. 552, 8:00 A.M.–5:00 P.M., Mon.–Fri.
New Hampshire		
Concord	(603) 225-5191	NWS
Massachusetts		
Boston	(617) 567-4670	NWS, 24 hours
	(617) 569-3700	Recorded, marine and general
	(617) 569-3701	Recorded, marine and general
	(617) 936-1212	New England Report
	(617) 569-1773	Pilot weather
Rhode Island		
Providence	(401) 738-1211	Recorded, general
	(401) 737-5100	Recorded, general
	(401) 737-6820	May 15–Oct. 15, marine
Block Island	(401) 466-5531	6:30 A.M.–2:45 P.M., Thurs.–Mon. 7:30 A.M.–3:45 P.M., Apr. 30–Oct. 29
Vermont		
Burlington	(802) 862-2475	9:00 A.M.–4:00 P.M., Mon.–Sat.
New York		
New York City	(212) 971-5561	NWS
	(212) 936-1212	Recorded, general
Long Island	(516) 936-1212	Recorded, general

PUBLICATIONS

Local Climatological Data. Monthly and annual summary. National Climatic Center, Asheville, N.C. 28801. $2.55 per station. Make remittance payable to NOAA; send to Asheville. Published for the following stations: Albany, Block Island, Blue Hill Observatory (Milton, Mass.), Boston, Bridgeport, Burlington, Caribou, Concord, Hartford, Mount Washington, New York City, Portland, Providence, and Worcester. Single copies available: per individual month, $0.20 each station; annual $0.15 each station. Also available for about 300 stations in the United States.

Climatological Data. New England. Monthly and annual summary. National Climatic Center, Asheville, N.C. 28801. $4.50 per year; single copies $0.35 each month, $0.30 annual issue. Make remittance payable to NOAA; send to Asheville. Contains daily data for about 300 New England stations.

Daily Weather Maps. Weekly Series. 52 issues per year; each contains seven daily weather maps of North America. Mailed Tuesdays. $16.50 per year; single copies $0.35. Send remittance to and order from Superintendent of Documents, Government Printing Office, Washington, D.C. 20402.

Storm Data. Monthly. National Climatic Center, Asheville, N.C. 28801. $3.60 per year; single copies $0.30. Make remittance to NOAA; send to Asheville. Contains details of severe local storms throughout the United States.

Weekly Weather & Crop Bulletin. Mailed on Tuesdays. Annual subscription $5.00. Make remittance payable to NOAA; send to Agricultural Climatology Service Office, South Building Mail Unit, Department of Agriculture, Washington, D.C. 20250. Contains temperature and precipitation data for past week and brief discussion of effects on crops, for New England and for other states.

New England Crop and Livestock Reporting Service. Weekly, issued each Monday, May 1 to October 1. Contains weekly weather and crop bulletins presenting a summary of the past week's weather and table of weekly and cumulative precipitation, temperature, and growing degree-day data for about 36 New England stations. Address requests for free subscription to U.S. Department of Agriculture, Statistical Reporting Service, 1305 Post Office Building, Boston, Mass. 02109.

Weatherwise: The Magazine about Weather. A bimonthly publication containing articles on the progress of the science of meteorology and descriptions of outstanding weather events, past and current. Presents a weather map for every day of the year and a discussion of each month's main weather features. Subscription $8.00 per calendar year. Send check or money order to Weatherwise, Inc., Box 230N, Princeton, N.J. 08540.

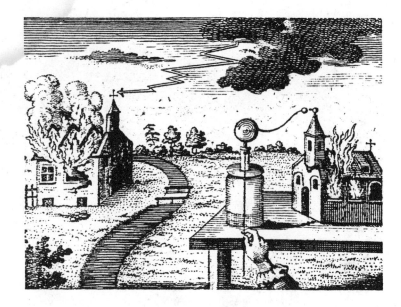

GLOSSARY

advection horizontal movement of any meteorological element, such as air, moisture, or heat.

air the mixture of gases forming the atmosphere. Dry air is composed mainly of nitrogen and oxygen, with small amounts of carbon dioxide, hydrogen, ozone, and the inert gases. Moist air contains, in addition, varying amounts of water vapor.

air mass a large body of air whose horizontal distribution of temperature and moisture is nearly uniform.

airstream a substantial body of air flowing with the general circulation [*see* circulation, below].

altimeter an instrument used to measure altitude above sea level, especially on aircraft; usually calibrated in inches of mercury, as on a barometer.

anemometer an instrument designed to measure wind speed.

anticyclone an atmospheric pressure system characterized by relatively high pressure at its center and winds blowing clockwise outward (in the Northern Hemisphere); also called high-pressure area, or high.

atmospheric pressure the weight per unit area of the total mass of air above a given point; also called barometric pressure.

backing winds shifting counterclockwise (e.g., from northeast through north to northwest); opposite of veering.

circulation the flow of air occurring within a somewhat circular wind system. General circulation is the large-scale flow characteristic of the semipermanent pressure systems; secondary circulation is flow characteristic of more temporary, migratory pressure systems.

coastal storm a cyclonic system moving along the coastal plain or just offshore in the Atlantic Ocean; it causes north to east winds over New England and is often called a northeaster.

cold front the interface or transition zone between advancing cold air and retreating warm air.

condensation the process whereby a substance changes from the vapor phase to the liquid or solid phase; the opposite of evaporation.

condensation trail a frequently observed cloudlike streamer that forms behind aircraft flying in clear, cold, humid air; also known as a contrail.

conduction transmission of heat through and by means of a material substance, as distinguished from convection, advection, and radiation.

convection the transfer of heat by movement of material bodies; especially, the thermally induced, vertical motion of air.

convergence a distribution of wind velocities that results in a net inflow of air into an area and, consequently, an increase in the vertical motion of air.

cyclogenesis the process leading to the development of a new cyclonic storm system or the intensification of a pre-existing system.

cyclone an atmospheric pressure system characterized by relatively low pressure at its center and winds blowing counterclockwise and inward (in the Northern Hemisphere); also known as a low-pressure system, or low.

deepening the decrease of pressure at the center of a storm system.

depression an area of low pressure.

dew liquid water droplets deposited on grass or other objects by condensation of water vapor from the air, usually as a result of nocturnal cooling.

dew point the temperature at which a parcel of air reaches saturation as it is cooled at constant pressure.

discontinuity a term employed in meteorology to describe the rapid variation of the gradient of an element, such as pressure or temperature at a front.

dry-bulb temperature the ordinary temperature of the air as distinguished from the wet-bulb temperature.

equinoctial storm a violent storm of wind occurring, in popular belief, when the sun crosses the equator; also known as a line storm.

evaporation the change of a substance from the liquid to the vapor or gaseous stage; the opposite of condensation.

extra-tropical cyclone an atmospheric disturbance that either originated outside the tropics or, having left the tropics, has lost the characteristics of a tropical storm.

eye of the storm a roughly circular area of comparatively light winds and fair weather found in the center of many tropical storms.

fastest mile the speed of the wind requiring the least time to move one mile past a station.

filling the increase of pressure at the center of a storm system.

foehn a warm, dry wind that is heated by compression as it descends from a mountain range.

front the interface or transition zone between two air masses of different densities and characteristics.

frontogenesis the process that leads to the formation of a front.

frost ice crystals formed on grass or other objects by the sublimation of water vapor from the air.

gale a wind speed from 32 to 63 mph, 28 to 55 knots, or 14 to 28 meters per second; it is classified as a storm if wind speed is from 64 to 72 mph and a hurricane if 73 mph or more.

glaze a sheath of transparent ice resulting from an ice storm.

graupel soft hail, consisting of white opaque grains of small diameter that have a snowlike structure.

gust a sudden brief increase in the speed of the wind. It is of a more transient character than a squall and is followed by a lull or slackening of the wind.

high a pressure system characterized by relatively high pressure at the center.

hygrometer an instrument designed to

measure atmospheric humidity.

ice needles small ice crystals suspended or falling slowly in the air at low temperatures, sometimes giving rise to halo effects.

instability a condition of the atmosphere whereby a parcel of air given an initial vertical impulse will tend to continue to move farther from its original level.

inversion a reversal of the normal decrease of temperature with increasing altitude; above the inversion level the temperature increases or decreases less rapidly.

jet stream a zone of relatively strong winds concentrated within a narrow stream in the upper atmosphere; usually the zone of maximum winds imbedded in the westerlies.

land breeze a light wind blowing from land to sea during night hours when the land is cooler than the sea surface.

mackerel sky a popular name for cirrocumulus or altocumulus clouds.

mean temperature the average of any series of temperatures observed for a period of time. The mean daily temperature is the average of the maximum and minimum temperatures for a 24-hour period.

mean wind speed the number of miles of wind passing a station divided by 24 gives the mean daily wind speed; the mean monthly speed is the average of the daily means.

millibar a pressure unit employed mainly in meteorology equal to 1000 dynes per square centimeter; 1 mb = 0.295 in.

mist a term used to describe a very light fog condition in which the visibility is not so reduced as in actual fog.

mountain breeze a usually light wind blowing downslope along the sides of mountains into adjoining valleys. It most frequently occurs at night when the air in contact with the mountain slopes is being cooled.

noctilucent cloud a very rarely observed cloud of unknown composition visible only after sunset at great heights (about 80 kilometers) above the surface of the earth.

northeaster a New England coastal storm in which northeast gales prevail.

occluded front a composition of two fronts produced when a cold front overtakes a warm front, forcing the warm air aloft.

overrunning the ascent of warm air over relatively cool air, usually in advance of a warm front.

ozone layer a layer in the upper atmosphere in which there is a relatively dense concentration of ozone, a gaseous form of oxygen (O_3).

peak gust the highest instantaneous wind speed recorded during a specified time, usually an hour or 24 hours.

polar air an air mass conditioned over the tundra and snow-covered terrain of high latitudes; it is distinguished from arctic air, which is colder and less moist.

polar front a semipermanent discontinuity separating cold polar easterly winds and the relatively warm westerly winds of the middle latitudes.

precipitation falling products of condensation or sublimation such as rain, snow, hail, or drizzle. Precipitation elements are usually larger in diameter than .02 centimeter; particles smaller than this usually remain suspended in the air.

prefrontal squall line an instability line of turbulence preceding a cold front at some distance, usually accompanied by thunderstorms.

radiation the transfer of energy through space without the agency of an intervening matter.

rain shadow an area of little rainfall in the lee of a mountain barrier.

recurvature a more or less sharp poleward turn of the path of a tropical storm.

relative humidity the ratio of the actual amount of water vapor in a given volume of air to the amount that could be present if the air at the same temperature were saturated. Commonly expressed as a percentage.

ridge an elongated area of high barometric pressure.

rime feather-shaped, white, rough deposit of ice crystals that grow out into the wind on objects exposed at below-freezing temperatures in a fog of super-cooled water droplets.

Saint Elmo's fire a brush discharge or corona of electricity that appears on sharp points or edges of objects during the presence of strong electrical fields such as exist during severe thunderstorms or some snowstorms.

saturation condition of a parcel of air holding a maximum of water vapor (a 100 per cent relative humidity condition exists).

scud a popular name for low, drifting clouds that often appear beneath a cloud from which precipitation is falling. They frequently appear along the shoreline with an onshore wind in a developing storm situation.

sea breeze a usually light, daily wind blowing from sea to shore when the land is warmer than the sea surface.

sea swell a long, regular undulation of the sea surface, usually caused by a disturbance some distance away, such as a tropical storm or cold front.

secondary cold front a cold front that may form behind the primary cold front and carry an even colder impulse of air behind it.

secondary depression an area of low pressure that forms in the trough of low pressure to the south or east of a primary depression.

semipermanent high or low one of the relatively stationary and stable pressure and wind systems of the atmosphere, such as the Icelandic Low or the Bermuda High.

source region an area of nearly uniform surface characteristics over which large bodies of air may stagnate and acquire a more or less uniform horizontal distribution of temperature and humidity.

squall a strong wind characterized by a sudden onset, with a duration of the order of minutes, and a rather sudden decrease in speed. A squall is usually reported only if the wind speed of 16 knots or higher is sustained for at least two minutes (thereby distinguishing it from a gust).

squall line a well-marked line of instability ahead of a cold front accompanied by strong gusty winds, turbulence, and often heavy showers.

stability a condition of the atmosphere whereby a parcel of air given an initial impulse will tend to return to its original level.

stationary front a front that exhibits little movement over a six-hour period on successive weather maps.

steering the process whereby the movement of a surface depression is influenced by the circulation aloft.

storm surge an abnormal rise of the sea along a shore, primarily as the result of the winds of a storm; also called storm tide, storm wave, hurricane wave. This is often the most damaging aspect of a New England hurricane.

sublimation the transition of a substance from the solid phase directly to the vapor phase, or vice versa, without passing through the intermediate liquid phase.

subsidence the descending motion of a body of air, usually within an anticyclone, accompanying divergence in the motion of the lower layers of the atmosphere.

tendency the local rate of change of a meteorological element, usually barometric change.

tropical air an air mass conditioned over the warm surfaces of tropical seas or land.

tropical cyclone a low-pressure area that originates in the tropics.

trough an elongated area of low barometric pressure.

typhoon the name applied in the western Pacific Ocean to severe tropical storms; their structures are similar to those of hurricanes.

valley breeze a usually light, but sometimes strong, wind blowing from a valley upslope along the sides of mountains. It occurs in daytime or early evening when the air in the valley is being heated.

veering winds shifting clockwise (e.g., from northeast through east to southeast); the opposite of backing.

virga streamers of precipitation visibly falling from a cloud but evaporating before reaching the ground.

warm front the line of advancing warm air at the surface that is displacing cooler air.

warm-front-type occlusion an occluded front formed when the air behind the original cold front is less dense than the air in advance of the original warm front.

warm sector the portion of the wave cyclone containing warm air, lying in advance of the cold front and to the rear of the warm front.

waterspout a funnel-shaped, tornadolike cloud complex that occurs over a body of water.

water vapor moisture in the gaseous, invisible phase.

wet-bulb temperature the temperature indicated by the ventilated thermometer, arrived at by evaporating water.

whirlwind a rapidly whirling, small-scale vortex of air, with its axis vertical or nearly so, usually seen on hot still days. The diameter and height may vary from a few feet to several hundred feet.

wind air in motion, occurring naturally in the atmosphere, in general moving parallel to the surface of the ground.

Staff for This Book

EDITOR
Richard M. Ketchum

DESIGNER
Thomas Morley

ASSISTANT EDITOR
Lynda Hobson

PICTURE RESEARCHER
Diane Hamilton

COPY EDITOR
Janet Meacham

ART ASSISTANT
Jennifer Richardson

PRODUCTION MANAGER
William Farnham, Jr.

PICTURE CREDITS